Making
Life Right
When It Feels
All Wrong

Also by Herbert Fensterheim, Ph.D. and
Jean Baer in Futura

DON'T SAY YES WHEN YOU WANT TO SAY NO

Making Life Right When It Feels All Wrong

HOW TO AVOID BEING AN EMOTIONAL VICTIM WITH LOVERS, MATES, BOSSES, FRIENDS, FAMILY

BY

HERBERT FENSTERHEIM, Ph.D.,
CLINICAL PROFESSOR
CORNELL UNIVERSITY MEDICAL COLLEGE
AND
JEAN BAER

Futura

From Jean: for Herb
From Herb: for Jean
with love

A Futura Book

Copyright © 1988 by Herbert Fensterheim, Ph.D. and Jean Baer

First published by Rawson Associates,
Macmillan Publishing Company, New York in 1988

This edition published in 1989
by Futura Publications, a Division of
Macdonald & Co (Publishers) Ltd
London & Sydney

ISBN 0 7088 4209 7

Printed and bound in Great Britain by
Collins, Glasgow

Futura Publications
A Division of
Macdonald & Co (Publishers) Ltd
66–73 Shoe Lane
London EC4P 4AB

A member of Maxwell Pergamon Publishing Corporation plc

☐ Contents

☐ Acknowledgments

So many people have contributed to and influenced our thinking on this book that we cannot list them all and must ask the forgiveness of those we omit.

Amazingly, no one exists in the field of emotional victimization whom we can acknowledge. Despite much concern with victims of crime, catastrophe, abuse, and discrimination, except for an occasional observation in the clinical literature (particularly in the work of the late Karen Horney), literally nothing has been written or studied about emotional victims. This book is a first.

On the other hand, there are theorists and clinicians working on the combination of behavioral and psychoanalytic therapies, the approach that forms the action core of this book. We are indebted to Dr. Paul Wachtel of the City University of New York, who helped form the Society for the Exploration of Psychotherapy Integration (SEPI), which held its first meeting in 1984. We would also like to acknowledge the work of Dr. Marvin Goldfried of the State University of New York at Stony Brook, and the stimulation and contact with many members of SEPI. Particularly important has been the continuing contact with colleagues at Payne Whitney Clinic—The New York Hospital, especially the Friday morning seminars where some of the concepts we present in this book were first discussed.

We would like to thank Dr. Helen Singer Kaplan of the New York Hospital—Cornell University Medical Center, Dagmar O'Connor of St. Luke's–Roosevelt Hospital Center, New York, and media specialist Dr. Ruth Westheimer for ideas influencing our chapter on "super sex." In addition, we would like to thank Dr. Kathleen M. White of Boston University, Dr. Robert J. Sternberg of Yale, Dr. Sandra Lipsitz Bem of Cornell University, and Dr. Gwendolyn Gerber of John Jay College of Criminal Justice, City University of New York, for concepts presented here on male-female relationships. Further thanks to Dr. Arnold Lazarus of Rutgers University for his thoughts, which we used in the chapter on doctors and therapists.

Our appreciation also goes to Dr. Lawrence Hatterer, Dr. Mary FitzPatrick, management consultant David McLaughlin, personnel counselor Lillian Roberts, Suzanne Prescod, editor of the newsletters *Behavior Today* and *Sexuality Today*, and the eminent lawyers Julia Perles and Norman Sheresky.

We would like to express special appreciation to Keir Dullea and Anne Jackson, who gave so freely of their time.

In the book we use a number of methods derived from the field of sports psychology, and we recognize the influence of Dr. Richard Suinn of Colorado State University and also the more direct influence of the directors of the elite athlete project in fencing of the U.S. Olympic Committee and of the athletes themselves.

We would like to extend a special note of thanks to Kathy Levine for her generous helpfulness. In addition, we would like to thank the network of one hundred and fifty interviewees we established around the country to probe the influences and consequences of emotional victimization in all major life areas.

We must give special acknowledgment to the work of Dr. Albert Bandura of Stanford University and former president of the American Psychological Association, who may well be the most influential academic psychologist of the second half of this century. His concept of self-efficacy, which we call "I can do it" thinking, forms one of the outstanding elements for change we present in this book.

And, finally, our appreciation to Grace Shaw and Eleanor Rawson of Rawson Associates for interest, professionalism, and loving concern about every thought and word in this book. This is our third collaborative book with Eleanor, and, with each book, we have gained an increased sense of her caring and creativity. She is an author's idea of what every editor should be like.

☐ Before You Begin This Book . . . A Very Personal Note by Jean Baer

I always believed my mother didn't love me, so I didn't love her. I felt her victim. She never praised me (my straight A report cards, my election to class office, my role as star of the drama club). She obviously preferred my brother (no honors) and gave her time and affection to the Mount Vernon Senior Citizens, not to me. In my head, her imagined lack of love didn't matter. I was daddy's girl. *He* thought I was perfect and I idolized him. A newspaperman, he taught me how to write a lead when I was eight. I followed him into a career in journalism. Later I boasted about my "father fixation" and rationalized that I married late because of it.

After my marriage to Herb, a therapist, whenever I went into my perpetual raves about "my perfect father," Herb would tell me in his analytical manner, "Jean, your problem is your mother." Whenever I said, "He should have been married to someone like me," Herb would laugh and say this father-fix solution was "much too obvious." Then, in the course of writing this book, Herb asked me to delve into my memories (we term such recallable memories the preconscious in chapter 4) and see if my need to make myself my mother's victim wasn't actually a fantasy on my part. Had she *really* not been nice to me? I thought a lot. I did remember events I had suppressed. Then I bled a little—for me, for her. I had misperceived everything.

She did praise me. Once as a child I made a doll dress out of red velvet scraps and cotton (ermine). She boasted about it to everyone who came into the house. Years later, when she lay dying and the household was in turmoil, I recall her begging me to have some friends over. I did. The next morning, she told me, "I'm so proud of you. I heard you pick up the conversation when there were lulls."

She did pay attention to me—just as much as to my brother. At eight, I starred in a school production of *Princess Tenderheart* and toured all of Westchester County. She gave me a present for each performance. Years later when I tried for a Cornell scholarship and took four exhausting exams in one day, she put me to bed and fixed my favorite meal—fried chicken and strawberry shortcake.

And yet I had forgotten she ever did *anything* for me. I saw only her caring for others, not the warmth that was there for me. I always blamed her. In my teens I had a new coat that I wanted to wear when my father was to take me to a special Easter event at NBC. That day it snowed. Mother refused to let me wear the lightweight coat. I thought she didn't want me to look nice and so get even more of my father's attention. Now I know she was thinking of my continual ear infections.

In relations with her, my motives were always for self-aggrandizement. I was in my late teens to early twenties during her long final illness. I was saintly because I thought I should be. After all, I was the oldest child, what we term the "responsible one." It was a sense of duty, not caring, that motivated me.

Obviously, because of some unconscious need—whether Freudian envy of my younger brother or fear of my mother's emotions in contrast to my father's reality orientation—I maintained a completely false idea of myself as her victim.

My actions and reactions had severe consequences that made me a real victim. I went around seeking alternate mothers. At work I always sought out women bosses whom I tried to turn into caring mothers. With one, I was truly thrilled when she gave me twelve beautiful dinner plates as a wedding present. I ignored the fact that she hadn't given me a raise for four years. The plates proved she cared.

I was always disappointed with women friends. A friend

could do ten good things and then one that was not so good and I'd think, "She doesn't love me."

As a result of the Behavioral Psychotherapy techniques I learned from Herb while writing this book, I know that all those years of my feeling hurt about my mother caused both of us pain. She loved me. I wasn't her victim but her victimizer. I didn't realize that what I wanted—the caring mother—was right there. The memories are still repressed. I can't recall anything before I was eight, but I'm trying.

However, clarification of previously suppressed memories has produced good consequences, which matter more in a gut sense than the assertive ability to demand a raise. My necessity to feel the victim has diminished. With authority figures—like women editors—I used to care about how they felt about me. I'd test. If one didn't do something personal like asking me to lunch, I'd feel unloved. Now I don't test. I just write. I can evaluate criticism without personalizing it.

With friends, I concentrate on what they do right rather than wrong. I never asked my mother to come to school to hear me speak and then I blamed her for not coming. I expected her, and later my friends, to be mindreaders. Now I ask my friends when I need or want something.

My new perspective has enabled me to change my attitude so that I can stand up to other members of my sex. Because of my unrecognized need to feel victimized, I had always let my childhood friend Margy put me down. Through Assertiveness Training I learned to answer her back, but I always wondered, "Is she right?" Recently, she said to me, "You're very manipulative." I thought of all those jobs I'd "manipulated" for her when she was unemployed. I also saw reality: In no way would I ever have the kind of friendship with her I would like to have. I didn't even attempt an assertive response to her putdown. My choice was to accept her hostility or pull out. I haven't seen her since.

I always used to tell my husband, "My father was perfect," meaning in a teasing but true way "You aren't."

The other day I impulsively said to him, "How my mother would have loved you!"—and then I knew how my emphasis had shifted. I wish I could tell her.

But I can tell you. *It is never too late to change your life.* You may imagine yourself a victim when you're not—or learn you've made yourself into one. In either case, you can learn a different pattern.

This book will tell you how.

In this book we are talking in general terms and not attempting to diagnose specific symptoms. The book is not intended to replace consultation with or treatment by appropriate professionals.

The substance and most details of the case histories presented in these pages are authentic. But the material has been greatly condensed to save the reader's time, and names and incidents have been disguised with great care to protect the privacy of patients and other individuals.

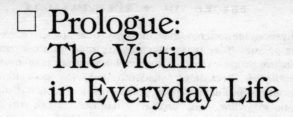

□ Prologue:
The Victim
in Everyday Life

You can learn new ways to make your life right when it feels all wrong.

And, with persistence, you can effect permanent change.

Psychology exists to help you attain this goal. As does any science, psychology continues to grow, develop, mature. During the past decade we have come a long way from Assertiveness Training and overcoming fears. We have found new courses of action to keep life problems from taking over your life, to help you conquer the problems on your own so that you can change from being a victim of others instead of a doer for yourself.

We have learned that it is possible to combine the psychoanalytic and behavioral approaches. Just ten years ago, mental health practitioners either dismissed the unconscious or worked exclusively with it. Today innovative therapists focus on interaction between behavior and the unconscious and their influence upon each other—and on your life. This provides a much briefer process of self-change than five-times-a-week analysis on the couch.

We have learned that a new category of individual exists—*the emotional victim*. The problem of emotional victimization is so pervasive in society that it is extraordinary to find it is virtually unexplored in professional literature. (To our knowledge, we are the first to introduce the term *emotional victim*.) Through ignorance, inefficiency, even hostility, other people (lovers, mates, bosses, friends, family) and life conditions constantly introduce problems that we must mobilize ourselves to meet in everyday life. Because of maladaptive behavior—poor adjustment to the problems we are posed—many of us are chronic emotional victims. The problem circumstances can run the gamut from a boss promoting a worker less able than you to the love of your life rejecting you for no apparent reason. Some of us feel such permanent victims that we expect others to tyrannize us—and set it up so that they do. Often we haven't realized what *we do* to invite victimization.

We have learned that you can change your reactions to the influences stemming from social structures (like your family) that tend to keep you in the victim role.

For example, Bob S. and Steve Y., two moderately successful middle management executives with fairly limited savings and with family responsibilities, each inherited several hundred thousand dollars. Each found a broker he trusted to invest it. Each got a series of buy and sell slips as the supposedly trustworthy broker churned the respective inheritances. Each ended up with most of the money gone.

Both Bob and Steve had grown up as family scapegoats, a role in which each was blamed for anything that went wrong. But in this situation, Bob took action. Steve, held back by self-perpetuation of his family victim role, could not.

At first Bob's initial reaction was that the fault was all his and he could do nothing but call himself names. Then he realized he was emulating his childhood role, and, with his wife's help, turned his anger against the broker. Recognizing Bob's helplessness in the situation and feeling his fury justified, they consulted with friends and with their help found a knowledgeable attorney who instigated a lawsuit. The case was settled out of court; Bob got back his complete inheritance. Because he possessed a realistic knowledge of his capabilities, Bob emerged the winner rather than financial loser. Aware of his tendencies to play the scapegoat, he stopped them. He also understood his limitations, realized he had to seek outside help, and had the emotional strength to work with his wife as a cooperative couple to remedy the situation.

On the other hand, Steve still behaved in the scapegoat manner he had assumed as a child. Furthermore, he had trained his wife to relate to him in the same manner his parents had. Steve found his adult scapegoat role comforting. In his distorted thinking, by taking responsibility for everything that went wrong, he achieved an inner sense of power as a person. So after Steve lost his money, he completely agreed when his wife blamed him for his "stupidity." He discussed the problem with some street-wise friends but didn't listen to their advice. He wasn't interested in money remedies, but wanted to prove how much he suffered, how bad he was for turning his money over to an unscrupulous broker. He acquired the name of a lawyer but failed to call him. To take steps against the broker (other than entertain fantasies of exposing him to the local newspaper) would have denied Steve the paradoxically comforting feeling of being a victim, which he needed psychologically. Unhappy with what happened, Steve continued to enact his emotional victim role because he lacked any conception of what steps to take.

We are going to show you the steps that lead to freedom from emotional victimization and teach you how to take those steps yourself.

You may be someone who can change simply by changing actions. Or you may have to delve into parts of yourself that prevent action change. You may have to address life-long fears and goal inhibitions, emotional blocks you may not even realize you have that prevent personal growth. To gain a perspective of what goes on now, still others may have to reach far back to early formative years. This may involve doing, thinking, creating, fighting back, feeling in ways that may seem strange to you. But *your new ways of action can stop you from being an emotional victim.* A basic guideline: *"I may not be able to control what happens to me in life, but I can control my reaction to it."*

We want to help you change your pattern, personality, and behavior so that you will feel right—not wrong—about yourself. In this book we will reveal to you a *new therapeutic method* that will enable you to start a program of self-change. Our goal: to stop you from ever being or feeling an emotional victim of others or yourself.

This self-freeing process involves five *R*s.

■ *Recognition* of whatever bothers you. The more

Part I

Emotional Victims: The Who, What, When, Where, Why

1 □ You Don't Have to Be an Emotional Victim

At work, Jill A., a successful copywriter, acts with competence and authority. In private life, however, when interacting with the opposite sex, she becomes dependent, self-effacing, and demands nothing less than total commitment. Jill's pattern: She becomes involved with dominant, aggressive, self-absorbed men and then worries about losing them and feels exploited when she does. This type of man will never provide Jill with the kind of commitment she finds necessary. Still, she always seeks the same kind.

Tim P., a thirty-year-old middle management executive, has always had an enormous sense of financial responsibility for his mother. Because he gives so much of his paycheck to her, he can rarely afford to date. Recently he discovered that his mother had been depositing her Social Security checks in a healthy bond fund while living off the money he had been giving her. Tim feels "taken" and resentful but cannot stop his unnecessary giving to mother.

John and Mary are a mutually exploitative couple. Their pattern: When John has a problem, he wants Mary to help solve it. When Mary has a problem, she craves sympathy and support. In real life, John gives Mary what *he* wants—practical help. She gives him the empathy that *she* desires. Each provides what the other doesn't want. Each feels empty, disappointed, betrayed.

Jill, Tim, John, and Mary differ in age, appearance, talent, and economic success but share the quality that affects their entire way of life. They are emotional victims. Aloud, they wonder, "Why did *they* do this to me?" On the outside, they feel martyred and miserable, victims of people and forces beyond their control. But often they suffer needlessly because they lack the realization that *they can change*.

Are You an Emotional Victim?

At some time or another in life we all become victims of some outside event—e.g., fire, bad business circumstances, illness, crime. The less fortunate of us will be victims of abusive or deliberately cruel people, sometimes even those we have a right to trust. These are sad, sometimes even tragic circumstances, usually filled with a sense of personal violation.

There is a second, even more common kind of victim: those of us who consistently set ourselves up to lose in the ordinary course of living, of being engaged with life, of interacting and relating to people. Our sense of defeat comes from the way we relate to other people and ourselves. If we tolerate the intolerable, cooperate with people who take advantage of us, imagine what is not true, bring about difficulties by our own behavior, or magnify a situation that is already difficult for us into something much worse, we are emotional victims, doomed to an experience of continual pain, suffering, anguish.

It is to this so common type of victim, rather than to the victims of crime, abuse, and misfortune that we address this book. We will take up the everyday problems of essentially normal people, as most of us are, and show how to deal with these problems in life through new psychological techniques.

Do you let your victim-proneness limit your life or your potential and often destroy you as a person?

Do you suffer when you don't have to?

The goals of this book are to teach you that you don't have to be a victim and how to accomplish your own devictimization.

The Four Types of Emotional Victims

1. THE EXAGGERATOR

In the life situation you actually are a victim, but you magnify the reality. In a company takeover, you lose your job and tell yourself, "I'll never get another one," yet most people do. Or you become a divorce statistic, feel "nobody will ever want me again," and ignore the reality that an estimated 85 percent of the divorced remarry. Sometimes you react to the trivial as if it were major. A date arrives half an hour late and you turn what was probably a traffic jam into a personal attack.

2. THE "KICK ME" VICTIM

You set yourself up for victimization. Because you so crave approval and love, you fail to do what's necessary to protect yourself. You sport a sign that announces, "Take me, hurt me, make me the nothing I believe I am." You may choose friends or lovers who will take advantage of you. You may trust the wrong people with the wrong thing. Often, even though you know you'll become a victim by doing so, you act in just the way that will produce that effect. For example, you constantly complain about feeling hurt, and when your friends beg, "Stop—you've told me that a million times," you're upset. You think others are victimizing you, but you're really doing it to yourself.

3. THE MISPERCEIVER

You see yourself as a victim when you're not. You spot unfairness, exploitation, duplicity, or rejection where none exists except in your imagination.

For example, Lenore D., a Chicago middle-management executive, dislikes her upstairs condo neighbors because they want no social relationship and refuse to do any of the chores necessary in a six-unit building with only a part-time super. She calls them "the stingies" because they won't spend money on areas shared by all. So Lenore buys the costly wallpaper and sulks. She won't realize that condo living represents a business situation and that the neighbors are not out to "get her" but simply acting the way they believe right by their standards, not hers. In actuality, Lenore would like everyone in the building to measure up to her concept of a kind, considerate family, even though her own family relationships bear no resemblance to her fantasy.

4 . THE KNOW-NOT VICTIM

You don't even know you are one. For example, when Joe M., an internist, comes home after a stress-filled day, his nonworking wife issues a series of orders: "Do the laundry" . . . "Pick up some coffee at the store." Joe obeys, not allowing himself even to experience his own resentments. To do so, he thinks, would show him how "selfish" he is.

If we think of ourselves as victims, we will act the victim's part, and, in time, we will become victims, unable to achieve love or a feeling of accomplishment.

The New Treatment Method for Behavioral Change

Our incorrect ways of thinking about things, combined with the actions we take, set our victim feelings in motion and maintain our victim psychology. The key to change seems simple: Change our behavior and thoughts and we will disrupt our victim pattern. However, in the past few years, theorists and clinicians have learned that while this method can work for some people, it also may prove effective only partially, occasionally, or temporarily. Eventually many of us revert to our old ways.

We have found an answer in Behavioral Psychotherapy (BP), a new treatment method that integrates two diverse approaches and which we introduce to the general public in this book. These two approaches are:

      1. *Behavior Therapy.* A person deliberately changes automatic patterns of actions and thoughts without probing the past.

      2. *Application of psychoanalytic concepts.* A person learns to understand unconscious needs, conflicts, drives, and memories.

For a good part of this century, Freudian thinking dominated treatment with the tenet that most problems, many dealing with sex and aggression and usually acquired during childhood, lie buried in the unconscious. As an individual brings these feelings and memories into consciousness—via free association, seeking to retrieve memories and gain "insights"—the person changes and becomes freer to love and attain personal growth. Behavior might change as a consequence, but that is not the focus.

Some thirty years ago Behavior Therapy (BT) came along. This had a different theory. As we noted in our book *Don't Say Yes When You Want to Say No*, Behavior Therapy followed the principle that "by changing your actions, you can change your attitudes and feelings about yourself." In other words, solve the problem and the person changes. Just as psychoanalysis pays little attention to behavior, so BT focuses little on wishes, motives, drives, or the unconscious.

In the past, little interaction existed between the various practitioners of these two methods. They ignored each other. But now a significant minority of leaders in each field have joined forces to use an integrated technique that utilizes the strength of *both* therapeutic processes. The sponsoring group is the Society for the Exploration of Psychotherapy Integration (SEPI), in which analysts and behavior therapists combine to work for clients' common psychological good.

To help you master the complex and universal problem of being an emotional victim, this book will present the newest findings in the integrated approach, applying them to major life distress areas that affect all of us.

WHAT YOU LEARN IN BEHAVIORAL PSYCHOTHERAPY

(Guiding principle: *Remember your past to control your present and change your future.*)

■ Use of the Levels Approach (changing behaviors, overcoming blocks, uncovering your unconscious)

■ "I can do it" thinking (acquiring both the can-do feeling and the ability)

■ Saying yes (to others and yourself)

■ How to stop being part of a punishing pair (becoming a cooperative couple emotionally/professionally rather than a couple working together for mutual destruction)

■ Acceptable aggression (to gain a goal, for self-defense, and for self-esteem)

■ Self smarts (development of creative talents you may not know you have)

■ Use of the preconscious (recalling past memories to use in the present)

■ Whom to trust with what (recognizing different trust factors with friends and in close relationships)

■ Thinking to win (exercises in psyching up and confidence building used by Olympics athletes that can work in everyday life)

■ How to be a relationship winner rather than loser (heightening intimacy, sharing love, knowing what to do when change occurs)

■ How to identify victimizers (the users, the bosses—including the egotist and those with the "Emperor" complex) and recognizing the warning signs

■ How to escape from paranoid thinking (getting the "they" factor out of your life)

■ How to recognize mutual victims (including doctors and patients)

■ How not to be a divorce victim the second time around (addressing the fears and facts about remarrying right)

■ Sexual confidence (through sexual self-assertion, overcoming myths, unmommying/undaddying yourself)

■ How and when to strike back and still retain your self-respect

Use the Levels Approach for Victim Change

Level One: Behavior

First we learn to identify behaviors, whether outward actions or inner thoughts, that turn us into and keep us victims. Then we systematically work to change them. Usually people do have an awareness of their basic problem. For instance, because a woman has the habit of always arriving late for work, her boss always yells at her, and she feels put-upon. Or an individual with a victim problem gives up without trying to change ("It's hopeless!") and allows victimization to proceed. Arriving late and giving up are the self-victimizing behaviors to identify and change in these situations.

If you change your action and thought processes, you *will* change your victim pattern. The cause or *why* you do what you do has no relevance.

Level Two: Blocks

Maybe we try to change and our attempt fails. This happens because people have developed emotional barriers like fears, a passive orientation, or bad habits that keep them from doing what they must do to alter their behavior. For instance, they know they should say yes to pleasurable things but their wait-and-see inaction policy and fear of novelty keep them from doing so. By not changing, we sometimes gain payoffs in the form of a psychological security blanket ("To make myself liked, I have to act like and be a victim"). As well as trying to take action at the behavioral level, you must work on personality blocks that prevent success with your target behavior.

Level Three: Unconscious

Sometimes we can't make the first two levels work, or perhaps any change in our victim pattern proves merely transitory. Then we can assume that some unconscious process/need (search for a caring parent, desire to be dominated by a hostile person) makes victimization psychologically rewarding to us. Because the sense of being the martyr to others or self fulfills a certain need, protecting us from certain thoughts and anxieties, we maintain the pattern. In some cases, victim behavior tells us something about ourselves that we can't express or face directly. For example, a woman acts helpless with her mate and can't/won't make any decisions. She is expressing her unconscious desire to be cared for as a helpless infant.

If we are able to change these triggering sources, we become able to see and do things *differently* and thus minimize victimization.

Personal Effectiveness: The New Breakthrough

The "personal effectiveness" concept (formulated by Professor Albert Bandura, a psychologist at Stanford University), so important for any self-change, represents a new major psychological breakthrough and serves as the levels linchpin. There are two connected points of emphasis.

    1. Being able to do what you have to do to effect change, though necessary, is not sufficient.

    2. You must know you can do it!

This does not mean you will necessarily win everything you want in life, but *knowing you can do what you must do* provides you with the best chance of overcoming any difficulty. For example, a woman may want to call a man and arrange a meeting; she realizes he may refuse her, but she can still *make* the call.

The more you acquire this inner sense of know-how, the more you will be able to face the risks and fears of your change program and keep going.

We can gain the necessary sense of personal effectiveness in four specific ways:

    1. Through a series of *successful performances*—the best way. Start at change levels you can manage and keep stretching. When you can do so legitimately, you want to attribute success to yourself and your competence.

Wrong way: You slough off a minor triumph at work with, "The boss felt good today, so he praised me."
Right way: Tell yourself, "I did a good job. I'm glad the boss recognized it, but I deserved the compliment."

    2. Practice *constructive voyeurism* by using others as models. See how coworkers, close friends, mates (yours and others) avoid victimization, and *copy* the technique. For example, one woman agonized because her two siblings "looted" the jewelry when their mother died. At the same time, a dear friend also lost her mother, and, within hours, her brother and his wife had invaded the mother's apartment and helped themselves to three valuable rings. The friend wasted no time agonizing; she went right to her lawyer and took her brother out of her will. Instead of obsessing, the first woman might have learned from others and figured out a strategy of action that would have relieved her misery.

　　　　3.　You can also learn from *reading*. If you find the material trustworthy, it will supply ideas you can apply to your own situation. Take this very book. From it, you can gain awareness that others have had the same or similar problems, mastered them, and thus you learn vicariously. This technique builds "can do" confidence.

　　　　4.　*Friends' exhortations*. When a friend tells you, "You don't have to endure that monster of a boss," he or she is really expressing confidence in your ability to get out of the situation—whether you decide to speak up to the boss or look for another job. The confidence of friends provides *you* with confidence: "I can do what I have to do."

Once you possess the conviction that you *can* do whatever is necessary to gain the outcome you crave, you will not be a helpless victim. Because you know you can search for a more satisfying lover, you are free to leave the hostile lover with whom you've unwittingly become involved. Because you know what you must do to climb to the next job rank, you can overcome your fears. *Just knowing you can do it makes doing possible.*

2 □ Why Me?

"Everyone picks on me. Why?"

"I'm like a football. The world just tosses me around. What I want doesn't matter. Why?"

"I'm smarter than other people, but I always end up the underdog and others win out. Why?"

These are just a few of the dark thoughts of able, nice, often extremely talented people who let themselves become victims. If they thought about it, they might discover the truth under their emotional camouflage: that they actually become victims because they gain from the experience.

Their gain may be *positive*. They increase their feelings of security, of being wanted, of belonging, of emotional safety. They know the victimizer is paying attention to them. Such people think that the victimizer, because he or she at least pays attention, is less apt to abandon them than someone who seems more indifferent, even though they realize the victimizer gets a kick out of putting individuals down.

Or the victims' reaction may be *defensive*. Because they are busy complaining about the "terrible" things the other person does, victims avoid the responsibility of examining their own conflicts and needs.

What Makes Us Victim-Prone?

People become victim-prone in different ways for different reasons. They do not do this willfully or out of free choice. They unwittingly make themselves emotional victims in order to achieve something important to them, something they need for their own emotional sustenance.

A series of forces—from outside or within—can act as motivators leading to vulnerability or a psychological predilection toward emotional victimization. The following quick quiz will help you determine your Inclination Quotient toward victim-proneness. If you answer yes to any of the following questions, you are a candidate for victimhood.

INCLINATION QUOTIENT QUIZ

Goal: To determine the traits that make you victim-prone.

1. Were you brought up to do unto others—and not unto you?
2. Do you seek love from the outside because you don't really love yourself?
3. Do you subtly encourage people to pick on you without realizing what you're doing?
4. Are you a good loser and bad winner?
5. Does your naïveté lead you into trouble?
6. Do you take on no-win situations as a way of life?

Here are some of the most common candidates to become an emotional victim in life.

THE CHILDHOOD-TRAINED VICTIM

For many people, their early family environment establishes a later pattern of victimization. Perhaps you had ailing parents and took on too much responsibility too soon, too young. As an oldest child, you may have had a ne'er-do-well father so that you had to become the breadwinner. You sent your younger siblings to college but couldn't go yourself. All your life you've resented the responsibility you believed you had to take and the lack of opportunity to get your own degree.

In many cases an adult male victim had a mother who was "too caring." Because she overprotected him, he acquired feelings of incompetency and helplessness. Or she may have constantly criticized his father, a friend, or a boss. Because the son wanted to help her and felt helpless to do so, he began to associate love with helplessness. Now his model of the close relationship contains that element of helplessness.

THE SELF-EFFACING PERSON

Deep down, this type of person feels unworthy, even feeling contempt for self, in the belief that only love from someone else will give meaning to life. Therefore, continually he or she seeks that love. As a result, the other person becomes of such importance that the self-effacer does everything to placate the other person to be sure of getting that desperately needed love. If the self-effacer were to act annoyed, assertive, or independent, it would be at the risk of withdrawal of that love, so self-effacers inhibit these expressions, always put the other person's needs first, and brush aside any resentments of exploitation. Eventually the feelings may come through in an outburst that destroys the relationship. The victim pattern goes on and on. The self-effacer *continually* tests everyone for evidence of love. Even a friend forgetting to call means lack of love.

THE PERSON WITH THE NEED TO SUFFER

As Freud pointed out, for survival, human beings must control certain masochistic feelings that usually develop during childhood.

Hostilities and Aggressive Needs

Many people who have conflicts about their aggressive urges find they must control the need to strike out and harm someone else. At the same time, they must express these desires to hurt. Their defensive solution: They turn these aggressive yearnings against themselves. By seeking out people and situations that will result in victimization, thereby turning the aggression against themselves, they can act out and relieve their self-inflicted pressure.

Example: Pete W., a young businessman, gets mad at his boss. This stirs up the feelings of *repressed* aggression he had against his father as a child. (These feelings are part of the normal developmental process that most of us resolve in the course of growing up, but Pete had not resolved them.) In his unconscious, Pete wants to tear his boss apart. He has fantasies of murdering him. However, because such feelings terrorize him, Pete must hide any aggression, assertion, anger against his boss. His solution: to blame himself over every triviality, getting angry at himself for his inability and insensitivity. Turning his anger against himself and making himself the victim of unjust self-criticism helps him control his destructive urges. Like most victims of this type, Pete has no idea he is doing this.

Guilt Feelings

In childhood, some sufferers develop guilt feelings because of fantasies, sensations, and desires they deem unacceptable. Unconsciously, they feel the need to be punished for these. In adult life, without recognizing the connection, they create conditions where punishment occurs.

Example: For his first wife, an opthalmologist picked a lively, blond copywriter who continually listed his faults aloud. After fifteen years, they divorced. For his second wife, he chose a dull, brunette teacher. While, on the surface, the two wives seemed different, actually the doctor made the same mistake twice. Each wife used (and uses) the same sentence continually—"You're a terrible person." The luckless husband continues to get the punishment his unconscious guilt, stemming from buried childhood fantasies about his mother, requires. So he finds punishing wives.

THE VICTIM OF THE
ABEL SYNDROME

In 1916 Freud described individuals who "seek painful situations to punish themselves or in which they are deprived of the fruit of their success." The term *Abel Syndrome* actually stems from the Biblical story of the brothers Cain and Abel. Abel was a successful farmer. Because of jealousy, Cain killed him. Some analysts suggest that because Abel possessed guilt feelings about his success, he cooperated in some way with killer Cain to absolve himself of those feelings.

Victims of the Abel Syndrome are individuals, favored by fate, who easily come by success in life but deep down suffer from it or are unable to enjoy it. Success in life arouses unconscious guilt feelings in them, which strengthens their victim tendency. They believe themselves to be imposters.

To expiate these bad feelings, they set themselves up as victims. They have a self-negating attitude ("People believe I'm more talented than I really am") and that becomes a self-fulfilling prophecy. They predict friends will desert them because they earn more money, so they desert their friends first. A major department head who has unrecognized guilt because she has such a good job arrives at the office at 7:00 A.M. to do clerical work because she thinks that's what *she* should be doing, rather than delegating it and going on to more important things.

Victims of the Abel Syndrome have trouble accepting compliments ("I'm not really that good"). Or at the height of success, they feel such guilt that they unconsciously or even deliberately pull a boner that can harm and destroy a career opportunity.

THE NAÏVE DEPENDENT

This is the person who automatically submits to any victimization. Because he or she hasn't learned to take safety precautions or even recognize the early signs that another person is a victimizer, the naïve dependent takes no measures to stop the process. For instance, a coworker claims credit for your idea at a meeting and you say nothing—then or ever—and thereafter go on telling her your ideas, instead of backing up, revealing nothing, and speaking out for yourself at meetings.

This type of victim lacks the ability to recognize the dangers of certain situations—such as overdependence on one person in business. For example, Maggie L., head of a small import-export firm, has a thirty-year-old accountant who serves as the key employee of the three-member staff. Without his expertise, certain projects would collapse. Knowing this, he comes in late, takes an excessive number of days off, makes too many personal long distance calls. Because Maggie has permitted herself to become so dependent on him, she thinks she must endure his behavior—rather than seeking a replacement and firing him.

This same sort of dependent insecurity can develop with women and domestic help (a career woman makes herself a victim because she fears firing an incompetent). It can also develop with couples (one or both partners feel, "Without him/her, I'll be all alone. I must take it [the mate's egotism, bad habits, tempers] without speaking out."

THE PERSON WITH SPECIAL VICTIM NEEDS

Some people want to be *saviors*, to take on losers like the alcoholic, boor, leaner. But the underdog may not want saving or may hunger after a different kind of protective partner. Sometimes being a savior works out; other times it does not and the savior ends up the victim, thinking, "I do so much and look what happens."

Others have a need to turn *crisis* into catastrophe. Any sort of misfortune makes them lose confidence, focus on what is wrong and what should have been rather than on what they can do. For instance, to ease the grief at the break-up of a relationship, a woman stays home and cries, making minimal efforts to cope or even desisting completely. The crisis victim may set himself/herself up for a life term in the emotional victim's prison.

Gaining Control of Your Victim Psychology

DEAL WITH THE BASIC FEARS THAT MAKE YOU A VICTIM

There are three major fears to deal with.

1. *The fear of being you.* Today our mass-production society pressures not only for standardization of products but of people. Conformity has become normality. You may be smarter than others in a similar job slot at work, more talented than others, more adventurous than your friends, but, because you fear what others think of you, often you hold yourself back. Because you fail to reveal your creativity and originality, you emerge a carbon copy of others, rather than what you might be. Because you hold back from being your real self, your life-style becomes defensive and you end up a victim—professionally, socially, emotionally.

Be glad you're not like everyone else! Seize the chance to capitalize on your individuality. As the late Justice Felix Frankfurter wrote, "Anyone who is any good is different from everybody else."

2. *The fear of doing frightening things.* When we have to do new things that will prevent victimization (like asking for a raise, telling friends they've done wrong), many of us feel frightened. We build up disturbing thoughts, keep thinking of the worst that might occur. Usually these imaginings far exceed what might happen in the actual situation, but the difficulty occurs when we have such a fear of being frightened that we avoid the situation completely.

If this fear is affecting you, do not tell yourself, "I won't be frightened." Instead, tell yourself, "Sure, I'll be frightened, but I can handle the fear and do what I have to do." With this "I can do it" attitude, you are more apt to make the "frightening" action and, in the process, to discover that even though you fear it, you can gain more confidence from *doing* it. Next time you won't find it so hard because you will have less fear of being frightened.

3. *The fear of being aggressive.* This fear may launch or escalate a victim pattern or inhibit you from relinquishing yours. Many of us think aggressiveness "bad," so repress our behavior and thereby make ourselves victim-prone. Others of us confuse the word *aggressive* with forcefulness. We believe a man acting macho is aggressive, or that a successful woman must be aggressive "or she wouldn't be where she is."

Until just a few years ago, many mental health practitioners also thought aggressiveness wrong and morally unjustifiable. Today we realize that in many situations the new "acceptable aggressiveness" serves as a constructive behavior. Social, situational, and self-respect–related needs may call for appropriate aggression.

Don't be afraid of *competitive aggression.* Fear of it may set you up to be a victim. Just use it at the right time. This type of aggression is routine in the sports world. In training, athletes learn psychological tactics to win advantage in competition. Use of psychological tactics in other competitive situations can also be perfectly appropriate. *Example:* You're in desperate need of a job. In the reception room sits another applicant, obviously just out of school and with a superior air. You would like to shake rather than encourage his confidence, so you say, "The ad didn't say it, but the firm wants five years' experience." (See chapter 5 for guidelines on use of competitive aggression.)

With *tactical aggression,* you try to achieve some goal. To accomplish it, you may have to hurt someone.

For example, Sally L., head of the promotion department at a major magazine, found her job jeopardized because her assistant, Lila O., an untalented but ambitious office climber, badmouthed her to the advertising director. The firm's publisher scheduled a meeting with himself, Sally, and the ad director to discuss the situation. Warned a savvy friend, "Promise him anything, Sally, but get rid of Lila." Sally succeeded. She got the assistant fired ("She just can't handle radio-TV placement"). Sally did not become the victim. The victim, quite deservedly, was Lila, the assistant who had tried to victimize her.

Sometimes aggressiveness is both justifiable and necessary (as when lawyers oppose each other in court). If you must choose between being an unnecessary victim or taking appropriate aggressive action, be aggressive. Protect your job, family, marriage, self. Just ask yourself, "Will this action increase my self-respect?" If it will, go to it!

SET REALISTIC, NOT SELF-DEFEATING GOALS

Essentially, much victimization occurs because we feel we should be able to control the uncontrollable.

We cannot change the world. Outside forces may interfere with achieving goals. Circumstances can make us a victim. You may not be able to stop your company from going bankrupt in a recession market. It may take you a year to find another job. Your spouse may have a heart attack. A car may hit your mother. Your best friend may move to Singapore. When you *feel* that you should be able to prevent this kind of outside circumstance, you heighten and maintain the actual self-victimization.

We may also end up the victim because we *imagine* people the way we want them to be, refusing to take them the way *they are.* You yearn for your boss to be a loveable, considerate father figure when, actually, he's the meanest man on earth. You can't change him, but you keep trying. You must realize that there are people and things no one can change.

We may feel that *our ailments*, real or fancied, give us the right to make demands, to act vindictive and manipulative. In doing so, we may gain power over everyone around us, but it is at the cost of our own self-development.

We must all realize that the victim habit just *seems* to provide benefits.

Traps to Avoid
■ Realize that when we use the distraction technique of blaming others or outside circumstances to absolve ourselves of responsibility we are arranging our lives so that we don't have to face or examine our own problems.

For example, Marge and Phil jointly conduct a customer relations class. Phil takes all the credit with management for its success, turns in reports under his name, and makes snide remarks about Marge in class. She complains constantly to friends about how "Phil hates me," rather than spending the same time figuring out how to protect herself in this corporate infighting situation.

■ Understand that we often convince ourselves that what people want from us is really what we want to do. Being a victim serves some process in our unconscious. This is subtle. Often we don't realize what's happening. As a young child, you felt no limits, but then your parents began to impose them. Imposed limits demand the recognition that you are not omnipotent and lead to what psychoanalysts call "a narcissistic wound to the ego."

To shield ourselves from the pain of this wound, we may have adopted the idea that "the things I am told to do are what I really want to do anyway." In this way we preserve the childhood illusion of no limits, but at the price of estrangement from our own true needs. You willingly fulfill the demands of others because you have persuaded yourself that their wishes are what you yourself want. You have no idea that you're a victim at all.

■ Guard against the victim goal of proving to yourself how terribly life has wronged you. Some people believe if they can prove to others how much they suffer, others will take care of them. Their fantasy is that through suffering they will gain caring. But they won't!

THE CASE OF THE UNCARED-FOR ADULT

David J., an oldest son and now a thirty-year-old bachelor, had a terrible childhood. His parents and siblings mocked him and blamed him for everything. His mother had a miserable relationship with her husband but, fearful of expressing her anger to her husband, she vented her unhappiness by punishing her son, David. Because of this harassment and abuse, David developed a fantasy: If he suffered enough, someone would eventually come along and care for him. As an adult, this fantasy virtually kept him in an emotional straight-jacket. He had not only brought victimization upon himself but, given his attitude, was completely unable to prevent it. David expected a savior would arrive to save him from his dull life.

Before he came to me as a Behavioral Psychotherapy patient, David had a series of unfortunate job experiences. An aerospace engineer, he wanted to be involved in jobs at the cutting edge of the field. Instead, he took jobs that worked out badly. In one, his work had little to do with his main area of interest. In the second, he became stuck in an "antiquated area." In both cases he quit. Now the same thing was recurring in the third job. David failed to realize that he had not investigated each position carefully enough. He blamed "the lying employment agencies" and was about to quit his job again.

In treatment, David came to realize at the very gut level that his fantasy was making him put himself in the victim position in career decisions. Through this perception, the fantasy lost its stranglehold. David realized no savior was going to come along—he had to be on his own. Conditions at his third job were so poor that he lacked even a telephone. In the past, he would have agonized over this—felt angry, depressed, and victimized and quit impulsively, no matter how destructive it was to him. Not so the new David. At lunchtime he used pay phones to set up job interviews. The first interview didn't work. At the second, he really sold himself. He told the interviewer, "You're not just hiring me; you're hiring a whole network," meaning his very valuable contacts in the industry. In a microsecond, the interviewer replied, "The job is yours." *David left his fantasy world for the real world.*

DON'T BE PART OF A PUNISHING PAIR

Unwittingly, we often collaborate with our victimizers to become or remain the victim. Essentially, openly wearing a gold chain on a New York subway represents a collaboration with a criminal. We may also select a boss, friend, lover who has the potential to victimize us. For instance, intimate matrimonial relationships exist in which, unable to leave each other alone or take off, the partners inflict lifelong torture on each other. Each knows the other's victimizing character but keeps on collaborating to satisfy his or her own needs.

Example One: A young woman begins dating a man and discovers that he is extraordinarily inconsiderate. He makes her feel foolish, weak, incompetent, but she can't break it off. Without being aware of it, her concept of femininity entails acting out the part of someone who is weak. As a result, she continues with the victimization, making it easier and easier for her lover to keep her in the thrall of victimization.

Example Two: For many years the boss of a major public relations firm has victimized a certain vice-president who, because of his own need to be the victim, has gone along willingly with every unreasonable demand. Now, planning to retire, the boss insists the vice-president prepare an "achievement scrapbook." So the obedient vice-president spends weeks doing a clerk's work while others at his level request—and get—raises. Then a new boss takes over, learns of the scrapbook, identifies the vice-president with the previous head, and fires him. Collaboration made the vice-president a casualty.

The punishing couple can be of either sex but *always* work together as a pair to make each other victims.

What actions do *you* practice to encourage victimization from your mother-in-law, exploitation from your sister, betrayal from a friend?

LEARN TO IDENTIFY A VICTIMIZER

Perhaps in your mind only an obvious sadist would have the need to make you a pushover, pawn, or even prey. However, many victimizers have conscious and unconscious problems of their own that prompt their behavior. As you become able to recognize different kinds of victimizers, you are less apt to become their prey.

Negligent victimizers have the acquired habit of never taking others into consideration. They probably behave the same to everyone else in their life as they do to you.

Habitual victimizers may act that way because in their youth they were victims. Now, in adult life, they want to reverse the situation. Or conversely, they may have victimized a puny younger sibling and so acquired the habit of pushing others around.

Impulsive victimizers do their act because on any particular day they feel angry, frustrated, or down—perhaps for good reason.

Compulsive victimizers have no control over their actions. They feel so unworthy that they must victimize others to reduce their own anxieties.

UNDERSTAND THE DOMINO EFFECT OF THE UNFAIRNESS FACTOR

In many situations we can be helpless without feeling a victim. For instance, a player who loses at tennis can accept the fact that he did his best but that his opponent performed better. Because no unfairness is involved, the player does not feel the victim. If he loses because of bad calls by an official, he does feel the victim. Unfairness has entered the picture.

Some aspect of unfairness often serves as the core of the victim feeling, along with a sense of being personally invaded, degraded, sometimes destroyed. The unfairness may stem from capriciousness, chance, or the stupidity, negligence, or actual malevolence of others. But many personalize this unfairness and feel they have been singled out, rather than see it as behavior by others that has little to do with who they are.

When we make ourselves the victim (through a wrong choice of career, mate, or friend), it hurts much more than when others victimize us. Then the unfairness and the sense of deep personal threat begin to dominate our life to such an extent that we distort reality and don't even try to cope with the problem. Our sense of worthlessness from unfairness leads to self-hate and we give up too easily on everything. The resultant depression, anxiety, and hopelessness all combine and build to make a bad situation worse. You become a double victim, *the victim of your own self.*

It doesn't have to be that way!

THE CASE OF THE COMPUTER PROGRAMMER

An attractive, unmarried woman in her early thirties, Julia T. earns $30,000 a year as a computer trainer. When she came to me, she felt depressed, unable to have good relationships with men, and a victim to some degree in all situations—least victimized by women friends, moderately victimized at work, and particularly victimized by men she dated. At work the boss would assign "unfair" tasks she found it difficult to perform. With men the situation became more serious. They made "impossible" demands: "Don't smoke" . . . "Do what I want, not what you want." Julia constantly pointed out the unfair requests of these male friends but never thought what she might do to prevent them and keep herself from becoming a victim.

Julia's life history had tremendously affected her present. When she was six, her parents had divorced. Her working mother had paid little attention to her, and for the most part neighbors and two older sisters provided care for this latch-key child. And the older sister picked on her.

Julia and I started on a Behavioral Psychotherapy devictimization program. First we focused on getting her to pay more attention to what she could do—like answer her boyfriend back. She tried to do this but could not. We both realized we were dealing with something deeper.

Then I gave Julia a psychological assignment to get her to probe her memories. I got her to think of times in her childhood when she felt the victim and to examine the similarities between then and now. She learned that the core of her problem was a strong feeling of unfairness about her father's leaving. Her helplessness in the here and now stemmed from her inability to do something about this unfairness. She felt that her father had been unfair to leave and feared other men would be similarly unfair to her.

We set about changing her victim pattern by introducing reality elements. (1) Julia figured out the justification of why her father had left her mother (actually a nagging, bossy woman) and realized the effect her mother had had on her (the development of feelings of insecurity and inadequacy). She thought, "If my mother had that effect on me, I can imagine what effect she had on dad." (2) She decided to get in touch with her father and ask him directly, "Why did you leave?" When she confronted him, he explained that the constant derogation had made him feel so low that he began to dislike himself for accepting such disrespectful treatment. Getting his point of view enabled Julia to realize that the situation had two sides, not just the one her mother had taught her ("Your father was terrible"). She felt an emotional load just slide away.

With her new perception, interpretation, and the emotional burden lifted, suddenly Julia's feelings changed, and she became able to change her whole victim pattern. She realized that *many situations that seemed unfair were not.* Understanding what had happened in her home life removed the feeling of helplessness she had associated with unfair situations. In life situations she now refuses to behave like a victim. She became able to tell her boss why she thought certain assignments unfair . . . to speak up to male friends . . . to answer back when anyone attempts to victimize her. Will one of her relationships work out? I don't know. But for the first time in her life Julia is in command of herself.

Decide to Change

You don't have to live with the heartache of remaining an emotional victim. In fact, being a victim can serve as an opportunity.

When budget cutbacks terminated Dr. Ruth Westheimer's associate professorship at Brooklyn College, she felt "angry, helpless, rejected." But she did not allow those feelings to overwhelm her. She kept lecturing on sex education, went quickly on to a career as "Dr. Ruth," internationally known therapist, television star, movie actress, and author. Courageous Mary Tyler Moore has two failed marriages, a son who shot himself at age seventeen, and a stint for alcoholism at the Betty Ford Center behind her. She has stated that she is coming closer to a desired "So what?" attitude about past troubles.

You don't have to be a famous or exceptional person to use victimization as a chance for growth and reevaluation. George R., an advertising agency executive, was fired twice— once out of spite, the second time because his firm failed. Taking stock, he realized that he had to become his own boss to attain true freedom and security. To amass capital, he worked at a prestigious firm for two years, then went into his own business. Today he's a happy millionaire. He used being a victim as a springboard to evaluate reality in his volatile field and take protective action on his own.

If you find yourself to be a real-life victim, tell yourself, "This is where I am now, fairly or unfairly. Where do I want to go? What are my first steps? And what is the process to get from there to where I want to be?"

Know that only *you can change yourself.* Whatever the past, *you control your present. You can change your future.*

3 □ The Family: Victims and Victimizers

Recently two middle-aged siblings met for their bimonthly lunch. Grace confessed she had always thought Claire, the younger by two years, to be the family favorite.

"Oh, no, you were the favorite," disagreed Claire. "They loved you best because you were so artistic and cute." More seriously, she added, "I always suffered. In school everyone asked, 'Are you Grace's sister?' I made up my mind to be as different and successful as possible." And she became a pediatrician. As they shared their memories, the closeness between the sisters was obvious.

Two other middle-aged siblings do not meet for lunch. In fact, they do not speak. Eleanor, the elder by four years, had been a star in school—class secretary, president of the dramatic club, columnist for the school newspaper. Chris, the younger sister, felt she was the victim of Eleanor's success. Insecure, she never tried to participate in high school or college activities, made a mediocre marriage, and has always told Eleanor, "Everything that's wrong with me is your fault." All her life Chris has put her energies into resentment of her perceived "victimizer," producing two severe consequences: Eleanor feels herself to be the victim of Chris's unreasonable hostility; Chris, in reality, has victimized herself.

Both sets of sisters come from middle class suburban homes with professional fathers. In Grace's case, a good relationship existed between the parents, leading to a warm, happy home atmosphere. Both mother and father treated the girls impartially and as individuals and encouraged each to find her own way. This respect and mutuality enabled Claire to see Grace's success not as victimization but as a challenge. Despite the usual competitive sibling element, the home environment also allowed Claire to feel close to her sister.

In the case of Chris and Eleanor, the relationship between the parents was not good. This resulted in a tense family atmosphere with a feeling of fragility, a sense that at any time the family might break up. At an early age, Eleanor emerged as the "responsible one," perceived by all—even though the parents may not have been aware of it—as holding the family together. The parents paid a great deal of attention to Eleanor, thus encouraging her in the role, and generally minimized Chris and a younger brother. The latter were victims, but they cooperated in the process because somehow the system they all had worked out provided an assurance of family stability.

Eleanor herself was a victim. Her parents brought their problems to her. She resented all the responsibilities she had to take over at too young an age—many counter to her own needs and desires—but behaved as if she had no choice. Rarely did siblings or parents express a thank-you or recognition of her efforts. The type of marital discord that existed between the parents and the solution they adopted for family maintenance led all of them to become victims.

The Family Hold

The family represents the most difficult area in which to change a victim pattern. A major thrust of Behavioral Psychotherapy is to make people understand why they (1) perpetuate family relationships that make them a victim and (2) cling to the same feelings with the same people that they had as a child.

It helps them learn how to adjust and shift their attitudes so that they can achieve a better relationship with their family—if it's possible.

Deep, primitive feelings characterize the various relationships within a family, and these relationships often are more impassioned than those encountered in marriage. With half of all American marriages ending in divorce, many men and women seem able to cast off a mate emotionally as well as actually. Yet the influence of siblings and parental attitudes seems to persist forever.

We deal with more than established habits. The very words *father, mother, sister, brother, cousin, aunt* produce a feeling of connection—whether good or not. We may have contact with a family member whom we haven't seen in years—or perhaps have never even met before—and yet we believe this person has some special relation to or claim on us.

The family structure develops its own characteristics, which influence family members. The family structure blocks and resists change. No matter how she tried as a child and teenager, Eleanor could not have stopped being the responsible one nor Chris the ignored, minimized one. If they had attempted to change, the family tension and disruption would have increased. The resulting pressures would have forced them to revert to the roles they yearned to leave behind, just to keep the peace.

But the family *has* to change. Parents age. Children grow up and move away. Circumstances alter. Because our ideas of family comfort and security persist and provide a sense of soothing (whether they are based on reality or illusion), we tend to maintain the same role in the family as we grow older—even when it's a painful victim role. For instance, a person may paradoxically experience a sense both of solace and enjoyment in being the family financial failure and getting $5,000 a year as a gift "to help out." Beyond this, we may subconsciously fear that if we or the others change, we will destroy the family—even if that family no longer exists.

When we were young, we could do little about our family relationships. We had to take on the roles demanded by the family structure, and if we were victimized, we couldn't do much about it. However, as adults, we don't have to let the pattern continue. Remember, we now have our own spouse, lover, children, boss. Ghosts from the past need not impact on them.

WHY A PERSON CONTINUES A FAMILY VICTIM PATTERN

Repetition of the Same Reactions as in the Past

The professional name for this kind of response is *reintegration*. In childhood a certain family situation would set off an automatic reaction—for example, anger would provoke punishment or obedience would result in approval. In the present, a situation or even some part of a situation resembling one from childhood still produces the same reaction. For example, now you're an adult, but when your father gives you the same kind of disapproving look he gave when you brought home a bad report card, you feel still eight years old and naughty.

Awareness of the pattern can help you change it.

THE CASE OF THE TWO BROTHERS

A five-year age difference existed between Jim and Phil. Older brother Jim grew up as a wild, macho kid and took delight in beating up the milder Phil. Phil learned to react to his older brother's treatment with surly obstinancy and to take his beating. Both became successful. Jim is one of Washington's most prosperous and respected lawyers. Phil runs a thriving business in New Jersey. Until recently, however, whenever the brothers met—a few times yearly—Phil always reverted to his surly obstinate manner, just as if he expected to get a beating.

A highly intelligent man, Phil has gained considerable awareness of this pattern. Recently Jim came to New York and the two brothers had dinner together. They argued over a triviality: Jim wanted Phil to drive him to the airport. Phil didn't want to and once again began to feel himself the same old underdog. But he caught himself, stopped the feeling, and stood up for himself. In a firm but nice way he told Jim that he had to be up early and could not drive him to the airport—Jim would have to take a taxi. Jim pressured but Phil insisted, "I can't," and Jim had to take a cab. Then Phil had a feeling of achievement far out of proportion to the situation. Not only had he resolved the problem, but he realized he could stand up for himself—he no longer had to be the younger sibling under-dog. Phil had finally broken his victim pattern.

Misconceptions About the Family and Its Different Members

Many of these beliefs may always have been untrue. You saw mother as "weak, helpless, and vulnerable," whereas mother, in reality, may have been a powerful victimizer, using her perceived weakness to control and dominate. You viewed father as a punitive disciplinarian, whereas father may have been and is a passive, benign man who simply goes along with mother's pressure to punish.

Or your beliefs may once have been correct but no longer are. Death has taken mother. Age has mellowed father. The sibling situation has changed. You're the oldest child. Your sister has become an investment banker, and you're still trying to find the right career. Somehow you feel, "She has usurped my role. As the elder, I should be the successful one."

Misconceptions can seriously affect our relations with family members and our responsibilities within the family. These are some common misconceptions:

■ That because these people are family, they will love us no matter what.

■ That even though we are grownups, our parents still have the power to punish us. Your father gives an order and even though you know it's silly, you still act as if he'll send you to your room if you don't obey. Even middle-aged, successful people provide their parents with this power. We have this belief because at the unconscious level we may still get comfort out of the thought "dad knows best." If we stand up to him, we destroy our illusion, take away the comfort, and may—because now we are in effect saying that we, rather than father, *know* best—end up the victim of our own feared inadequacies. Ask yourself: Are you obeying your parents out of remnants of childhood fear or out of adult, mature respect and an understanding of *their need*? The latter does not lead to victimization.

■ That our family is warmer and more caring than it is or, conversely, that other families are more warm and caring than ours. We often have illusions about our family or others' families. For emotional needs of our own we may distort the reality of our family relationships. For instance, every year some fifty members of the Jones family gather for a family picnic. Alternating locations, first, second, and third cousins come from all over to share a day of family togetherness. Few realize the hostility, even agony that lurks in this seeming family paradise. Aunt Martha puts down her sister, whom she hasn't seen for years. A daughter does not speak to her father, who has remarried. In actuality, the family is bound by feuds rather than by warmth and closeness. However, insiders and outsiders maintain an illusion of an idyllic family situation, an illusion fostered in part by the need to see it as such.

Perpetuation of Old Family Roles

We often hold on to roles of the past, even when they are no longer appropriate. Some common roles:

■ *The responsible one.* From childhood you've always taken on every burden, been the family doer, and you still fall into this assigned role. You feel that without your doing, the family would collapse. Your family encourages your behavior. But you can never do enough! For example, one of your sister's children becomes ill. At her request, you find a doctor who will come to the house. But your sister doesn't like the internist and blames you. You feel yourself to be the victim of her blame, and she feels herself to be the victim of your "incorrect choice." So the relationship with your sister becomes one based on mutually held bad feelings.

The *listener* represents a variant of the responsible one. Because you have a sympathetic quality, family members turn to you for sharing bad feelings. As an adult, you become the victim for two reasons: (1) You feel you have no choice; you must listen to your siblings' and parents' complaints; (2) when you try to express your own problems, the others don't listen—no reciprocity exists.

■ *The star.* This person is the favorite, the one who brings attention to the family, usually by a record of accomplishments outside the home. Often children carry out a parental fantasy; thus one sees the stage mothers who push their offspring to modeling, acting, or television fame. Thriving on the recognition from within the family or others, a child's own motivation to gain glory develops. Sometimes this may work. At other times it becomes both a burden and a pressure.

Siblings can compete for stardom. For example, one sixteen-year-old became a high school basketball star. But by doing extraordinary academic work, his younger brother also became a star. In other cases, the siblings of a star can feel helpless or ignored and give up. The family atmosphere and interplay determine the response.

■ *The forgotten one.* This person is the very opposite of the star, an individual who rarely receives notice. Even if you achieve something good, you're overshadowed by the star. Comments one teenager, "I get A's, too, but nobody talks about me. They just talk about Katy." However, this teenager, trained by family habits, perpetuates her victim role by never calling attention to her accomplishments.

■ *The clown.* You crack jokes and do funny things, especially when a difficult situation confronts you. As a child, you learned this technique to get the family to pay some attention to you. In later life, this becomes a habitual way of relating to people and often inhibits expression of feelings.

■ *The manipulator.* You want to control and manage other family members to get them to do what *you* want them to do. As a child you tried it by being seductive (girl to father, son to mother, siblings to each other), feigning illness, weakness, using charm. For example, one competitive and highly verbal younger brother manipulated the situation so that he could deliver a speech at his older brother's high school graduation party—and he stole the show. Perhaps you're still manipulating, victimizing family members by exploiting them. Some may revolt and hit back.

■ *The critic.* You find fault with everyone and everything. Using complaints, sarcasm, and teasing, you focus on the unfairness demonstrated by family, friends, teachers. You victimize others by showing them what they've done wrong. You gain strength not by building yourself up but by tearing others down.

■ *The scapegoat.* You are often the true family victim. You tend to get blamed for everything—sometimes directly, sometimes subtly. Mother has a cold because you left the window open, or sister arrived late for school because you lingered too long in the bathroom you share. The scapegoat serves a family function. As long as the rest of the family has him or her to blame, no one has to look at the real problems that exist. (Some evidence suggests that a relationship exists

between being the family scapegoat and becoming anorexic.)
The scapegoat sometimes can turn into the *black sheep* by doing
something so "shameful" that the family abandons or exiles him
or her.

Why do we perpetuate these family roles of the past when
they may no longer be appropriate—or even true?

Comments Dr. Mary FitzPatrick, clinical assistant professor at
Cornell University Medical College, "The role becomes part of
your heritage. It turns into the way you deal with difficulties. As
an adult, if you don't act in the role, you experience guilt and
anxiety. It relieves you to fit into the pattern."

Fulfillment of the role can also spur guilt and anxiety. In the
responsible role, you may take on an unrealistic responsibility.
For example, an older sister took on the responsibility of raising
a much younger brother. At age six, he died of an incurable
liver disease. Not only did she find it difficult to accept life
without a family member to care for—the role she had traditionally undertaken—but felt she should have saved him. Now
she lives with the burden of guilt, resulting in a depressed life-
style and increasingly unrealistic self-expectations.

If you now recognize that you are perpetuating an old role
that is no longer appropriate, don't be discouraged. *You can
change.*

THE CASE OF THE WOMAN WHO FEARED PARENTAL SEPARATION

Louise G. grew up as the "needy one," an only child, extremely
attached to her family and encouraged to make constant demands for time and attention. She had been living with George
R. for two years and they decided to marry. Suddenly Louise
found herself apprehensive and doing peculiar things. She was
spending much more time with her family and, when with
them, criticizing George, whom she really loved. Her parents
were getting upset, thinking the envisioned marriage a mistake.

"Is the problem between me and my parents?" was the first
question she asked me. Talking proved she was right. Using the
levels approach of Behavioral Psychotherapy, we found that (1)
at level two *(blocks),* she irrationally feared that marriage would
lead to a rift with her parents, and she couldn't imagine any

kind of separation; (2) at level three *(unconscious)*, her marriage to George would mean a sense of aloneness in the world without parental protection. They had trained her that whenever she became upset they would provide reassurance. She had maintained this childhood pattern, never sharing anything good with her family, only her weakness, suffering, and emotional fragility.

The goal of the Behavioral Psychotherapy treatment we devised was to give Louise and her parents a way of relating to one another based on strength, not weakness. We worked out a three-part action program for Louise. She was to

    1. Share more and more good things about her times with George with her parents. She was given the assignment to call every night and reveal some joy or triumph that had occurred during the day. She was not to report anything negative.

    2. Stop badmouthing her lover (in her distorted thinking, she had viewed this as loyalty to her parents) and increase all possible contacts between George and her parents, thus fostering closeness between them.

    3. Set a date for the wedding.

The treatment worked. Her parents began to view Louise as an independent adult. She began to see herself the same way. Louise and George married. Now she has completely reversed roles. No longer the needy child, she deals with her parents with the aim of fostering closeness rather than prompting care and attention through emotional demands.

The following quiz may help you correct your misconceptions and gain a better idea of actual family roles.

FAMILY VICTIM QUIZ

Goal: To help you see how your earlier family atmosphere affects your present life

    ■ Was your family mainly *authoritarian* (rules were laid down and you had to follow them), *laissez-faire* (permissive, you could do as you liked), or *democratic* (with limits and responsibilities but rational ones that you could discuss and challenge)? The greatest chance of being victimized occurs in an authoritarian atmosphere, the least in a democratic one; the laissez-faire atmosphere falls in the middle.

■ To what extent does this atmosphere exist today in relations with your parents and siblings? The authoritarian atmosphere, for example, may endure but in a different way. Today, instead of the parent, the oldest child may have taken over the authoritarian role.

■ What is the atmosphere within your current family (your spouse and children)? Do you see a similarity between your own current family and your childhood one? Is this the way you want it to be or just an automatic carryover?

■ As a child, who did you believe had the most power in your family?

■ Thinking back, did that person really have the power *or did someone else?* Does this person still have the power and use it in the same way? If so, does your response to the situation remain the same?

■ When did you feel you were the victim of family members? What circumstances set you up at the time for victimization? Are these forces still at work? For example, as a child you felt your parents were so involved in one another and their work that they had no time for you. Now you and your children still feel victimized by your parents' obsessive self-involvement.

Your answers may help to point out *how much you sacrifice in adult personal life to maintain your childhood role.*

When Everyone's a Grown-up

Understanding the past will not be enough. We must understand family victimization in the present. We, our parents, and reality all play major parts.

Parents may continue to use power tactics. When we were children they did have more knowledge and the responsibility for us. Now, despite radically changed circumstances, they may continue to perpetuate a situation that no longer exists. They may seem to do this out of good intentions, but in actuality, they still feel they hold parental power and deny our grown-up status.

Or they may have *mixed motives*. For example, one father, a third generation lawyer, felt his middle daughter to be the brightest of his four children and insisted she carry on the family tradition and become an attorney. She did, and hates it. Rationally, her father thought he was exerting his influence for his daughter's good. On another level, however, he also wanted to show *his* pride in the family profession and carry on the tradition. If you are in such a situation, think through the parental considerations but make a decision based on *your* motives, not *theirs*.

Parents may have a need to *continue the control* they had over us as children and thereby make us adult victims. They offer advice about things they don't understand (for example, "You should get married . . . Why don't you have a job with a weekly paycheck?" to a respected documentary film producer). A mother may visit a thirty-year-old daughter and rearrange carefully collected antique furniture. To mask their desire for power, such parents frequently use anxiety and concern to exercise their control. They ask adult children to telephone after they arrive at a destination; they even call in stormy weather to advise, "Wear your boots."

To gain or maintain power, they may use a weakness of their own—either imagined or real. For example, the mother of a married thirty-five-year-old makes him travel to her suburban condo every weekend to perform her carpentry chores. Or, refusing to do what she must do to establish a new social life for herself, a comparatively young widow insists that social life stem from her son and his Saturday visits. Unconsciously, she uses her needs to maintain control.

Whatever their motives, parents often continue to feel responsibility for their grown children as if they were still young children. This may make the children victims because the parents continue to do too much.

Because they have their own current motives, adult children can turn parents into victims.

Grown offspring may continue to make financial demands. For example, one woman got divorced in a messy case with suits and countersuits. The woman's mother, a fifty-seven-year-old widow who had recently been fired from her advertising agency executive post because of age discrimination, used her only capital—the company stock she had acquired from twenty years of hard work—to pay for the daughter's expensive lawyer. The daughter is making no effort to pay back the money. The mother barely manages to make ends meet. Through her efforts to help her daughter, the mother has become the victim of the daughter's selfishness.

Other immature grown children resent it when parents stop supporting them. Or they frown on parental behavior. Just as parents have fantasies about or set standards for the way their children should live, so grown children have similar fantasies and set standards for their parents. They expect mother and father to conform to these fantasies, particularly when they concern the "ideal family." The idea of a parent remarrying may make a son or daughter feel completely victimized. One thirty-year-old man felt heartbroken when his father remarried. He refuses to visit the father's new home and the father feels rejected and abandoned.

Some grown children refuse to take any legitimate responsibility for aging parents. Forgetting what their parents did for them in their youth, they display only meanness, negligence, or power needs. "Let them live on their Social Security," they chorus as they head for a European vacation. They rationalize their irresponsible, ungenerous behavior with all sorts of reasons—some true, some false.

RIGHTS: A MATTER OF "YES" OR "NO"

With family members, we must possess an understanding of our rights. Usually this means when to say yes or say no. Either response may disrupt the family system or run counter to our conscious feelings. The consequences may run the gamut from joy to perpetual hatred as a result of a family member's decision. Sometimes it's hard to say no within the family unit because then we refuse a person for whom we care deeply, not just an acquaintance or coworker. Conversely, saying yes may at times make us feel like a patsy. A good guideline to apply is: *"Will I respect myself more if I say yes or no?"*

Here are three family situations. How would you have handled them?

Example One: Mary A. had a good future at a well-known

brokerage house but wasn't earning a lot at the moment. Her entrepreneur father, Doug A., had an apartment in a new Denver condo for which he paid more carrying charges than he could afford. He had some savings but no job at the moment. Every month he dunned Mary for the next month's mainte- nance. Despite knowing how he exaggerated his plight, she still said yes and paid the condo charges for eighteen months, giving up all entertainment and vacations for herself. Then her father acquired a wonderful job as a traveling sales manager and promised to repay her out of future earnings. Mary really loved her father and experienced only delight at his long- delayed success. She experienced no sense of sacrifice, only pride that she had helped.

Example Two: Eugene S. had not been a ne'er-do-well but had come close to that. A salesman, now forty, he had lost a series of jobs until he married a shrew of a woman who talked him into going into business for himself. He did well, but when the couple wanted a very expensive Michigan Avenue co-op in Chicago, he couldn't come up with enough money to satisfy the board and bank. He asked his older sister's monied husband to cosign a loan—"We're family," he emphasized. His sister felt that, family or not, she did not want to subject her husband into taking a possible loss. She insisted he say no to her brother.

Two years later, Eugene had developed a highly successful business and become far more responsible. He didn't need anyone to cosign when he bought a co-op.

Example Three: Virginia R. had a sister, Ro, and brother, Bill. When they were all in their mid-forties, there was a flap over two family businesses. Ro kicked Virginia out of the one in which they had shared co-ownership. Bill kicked them *both* out of the second business. For four years silence existed among the three of them. Then Virginia decided to make two peace ges- tures. She wrote her brother in Seattle, suggesting, "Can't we forget the past?" She called her sister nearby, making a childish forgiveness gesture by asking, "Will you water my plants while I take a vacation?" Both said yes. All feel better, although Vir- ginia comments sadly, "Too much has gone on. We love one another but don't *like* one another." However, they have ac- cepted the idea of a superficial sibling relationship, glossing over the rage they still feel, and Virginia admits to an awareness that Ro and Bill may play repeat performances.

THE FAMILY BILL OF RIGHTS

Do you have the right to evict your adult child who refuses to get a job and wants you to support him?

Do you have the right to give or not give a contribution to a favorite family charity?

Do you have the right to turn down the request of a parent who brought you up?

Each family bill of rights should be individual, but it should have respect—both for yourself and family needs—as a base. It might read something like the following:

I feel I have the right to feel any way I do about a family member. No law says I have to love each and every one of them.

I have the right to choose the way I act toward each family member. I have the right to get along or not get along with any of my siblings the way I choose to do at that moment. And I have the right to change my mind.

I have a right to consider my own needs rather than my family's needs. My aim is to find an acceptable balance between the two and thus lessen the chance of being a victim. Under this category falls the right to avoid certain family functions—such as the wedding of a third cousin whom I've always hated.

I have the right to do things with my life that other family members will disapprove of—spend all my savings on a year in India, switch careers, marry the person of my choice, whom my parents don't like. I have the right to be myself and fulfill myself *my way*, even though this differs from the way my family wants me to be.

I have the right to prefer friends to family.

I have the right to apply the above rights, not just to parents, siblings, and cousins, but to my own children, spouse, and in-laws.

Family Reconstruction

The following action guidelines involve everything from your own behavior and thinking—spasmodic or continual, conscious or unconscious—to family reality problems. How you handle yourself will determine whether or not you are or become the victim.

SET LIMITATIONS FOR
YOURSELF AND OTHERS

Above all, you must have realistic expectations of the members of your family. That includes realizing that a lifelong "hate you" problem will not change suddenly to a "love you" situation.

For instance, Jan, the elder of two sisters, always behaved like the good sister. She had bought her sister clothes for college, given her a key to her apartment before each married, then over the years bestowed present upon present on the sister's two sons. When Jan became seriously ill, Norma did not phone, even though her two sons, by now grown, briefed her about Jan's illness.

Suddenly, Jan realized her hopes were unrealistic. Norma had never done one nice thing for her. Instead she had been sarcastic and critical ("Why do you wear black—it makes you look like grandma"; "Don't come to me for help when you're old and sick"). Jan finally realized that she was the emotional victim of her own expectations, not of her sister, who was just as selfish in middle age as she had been as a child. Jan has learned she can cope with the meanness—and now with the false hopes that had previously victimized her the most.

Realize the limitations of your family members as people. To maintain a good relationship, you may want to ignore certain aspects of a sibling's or other relative's personality. For example, Tom is a Boston internist, his brother Mark a Hollywood lawyer. The former is honest, the latter cuts corners. Yet straightforward Tom loves his brother and wants the relationship to continue to be a close one. He feels he must ignore the less pleasant aspects of his brother's personality. He explains, "When my wife tells me, 'Your brother does crooked deals,' she isn't telling me anything I don't know. But voicing these thoughts disrupts my relationship with my brother, and I become *her* victim. I choose not to. I would rather ignore my brother's business behavior and continue to see and care for him."

In this case, the brother won't change, and the marital happiness Tom and his wife enjoy has more chance of enduring if she keeps quiet. She should respect her husband's needs.

You can limit your listening to family problems. The habit of telling all can victimize you far beyond time pressures. You can

become a family emotional victim through being drawn into
problems that are just none of your business. For example,
when twenty-four-year-old Jane S., a young social worker in a
New England city, returned home for weekends, each parent
took her aside to relate separate versions of a miserable marriage. Jane admits sadly, "They told me things about each other
that no one should hear."

Jane tried to take action by suggesting marriage counseling.
Neither father nor mother would listen. Then she said frankly,
"I won't listen any more. You keep telling me you stay together
because of your own neuroses. Work it out between you, and
don't make me your victim."

Limit the choices you take on. Ask yourself: "What will happen if
I don't do it? Is there another way? Will someone else take
over? Does it really matter?" A difference exists when you
perform a chore because help is needed or do it because you
yourself have some inner need—to relieve guilt, to give yourself
a certain image, to show up your siblings. *You* may be the basic
problem because you make yourself feel worthy by being put
upon.

It's never too late to set a limitation. The elements that affect your
choice may change. For example, while he looks for a job, your
younger brother comes to live with you. You say, "Come." Your
spouse resents the intrusion. Brother treats you like an outsider
in your own home. He does little to seek a job. If you still keep
him as a boarder, you are paying too big a price. You're a victim
of your emotional choice to do too much for a sibling. Ask
yourself, What is a reasonable price to pay for the sibling
relationship—or any family relationship?

Tip: In situations like this, listen to friends who say, "I don't
know how you can stand it." In your case, your friends may be
wrong, but take them seriously and also take a new look at your
behavior.

BE DIRECT

Indirectness with your family can often produce
unhappiness and resentment. *Ask for what you want.* For example, at the relatively young age of thirty-five, Mary S. had a

heart attack. Her mother, who lives a thousand miles away, had always told her, "If you need me, I'll come." In early May, when a weak Mary returned from the hospital to her home, she called her mother and suggested, "Why don't you come up?" The mother said yes, but as she was involved in a bowling tournament, said she would arrive at the end of June. Mary was upset. The very next day, she called again and emphasized, "Hey, Mom, I need you *now*. Are you coming or not?" Her mother's response: "Of course, why didn't you say so?"

Because they think parents and siblings should volunteer to do things, some people won't ask. To ask spoils your fantasy, so you remain indirect. The other person doesn't realize your need and does nothing. You feel more and more of an emotional victim.

The direct approach will not always win. Simply to say an honest "I want you to" or "I don't want you to" to a resentful parent or sibling doesn't always achieve the result you want.

Sometimes the *feeling of being a victim keeps you from solving the problem* when the direct approach has failed. You may have to settle the matter via an outside source. For example, two sisters who had always been unable to get along, had a terrible fight over a gate-leg table, a worthless piece of 1925 mahogany that was in a hall in the vacation home they shared jointly with their two brothers. When they sold the house, the brothers wanted none of the furniture. Jill and Laura wanted only one piece— the worthless gate-leg table, because it had belonged to their mother as a little girl. After an exchange of vituperative letters, Jill gave in—and then stopped all contact with her sister. Their victim feelings kept them from solving the problem.

A year later Jill's husband thought of a solution. "You should have said, "Let's get someone in—a mediator—to make the decision. You both took things from the house through the years. Let a paid expert decide."

"Why didn't you think of that at the time?" asked Jill.

Said her husband, "Jill, the fight was about more than the table. You were too involved in the power struggle and the unfairness of it to have thought through a fair solution."

After further analysis, the gate-leg table now sits in Laura's house. The two sisters have reconciled.

RECOGNIZE THAT SOME FAMILY PROBLEMS HAVE NO SOLUTIONS

Realize this and you won't feel the victim. However, often there are some steps you can take to try to cope with seemingly unsolvable realities like sick or aging parents.

You can try to make a deal. The key word is *try.* Deals don't always work. For example, your father has a stroke and you, thinking he will recover fairly soon, agree to care for him. You overcommit yourself. The situation becomes prolonged. You realize you've made a deal you can't keep and try to back out. Your siblings become furious with you and won't negotiate. You can keep trying to effect some sort of deal, but remember, family members don't look at the problem objectively as they would at a business deal. Laying out money for another family member may symbolize something to you (hurt, rejection as a child). Even though you can afford to give financially, you can't or won't do it. Sometimes one family member gains enough gratification to assume the responsibility. But with all those phantoms from the past present, making a deal over a major family problem may not be easy.

When you have a severe family problem, take every action you can to solve it. Get information from organizations like Cancer Care and Alzheimer's Disease International. Seek professional help from social workers and geriatric counselors. Figure out alternatives. Do what you can do. Face the fact that there may be nothing you can do. You may have to live with it as best you can or choose the lesser of two evils.

THE CASE OF THE RELUCTANT PARENTS

Everyone in the Powell family felt like a victim. The elderly parents had retired to Orange County, California, where Paul Powell, the elder married son, lived. The other two grown children resided in the East. All the care for the septuagenarian parents (they both had weak hearts and high blood pressure) fell on the elder brother. He was also the sole sibling with money. His brother and sister made just one contribution: Each came for an annual two-week visit to spell him. Feeling exploited, Paul constantly berated the others on the phone: "This just can't go on." Their reply: "We can't do more." Because of the fact that he spent more time with his parents than his wife, Paul's marriage was rapidly coming apart.

Paul consulted a social worker. The obvious solution: to put the parents in a nursing home to relieve the daily care, with Medicare picking up part of the expenses. But the parents didn't want to go. They wanted their son as daily nursemaid. Paul was faced with a clear-cut choice: keep his marriage or keep his parents happy. He couldn't do both. This is a highly individual matter, but Paul picked his wife. He put his parents in a home with their own room, a schedule of daily activities, and twenty-four-hour health services. He felt he had no other choice. Now they are doing very well, and so is he!

START PRACTICING INDEPENDENCE OF THOUGHT AND ACTION

Many people confuse independence with isolation or rebellion, but often rebellion represents the opposite of independence. The family still controls you, but instead of automatic compliance with the wishes of family members, you automatically act *against* them. Your response is not the result of a mature decision. You are still acting the part of a victimized child.

Some Independence Basics

■ You can call on your family for help, advice, or guidance when you need it, but avoid feeling that without their counsel you are a helpless nothing. Learn to evaluate what they tell you and then make your own decision. Recognize that the family serves merely as a supplementary source of practical and emotional support.

■ Keep in mind that often the dependency you have learned within the family carries over to many other situations. If you learn to become more independent within the family, this may generalize to other situations, and you may find yourself less of an overall victim.

■ Relinquish that childhood feeling that family knows best. In actuality, your judgment may be better than theirs. If nevertheless you do as they say, you will feel resentful and end up the victim—not of them, but of your own misconceptions and thinking. No matter how your family pressures you to be dependent, you are the one who goes along with it. You say yes when mother selects your clothing and follow dad's business advice even though he knows nothing about the stock market. *You are the one—not your mother or father—who has to change.*

■ Give yourself *independence assignments* as part of your independence program.

Isolate one area where you feel unsure of yourself and usually seek advice. For example, you usually ask your father how to lay out your garden, your mother for a dinner menu. Think about a particular area like that and decide first what is best for you. Then go and consult the family. Take time to evaluate their advice. It may turn out to be good; in that case you've learned something. Your ideas may turn out to be better. This enables you to see your family's limitations. Do not try to convince them you are right. *Just do what seems right to you.*

REALITY PERCEPTION QUIZ

Goal: To help you see your family as it is today

Step One: View each family member as that person is today.

What would his/her best friend say about that person?

What would his/her worst enemy say about that person?

If you were not a family member, how close a relationship would you want with that person?

Step Two: Ask yourself "now and then" questions to see how you look at things today compared with how you perceived them when you were young and helpless.

How much could you confide in that person?

How much did/does that person interfere with your life?

How much did/does that person respect you?

How much did/do you respect him/her as a person?

What you can learn from this quiz: To see your childhood family realistically for the kind of people they are today. Once you understand the current realities, you can work out the kind of relationship you want with the kind of people you know they are—or have become.

How to Cope with Family Growth and Change

As a family grows and changes, a different kind of family may emerge. For example, Alex and Tina married and merged families—his three children, her two. In their Ohio Victorian house, life seemed idyllic. At Christmas the family living room resembled a scene from a magazine cover—all togetherness, cheer, love, a giant tree.

But as the family grew up, a new organization emerged with changed feelings and values. Alex and Tina are Catholic; it upset them when his son got divorced. His older daughter married a man who stole her painfully acquired savings. Tina's daughter married and moved many miles away. Her son can't keep a job. Nowadays, at Christmas, even though some of the children are always there, the living room seems lonely. Because their expectations have not been fulfilled, Tina and Alex feel victimized. But life can do this. The old family unit changes, giving place to new.

Or, as we get older, we can change our position in the family structure completely—and not even know it. But we have the power to adjust to these changes.

THE CASE OF THE UNAWARE ACHIEVER

Sally S. grew up in a comfortable suburban home, where her family always petted her. There was a reason for this. At seven, she had come down with "incipient tuberculosis," and for the next three years rose at 10 A.M., napped after lunch, got up, went back to bed at 5 P.M., and had a private tutor. She remembers, "I thought of myself as a fragile person, a victim of circumstances. That's how my family saw me. This feeling of being helpless warped my life."

Sally went to a progressive college where she had a breakdown because "this school was such a departure from my previously structured life."

She married young and chose magazine writing as a career. This is how she explains her choice: "Writing didn't require aggression of any kind. I always felt I couldn't do anything. I had no mental or physical strength. Even when I became a mother, my father thought of me as 'that sick little girl.' He would listen to my brother's advice, not to me."

At work, through a series of regimes at different publishing firms, people complimented her, "You're a survivor." She says simply, "I couldn't believe it."

Her basic family unit changed. Her mother died painfully of cancer at age fifty-five. Sally was there for her. Her father became "my dependent" for twenty years ("I took care of his every need"). She has seen her brother through three marriages and coped with his feelings when the children from his second marriage sided with their mother.

Promoted at work, Sally became the head of a firm that collapsed. Three weeks later, at fifty-four, she had another job.

She tells of a recent weekend: "I was thinking about my life and remembering that emotionally frail girl I had been. Suddenly, I knew that in my mature years I had become the Rock of Gibraltar. My son says he's always seen me that way. From the little girl in bed that everyone took care of, I now take care of everyone. Suddenly *I've* become the matriarch."

But, thinking about it, Sally realizes that it is not a case of "suddenly." ("There was no one else to take on the family responsibilities. I did them by sheer will. I felt I had to.") She claims she survived at work because she realized "that the nicey-nice way I had been brought up didn't work in the professional world. I stopped letting myself be everyone's victim, took more risks by asking for more difficult jobs, and felt much more secure." She adds, "When my cousins criticized me because I was a working mother, I felt strong because I could handle the two jobs well, even though I got up at five in the morning to do so. I always tried to leave my job in time to have dinner with my son. Somehow because I *had* to do certain things, I learned to do them. In the process I became confident." The fact of success in itself did not bring about emotional change. It came because Sally *allowed* herself to realize she had ability and developed an "I can do it" attitude.

As you deal with emotional victimization in your family, you must realize that change takes place continually with you, them, and the relationship. If you don't like what they have done to you in the past or do in the present, you can effect a change that works *in your favor.* Your own permission and desire are all you need. Change your behavior to yourself, and you will change your behavior to your family.

4 □ Getting Started in Behavioral Psychotherapy Training

Use the 5R approach to change your actions and psychology—even if they represent a lifetime pattern. In Behavioral Psychotherapy terms, this means *recognition* of the problem, *remembering* childhood experiences that make you victim-prone, then *rethinking*, *retraining*, and *reevaluating* the ways you react to people and the world around you.

We have seen numerous people do this. You can, too.

Begin Retraining

Buy a looseleaf notebook. This will serve as your Behavioral Psychotherapy Workbook. Keep it in a convenient place—at your desk or bedside table. You will be using it for the two quizzes in this chapter, for many exercises throughout the book, as a memory recall bank, and to learn new ideas and ways to do things.

Recognize Your Victim Areas

Admittedly, it's difficult for all of us to change a lifelong pattern of being the victim. Before you can improve any situation that bothers you, you should know what kind of victim you tend to be (an exaggerator, a "kick me" person, a misperceiver, or a know-not victim), and your typical reactions under certain circumstances.

VICTIM PROBLEM INVENTORY

This Victim Problem Inventory should help your self-diagnosis and help you understand the typical victim situations that we all deal with and react to in our everyday lives.

Situation One: Your college roommate of twenty years ago moves in a mere five blocks from you. You expected to have a close relationship, but she rarely calls. Upset, you convince yourself she is being deliberately inconsiderate. Obsessing on this "slight," you feel worse and worse.

Analysis: You exaggerate reality. It's easy to see why you feel disappointed, but the victimization and "unfairness" stem from the fantasy that you and your ex-roommate should have the same relationship you had back in college. Because you insist that reality should fit that fantasy, you make yourself miserable.

Situation Two: After twenty years of marriage, your husband leaves you for another woman. You refuse to see friends and instead sit home and cry. Your new refrain becomes "There are no men around for me."

Analysis: Yes, you're a victim. There's nothing you can do about your departed spouse. But you *can* rebuild your life. Abandon the paralysis and *act*.

Situation Three: You're a very attractive woman and fall in love with a thrice-divorced man. He makes it clear that he has no desire for remarriage. Still, you have hopes. Eventually he leaves you for another attractive woman. Feeling his victim, you wonder, "What does she have that I lack?"

Analysis: This is a "kick me" situation. The new girl friend knows just what to expect: no marriage. Because she has no false expectations and accepts what he offers (looks, money) she does not end up the victim.

Situation Four: At a meeting of department heads, you bring up a good point, but your boss ignores it. You feel resentful.

Analysis: Because you misinterpret the situation, you think you're a victim when you're not. In reality, the boss wanted to follow his own agenda and deferred your suggestion for another time. Another example of this kind of rejection: You smile at a coworker who fails to respond. *You* don't know he has just been threatened with loss of his job. Or, close friends who give a Valentine Day's party every year did not invite you this year. "What did I do wrong?" you ask yourself and feel terrible. What you don't know, because you failed to keep in touch with them, was that this year your friends didn't give their annual bash. They took a trip to Japan instead.

Situation Five: For years you've been in charge of admissions at your local annual bazaar. You're tired of the chore but feel committed. This year the group president offers you the chance to take over journal sales. Fearing you can't do it well enough, you say no and agree to continue the annual chore that bores you.

Analysis: You are a victim who does not know it. Because of your need to avoid challenge, you miss out on the chance to meet new people and do interesting new tasks. If you liked your annual assignment, the refusal to take on a new one would be okay—but you don't.

Situation Six: You have a wife who constantly criticizes you. You don't realize how inappropriate her behavior is. But when a friend fails to return a book he has borrowed, you do get mad and feel abused.

Analysis: Again, you're a know-not victim. Unable to admit to anger at your wife, you deny and *displace* it. For a variety of reasons, you can't let yourself recognize the bad behavior of your wife. (1) It might disrupt the relationship and you require the stability of the marriage. (2) On a deeper level, to attack your wife might be like attacking mother, which is sinful. How can a little kid stand up to mother?—it's dangerous. Mother will tell father, who will punish you. (This may sound melodramatic, but some people actually function in this way.) You displace the victim feelings aroused by your wife's behavior—feelings that you're unable to admit—to some trivial, safer situation—in this case, getting angry at your friend who didn't return the book.

Situation Seven: You and your spouse work at full-time jobs and attend night school. On weekends you must each tend to your own chores. Meanwhile both sets of able, middle-aged parents press you into mowing their lawns, washing their cars, and fixing up around their homes on Saturdays and Sundays.

Analysis: Again, you're an unknowing victim who thinks that you have no alternative but to say yes. Possibly, you're still going along with the childhood dictum "Obey your parents." However, as an adult with your own needs and pressures, much as you desire to be respectful to your family and feel responsibility for them, you must find a balance between their needs and yours.

You may have a constant sense that you're a victim or pushover, but it's vague. Before we get to work on any deep emotional difficulty, it will help to spot the major trouble areas.

The following quiz serves as a warm-up exercise to sensitize you to your own problems.

QUIZ ONE: VICTIM ALERT

Goal: To help you define the specific areas where you have problems, so you can handle them better

Step One: In your workbook, take a separate page and note down the following list, leaving plenty of space between entries:

      Situation One: Impersonal
        ■ Salespeople

- Service people
- Doormen, taxi drivers
- Strangers

Situation Two: At work
- With superiors
- With peers
- With subordinates

Situation Three: Social relationships
- Same sex acquaintances
- Opposite sex acquaintances
- Same sex friends
- Opposite sex friends

Situation Four: Personal
- Spouse/lover
- Children
- Family
- In-laws

Step Two: For each of the situations, answer the following questions:

- Do you ever feel the victim with any of these people in the indicated type of situations? Consider them carefully one by one. (*Caution:* Be careful not to give a quick *no* answer. Stop and think. In any case where the answer is yes, follow through with the balance of the questions below.)

- Does the victim reaction happen rarely, sometimes, or frequently?

- What kind of victim are you most frequently in the situation? Do you exaggerate the rudeness of a waiter in a restaurant just as much as you do that of your boss? Do you feel that the whole world has combined forces to constantly put you down?

- Does the victimization produce a major impact on your life? For example, does it lead to avoidance of certain areas or influence your relationships with the people involved? Or, do you lead a limited social life where others always take advantage of you and then opt to stay home rather than risk this victimization?

- How does the mood you happen to be in at the moment influence your victimization? For example, when do you tend to be a victim—when you feel down . . . kindly . . . angry?

- Does being a victim have a large impact on your feelings about yourself? Does being a victim influence your self-image? Would you feel differently about yourself if you weren't so often a victim?

Step Three: After you answer these questions, analyze your responses.

■ Where is your area of greatest difficulty? It may be with the opposite sex in a close relationship; at work it may happen in a peer situation.

■ Where is your area of greatest freedom?

■ Which area would be easiest for you to change? For instance, it might be easiest with a same sex friend.

■ Are you the same kind of victim all the time or do you vary? For example, with peers on the job, you may exaggerate reality, while with the opposite sex, you may set yourself up to be a victim.

What You Can Learn from This Quiz
1. *Identification of the less important situations.* This is a valuable determination because the new knowledge may help you recognize the more important situations and thus find a link that affects your entire life-style and personality.

2. *Whether your victim behavior varies or stays the same.* If it varies in different situations—you're an exaggerator with superiors, a "kick me" victim with opposite sex friends, and a know-not victim with your lover or spouse—you may have to work on a series of different problems, thinking styles, or behavior deficits. If, for instance, you're a continual exaggerator, chances are you are dealing with an overall pattern that, while it varies in intensity, remains basically the same in all areas. You will have fewer problems to work on, but over the years they will have become set and may require greater persistence to change.

Remember: Use the Preconscious

According to the *Comprehensive Textbook of Psychiatry/II,* "The preconscious includes all ideas, thoughts, past experiences, and other memory impressions that can consciously be recalled with effort."

In other words, we are able to *recall* certain memories from our past that we can use to change behavior in the present. To distinguish between the preconscious and unconscious, authorities often use the following example. Think of memory as a piece of wood in a basin of water. Two things can happen. The piece of wood can float on top of the water and we just *have to look* and see it. That is the preconscious. Or our hand may hold the piece of wood under the water's surface, preventing it from rising to the top. That is the unconscious. The hand represents *repression*, which keeps us from remembering.

We all can benefit from an *investigative reporting job on ourselves*. The following quiz should help you to dig into your preconscious, uproot long forgotten memories, and understand the effect.

QUIZ TWO: YOUR CHILDHOOD HISTORY

Goal: To use preconscious memories as aids in understanding your present victim behavior

Step One: In your workbook, take a page and make headings for each decade of your life. Under each write a situation you can remember in which you were a victim: childhood (teacher unfairly punished you); teens (dad didn't let you have the car on Saturday night); twenties (your friend got the job you wanted even though you deserved it—he had pull); thirties (a friend went for and landed the job you wanted after you told her about your hopes of getting it).

Step Two: For each incident, note:
- Who or what made you the victim
- What your predominant feelings were at the time
- Any fantasy you recall connected with the incident
- How you attempted to cope
- Whether you think it had any lasting effect on you

Step Three: Contrast the changes as you grew older and in the present. Have changes occurred in who victimizes you and how you respond?

Step Four: Reminisce about people in your life at any early age—in relation to you and among themselves. In the process of calling up memories we have not thought about for a long time, we sometimes find ghosts remain, hidden but there, recallable and extractable.

Use the following three points as memory triggers:

1. *How your parents acted with others.* If our parents were strong, assertive people, we tend to model ourselves on them and have only a minimal chance of ending up a victim. If they coped only by compliance and placating, we are quite apt to absorb their habits and in turn wind up as victims. For example, if they complained constantly about the "unfairness" of their friends, we may have learned to do the same thing. Or we may react in a different way and constantly fight our friends' "unfairness" even when it does not exist.

2. *How your parents acted toward you.* If our parents handled us in an irrational way, we may experience *learned* helplessness that influences our whole concept of life. As a child we saw that no matter what we did, our parents responded only on the basis of their needs and moods. We learned that there was no point in trying to cope with such an unresponsive environment, so we stopped trying. The constructive adjustment would be to realize the irrationality of our parents. Most of us can't do that. Instead we just believe we're helpless.

3. *The manner in which your parents punished you.* The punitive responses of our parents may affect the way we punish ourselves as adults. If they were sharp and quick to punish, paying attention only to the negative, we very likely learned to become punitive with ourselves, to accent what *we do wrong* rather than what we do well.

What You Can Learn from Your Childhood History Quiz

1. Pattern clarification. In the present, your main problem may seem to be with your boss, but your childhood history shows little trouble with authority figures. Instead it reveals much victimization with people of the opposite sex. Thus, because of a knowledge of your own past problems, you know you need to look into the problem with your boss, who is of the opposite sex, in terms of your relations with the opposite sex rather than in terms of relations with authorities.

2. Change. By studying early forms of victimization, you may learn that even though your present victim pattern *seems* quite different from the early one, it really represents only a variation of the childhood form with the same key core. For example, your mate makes a simple request and you resent it. In looking back, you remember how your siblings forced you to do unreasonable things. Now you apply this sense of victimization to your mate.

You may discover that you've become a victim in situations that you never were in before or have become a different type of victim. Often you can pinpoint the reasons for this. You may have experienced a great life change (first job, first serious long-term relationship) that makes different behavioral demands on you or stirs up previously controlled conflicts.

Do an investigative reporting job on yourself by exploration of your preconscious memories. The beginning will stay the same but you can change the end.

THE CASE OF THE LAWYER WHO USED HIS PRECONSCIOUS TO FIND HIMSELF

When Joe B. came to me for Behavioral Psychotherapy treatment, he complained about assertiveness problems in dealing with the senior partners at his law firm. Even when he was right, Joe couldn't stand up for himself. He possessed the skills, but his feelings of unworthiness kept him from using them with authority figures. In discussing this, it seemed that this feeling of "unworthiness" stemmed from his own comparisons of himself with his adored deceased father. Even when Joe talked about himself at work, practically every other word concerned his father, who also had been a lawyer. As a child, Joe had felt such enormous pride when his father took him to court, and he loved the subsequent luncheons at which his father walked around the restaurant greeting people. He felt his father had been perfect.

Clearly Joe's problem in the present related to his father in his past. I asked him to reminisce about his father. Was there any time his father had *not* been perfect?

At first Joe had trouble recalling anything about his personal god. Then he remembered how, at age eight, he had returned home from a visit to a friend one day and found his father reading his diary, which he had left beside the bed. Joe had been horrified. His father had just laughed.

This memory triggered others. Looking back, Joe forced himself to recall how unfairly his father had dealt with all his children, never listening to their side of things, only to their mother's complaints. Joe also remembered a conversation in which a neighbor called his father "obsequious" and that, in the restaurants where Joe had been so proud of him, in fact his father had made all the overtures. With sorrow, Joe remembered a detail he had pushed to the back of his mind: His father had barely achieved partnership in his law firm.

Through these preconscious reminiscences Joe saw that he had (1) some unconscious need to glorify his father and (2) a fear of seeing his father's weaknesses. He had maintained the fiction of his father's strength by exaggerating the fiction of his own weakness in comparison with his father.

As so often happens when we face our fears as Joe did, the fear lessened. With treatment, Joe found he no longer had the need to make himself feel weak and helpless with authorities. He understood that his work insecurities stemmed from a false goal of trying to live up to a man who existed only in Joe's head. Thus he overcame his inhibitions in dealing with his senior partners and became able to use the business skills he already possessed. From a personal point of view, Joe no longer admires his father in the same way, but because now he sees his father's weaknesses, somehow he loves him more.

Caution: Do not take your preconscious recall as revealing feelings about the unconscious. The defense mechanism of *isolation* may distort things. This technical term means we remember only part of a specific incident and fail to see its application to our current lives. For example, Joe remembered all his adoring feelings about his father but had to repress those feelings that made adoration of his father so important.

Remember: Find Clues to Your Unconscious

With the preconscious, we may have forgotten events, but we can call them back.

With the *unconscious*, we deliberately keep memories and feelings buried (like pushing that piece of wood under the water) because allowing them to surface produces terrible feelings that make us feel anxious and guilty. This need to *repress* serves a protective function. Many people claim the whole course of psychoanalysis is the analysis of *resistance*. Understand that resistance protects you; it blocks out recall of some aspect of reality that is too painful or distressing for you to deal with on a conscious level. But that self-protective response may be contributing to a pattern of victimization.

It is not easy to take your hand off that piece of wood! Uncovering your unconscious is hard. That's why psychoanalysis takes so long. It would be grandiose or fraudulent to say that this book or any book will provide a direct path to deeply buried material. If you find yourself persistently blocked in any attempt to change, awareness of the previously stated victim gains may help you reach down to the deep feelings that lie far down in Level Three—the unconscious. Ask yourself:

■ Do you gain good feelings like superiority, safety, or comfort from remaining the victim?

■ Does being the victim serve a defensive purpose? For example, does evasion of responsibility let you focus on external problems rather than on confronting your own problems?

■ Have the feelings or actions that result in victimization been *transferred* from important relationships earlier in your life? When a mate victimizes you, do you have the same feelings you had toward your parents as a child—feelings you can't admit to?

THE CASE OF THE UNHAPPY HUSBAND

When Fred T. came to see me, he felt the victim of his wife, Gwen's, silver cord tie to her mother. To him, this "excessive mother love" and those "constant" weekend visits seemed the major problem in an otherwise happy marriage. The pair agreed to a marital decision contract—each would make a deal for specific behaviors from the other. Gwen would call her mother just once a day (when Fred was out of the house) and restrict the maternal visits to once a month. Fred promised he would not discuss his mother-in-law with Gwen and would "behave" when she came.

The contract failed. Gwen kept up her part of the bargain but Fred did not observe his. A highly intelligent man, he began to analyze his feelings toward *his* mother, whom he saw rarely. He recalled that his mother—of whom he thought so kindly in the present—had always acted unpleasantly and made him feel like a victim as a little boy. Consciously, Fred thought he avoided her now because she dumped too many "do for me" chores on him. Unconsciously, he figured out, he wanted to get even with her because she had treated him so horribly as a child. He had buried his rage.

Fred decided that this psychoanalytic perception formed the basis of his reaction to Gwen and her mother. Thereafter, whenever he found himself urging Gwen to fight with her mother, he would prod himself: "Hey, it's *my* mother I want to fight with." Now he could carry out his part of the contract.

Fred changed in two ways. *By learning to deal with his unconscious, he became able to deal with his conscious!* By facing his deep angers at mother, he became able to change his relationship with his wife. Fred had to dig in deeply to achieve Behavioral Psychotherapy success. He had to make certain assumptions and act as if they were true. For him, the technique worked.

Reevaluate Societal Conditioning

We've been brought up with certain beliefs that make us lose out in life and with false or idealistic expectations that can turn us into self-victims. To conquer them, we must identify and rethink them.

THE GENDER CURTAIN

Society teaches us to look at ourselves and others through a "gender filter." The phrase is that of Dr. Sandra Lipsitz Bem, professor of psychology at Cornell University and an authority on sex roles, who begins her lectures with the provocative question, "What would life be like if you were a member of the opposite sex?"

From childhood, we learn to assign certain characteristics and ways of behaving to men and boys, others to women and girls. Basically, society assumes the male is the doer. He is aggressive, forceful, has leadership qualities, a willingness to take risks. Tender feelings play little part in his role. He wants to repress them or not express them at all. Feminine qualities signify affection, gentleness, and sensitivity, with a main emphasis on contact and union with others. Women strive for openness and the full expression of tender feelings.

We have learned these traditional sex role attitudes and may cling to them. Comments Dr. Bem, "Roles smooth interaction. When you lose the roles, you lose the scripted way to behave. At a personal level, taking the sex roles away increases uncertainty. You lose options. You have to *figure out* what to do."

Just as we have learned these sex role attitudes, we can unlearn them. Twenty years ago blatant sexual discrimination existed. Today the change shows not only in women's rise in business but in academia. According to Dr. Bem, there has been a role reversal in faculty positions. Today the wife may lead the way, take a new job in another city, and then her husband hunts for one in that location.

However, many people still think in terms of traditional sex roles; thus they set themselves up for or perpetuate victimization.

By using the sex role stereotype to evaluate another person, you influence what you expect from that person. You may overlook a certain part of that person to which you would like to relate. One man married a young buyer who left her work and had three children—she became a full-time homemaker. He thought that should be her role, but he became miserable in the marriage. When she returned to work, he understood that he actually wanted the successful woman he originally married, someone with whom he could share talk of the working world, not a homebody.

In cases like this, the sex role attitude becomes a screen between your conventional expectations and the real, inner you. You dare not let yourself act or think in certain ways because to do so counters the stereotype you have let society force upon you.

Sex Stereotype Example One: A stunning thirty-three-year-old divorced mother of three complains bitterly, "Because I'm a woman who got married at eighteen, I'm not comfortable in social situations. I just can't start a conversation with an attractive man I don't know. If the man doesn't talk to me, I go chat with some woman. If I were a man, I wouldn't sit home so much. I'd have more options."

Sex Stereotype Example Two: Mary M. was running a small company where a group of malcontents revolted against the established order. She recalls, "They used to buzz around about my stupidity. I gave them too much leeway because I thought they were just kids, but word of what they were saying got back to my management. I got in trouble.

"Unlike men, women have been brought up to be fair. If I were a man, I would have wiped the opposition out at the start. I should have said, 'I am in charge. If you don't like it here, go!'"

Sex Stereotype Example Three: A thirty-five-year-old architect recalls, "I was a small kid. The other boys used to pick on me and hit me. One stole my bicycle. I used to cry a lot, and that made me very uncomfortable. If I'd been a girl, I would have felt those guys were mean and wrong. As it was, I felt terribly ashamed of myself. This pattern has continued all my life. I'm afraid showing emotion will make me look like a sissy."

By keeping the gender curtain closed, we limit our spontaneity and curtail our flexibility in problem-solving because we cannot consider counterstereotypical actions that might help.

Ask yourself the following questions about gender typing. It may help to write the answers in your workbook.

      1. What would you have done differently in a past victim situation if you were a member of the opposite sex?

      2. What would you do differently to change a victim situation *right now*?

THE NICENESS FACTOR

The old-fashioned word *niceness* still possesses the power to twist us into emotional victims. Its importance lies in the way we translate our ideas into action.

Wrong Concept One: Expectation of a *quid pro quo*—that is, when you make a nice gesture to someone else, you assume that person will return the favor in a similar manner. For instance, a friend gets sick; you cook and deliver a pot of chicken soup. When you succumb to the flu, you expect the same culinary compensation from that friend.

Wrong Concept Two: The belief that doing something *you* want for someone else constitutes niceness. For example, you love breakfast in bed, but your mate detests all those toast crumbs. When you want to express fondness, you bring the loaded wicker breakfast tray he or she does not want but that, in the same situation, *you* would want. Then when you receive the barest of thanks, you feel wronged.

Wrong Concept Three: That you can buy friendship through doing little favors (picking up luncheon checks, offering to return library books). When your "unselfish" behavior fails to buy you the friendship, you feel betrayed. This failure affects your self-image.

Wrong Concept Four: The denial of niceness. At great inconvenience to yourself you act very nice to a person but minimize your service. Your friend enthuses, "Great!" You respond, "It was no trouble" rather than "It was inconvenient, but I was glad to do it." The friend takes the action at the face value *you* put on it. Then you feel resentful.

All these errors can make us continual self-victims.

Effective Niceness Tactics

■ *Let people be nice to you.* This is important. If you do nice things for friends and never let them return any kindness, you make them uncomfortable. One professional woman grew up hearing, "Don't sponge off of people." With a false sense of independence, she does nice things for others but never lets them do for her. Secretly, she feels they don't care about her. They care but feel uncomfortable and tension enters the relationship. Eventually the friends stop offering.

■ *There's nothing wrong with being nice if you want to do something from a sense of self-pride and expect nothing in return.* A woman with two teenaged children took in her husband's mother, who spent three pain-racked years dying of cancer. When friends commented on Betty's "niceness" in not placing the mother in a nursing home, she replied, "I did it for myself. I thought it the right thing to do."

■ *Realize that people repay in their own way.* Marie, a lawyer, may not return the chicken soup you cooked for her when she was ill, but she'll spend hours checking a contract for you without a fee. Ray, a merchandise expert, does not run errands for you when you're sick but will draft an endless stream of touchy business letters for you. Alfred, a professional peer, will never pay the check but has supplied emotional support through a series of work traumas.

■ *Set niceness limitations.* Ask people what they want and comply. One woman with a sick husband asked a couple to dinner. Concerned about the work the dinner would cause her already beleaguered friend, the female half of the guest couple said, "I'll bring the food." The hostess replied firmly, "No, I'll cook it. I want the company."

■ *Understand that always being nice can interfere with closeness.* Times exist when you should bring resentments out into the open and discuss them ("I resent it when I take you out five times and you never call to thank me"). If you're always nice and fail to disclose your feelings, you won't achieve the kind of closeness you crave and you will end up an emotional victim.

■ *Above all, don't spend so much time doing favors for others that you have no time for your own life.*

Rethink Your Behavior

If you want to change, *do something about it.* Pick a specific target behavior, an area where you yearn to behave differently. It should be specific and limited: something as easily identifiable as responding to friends who take advantage of you or finding a way to increase confidence in a frightening situation.

Start today. Just take a small beginning step that will make you feel right, not wrong, about yourself.

□ Part II

The World Around Us

5 □ A New Kind of Workshop for Emotional Victims

You have the power to boost your self-esteem! Scores of noted athletes have proved that *confidence is a learnable skill*. You can adapt the same methods to achieve success in whatever life task or trial you face.

In the last few years the psychological field has changed completely. New methods emphasize enabling *healthy people*—rather than problem people with neurotic behavior patterns—to enhance their lives in order to work and live at their best.

In this chapter you will learn new habits and techniques in self-assertiveness. You will learn specific exercises that can change both your attitude and behavior and help you discover what you may be doing that encourages others to take advantage of you and how you can prevent that.

This chapter provides two major concepts.

    1. Your aim must be far more than preventing others from putting you down.

    2. The more you use your own strengths, the less you will fear what might happen.

Here is an action plan that works.

Advanced Assertiveness

We must have assertiveness skills and the knowledge of when and how to use them. We still need the basic skills my wife and I taught in our award-winning book *Don't Say Yes When You Want to Say No*—saying no, appropriately expressing feelings, handling criticism, making requests—to change a victim pattern. However, because of life's complications, having basic skills is not enough. We also need more advanced assertiveness skills.

Advanced assertion as we now use it in Behavioral Psychotherapy, covers changing interactions with others, dealing with alternatives, and confidence in our ability to change.

Most important, we *must learn to say yes as well as no*. While saying no keeps bad things from happening, saying yes adds new dimensions to our range of experience and can prove a major impetus to feeling happy in our lives.

LEARN TO SAY YES

Fred won't take a promotion because he fears he lacks the ability to do the job.

Because she always sticks with the familiar, Jane refuses to try a new vacation place.

Despite her strong desire for marriage and a family, Ellen stays single. She must avoid intimacy.

Whatever their life-style differences, Fred, Jane, and Ellen have a common problem: They don't know when to say yes. In the years that Assertiveness Training has been broadcast throughout the world via books, lectures, and courses, many people have learned that they can gain respect and circumvent exploitation by saying no. To do this, they maximize their defensive tactics.

However, more people have difficulty saying yes than no. They may know how to say yes, but somehow can't do it. The result is worse than just the loss of specific opportunities. The net result is a narrow, constricted, unsatisfying life. They limit their potential for growth and self-expression. Many people just don't know the wonders that saying yes to life can produce.

What keeps us from saying yes? Why do we say no instead?

We may say no almost automatically for a variety of reasons. We may want to preserve the status quo. Anything that threatens the security represented by the status quo makes us feel the victim, so we say no—and then complain about the sameness of our life. We may feel saying yes represents pleasure and that pleasure should have little or no place in our life. This attitude may stem from our childhood training, in which our parents taught us that duty and responsibility are the factors that count and that pleasure will detract from performance. Or we may feel undeserving of pleasure.

We may fear the unfamiliar. Saying yes often commits us to doing something different, whether fishing in Australia or attending a party where the hostess is a virtual stranger. Because of our own uptightness and worry about disruption of routine, we say no and thereby lose the chance for a new experience.

A TRAINING PROGRAM FOR SAYING YES

1. Know Your Yes Pattern

Are you a basic yes or no person? What kind of yes person are you? A yesser who *never learned to say no? A practical yesser*—you say yes to the boss because you want future promotion? A *situational yesser* who seeks out opportunities for new experiences? A *caring yesser*—you say yes to others because you have true concern for their feelings and needs but often do this at the expense of your own needs? A *service yesser*—you are so committed to a principle, ideal, or cause that you knowingly and willingly say yes even when it is at your own expense. You don't even try to find a balance. A *foolish yesser* who doesn't evaluate the situation first?

Analysis of your past pattern helps. Take several situations in the past six weeks (they can be trivial) in which you might have said yes but didn't. Review and answer these questions as if you *had* said yes:

■ If the situation had gone wrong, what reasonably is the worst thing that could have happened?

■ If it had gone right, what reasonably is the best that might have been expected?

■   Taking these two elements into consideration, was saying yes worth the risk?

2. *Rank Your Priorities*

In any given situation, you probably have a number of different goals, some incompatible with others and each possessing a different importance for you. At times you may have to prioritize your goals, relinquishing certain ones to gain others that matter more.

THE CASE OF THE RE-ENTRY WOMAN

After years as a homemaker, Mary K., with great difficulty landed a plum training job with a noted interior designer. One day the boss asked her to stay in at lunchtime to cover the office. Mary saw this as an unfair request. To avoid feeling the victim, she yearned to answer, "No, I want my lunch hour and will take it." She could have stopped her feelings of victimization by refusing the request, thereby risking the far more important goal of keeping her job. Knowing she needed the job for income and self-respect, she said yes. A savvy woman, she also realized that when and if such requests became a pattern on the boss's part, then she would have to reevaluate the job.

3. *Evaluate the Alternatives*

Decide upon your goal within the context of the whole. Alternatives can prove complex, with no single, simple solution. Often we land in the either/or trap: the idea that you must do it either one way or the other. In this kind of situation, the thing to do is apply your creativity.

For example, because of mounting job chores, Allan M. wanted to cut back on his volunteer activities for a local goodwill group. He had a problem. The current president, a tactless, boorish man, had failed to raise enough funds. The group wanted Allan to become president. Allan viewed this as a choice where he'd lose either way. If the other man remained as president, the organization, which Allan retained a commitment to, might fall apart. On the other hand, if Allan accepted the post, he would increase the very involvement he wanted to reduce. Fortunately he was able to devise a creative alternative: He committed himself to a one-year term as president. During that year he would groom someone else to take over the job.

Evaluating alternatives means applying techniques to open up the widest range of alternatives for yourself—or to identify alternatives you might otherwise miss.

Affirmative Action Technique One: Say no to the specific and yes to the general. For instance, a long-term friend invites you to a party you know will be full of bores. A blunt refusal will hurt her. Try this approach: "Look, I can't attend your party, but you and your husband come for dinner next Wednesday." You have said no to the party and yes to the relationship.

Affirmative Action Technique Two: Realize that many invitations are implicit rather than explicit. Because you fail to understand this point, in the actual situation you answer neither yes or no. You may say nothing, say the wrong thing, or change the subject and lose your chance. The opportunity may be business or social. For example, a friend says, "There's a great Renoir show in Boston. I'm going to fly up for the day." A shy woman, she really means, "Won't you go with me?" Missing the cue, you answer, "I read about it." The friend goes with someone else.

4. Learn to Say Yes to Yourself

The inability to do what you really want to do may stem from a series of fears.

You fear *doing things alone,* so often you sit at home alone and watch TV. Stretch your own life. Doing things can bring about many happy repercussions, such as an accidental meeting with a friend or even with an attractive stranger at a museum where you've gone on your own. If you had stayed at home, nothing could have happened.

Some people may *fear commitment.* For instance, Gerry M.'s relationships always went wrong. This hardworking obstetrician believed that if he acted like a saint—did all the right things with a woman ("his share" of chores even after he'd performed three deliveries that day) and ignored his own needs (for example, attending optional weekend professional meetings)—he would feel victimized and trapped. If he acted "selfishly"—insisted on "my time" and kept his bachelor slovenliness—he would be the kind of person he would not want to be and, of course, any relationship or marriage would fail. No matter what route he took, he would not like himself. His solution. Avoid the situation. He worked hard to make all his relationships go wrong because he could not say yes to commitment.

Even though we have a new set of circumstances, we may fear a *repetition of victimization.* Alex M. wouldn't marry Karen, a sweet woman whom he really loved, because he thought she'd use him in the same way his former wife did. Karen handled the situation with great intelligence. She volunteered to sign a contract, relinquishing any claims on Alex's estate should they marry and subsequently separate. This gave Alex the confidence to remarry. Six months later his confidence had increased to the point where he tore up the agreement.

Overcoming the fear of saying yes to self can produce more than action and growth. We can gain a sense of self-value. When John D. received an invitation to the twentieth reunion of his posh prep school, he hesitated to accept it. He had not gone on to college, had become a builder of suburban homes, and thought all his fellow graduates—now doctors, lawyers, and bankers—would look down on him. To his surprise, upon attending he discovered that the professionals and corporate executives present envied him because he had his own entrepreneurial business. Furthermore, because of his physical activity and work in the open air, he looked younger and slimmer than most of them.

5. *Realize That You Can Change Your Mind*

You may believe that if you say yes and matters don't work out, the end result will be a catastrophe. Sometimes it is. You can't win them all. However, more often, the negative result is really little more than an inconvenient mistake. If you hate a course you've signed up for, try switching. If you despise the vacation spot your friend chose, figure next time it will be better. If you say yes and don't like what happens, you can alter your decision. But if you say no, you may never have the opportunity again. *When in doubt, say yes.*

Acceptable Aggression

Traditionally, the old concept of aggressiveness meant people were out to hurt others, with any other considerations secondary. Today's new acceptable aggressiveness means we may *have* to perform an unfriendly, hostile, or antagonistic act in our own best interest. Not to do so could cause us irreparable psychological, professional, or emotional harm.

The psychological field rarely differentiates between different kinds of aggression and circumstances. However, professionals do accept that unassertive-*seeming* behavior may in fact be assertive. For instance, if we choose not to respond to a put-down (meaning we know we can answer but elect not to), that falls under the assertive category. We have deliberately kept silent because in this situation it makes us feel good about ourselves.

Following that line of argument, we see that aggressive behavior is not always a no-no. If we strike out at someone else for whatever reason—assuming that if we wanted we could refrain but that it is *our choice* to do so and will increase our sense of self-respect—this, too becomes acceptable aggression/assertive behavior.

To employ aggression acceptably, we must:

- Realize that under certain circumstances aggression can be morally justified as well as rewarding
- Consider our intention. Do we have good reason to hurt the other person?
- Decide whether we can live with ourselves if we do hurt the other person

When an assertive technique does not work, some form of aggressiveness may be the only way both to achieve our goal and to maintain a sense of self-preservation.

A GUIDE TO ACCEPTABLE AGGRESSION

It's okay to strike back to restore your self-esteem. Lillian H., who worked for a major fund-raising organization, produced an extravaganza that brought in a huge sum of money. For this she expected not just praise but a raise. She got neither. Giving no recognition to her feat, her superior asked, "What are you planning to do next?" Lillian felt victimized, put down, demeaned, exploited. Frustration will often produce aggressiveness. To get even, she walked out that day, leaving her office a mess. Lillian knew that would make things difficult for the firm but felt it was the only way she could restore her sense of self-worth. She was lucky. Outsiders heard about her achievement; by the next week, she had a better job. Job, or no job, she couldn't have lived with herself without hitting back in some way.

Practice time-limited aggression. This takes place within the context of negotiating and similar adversarial situations, and is not only accepted but expected. Lawyers do it all the time. In cross examination, they try to confuse or undermine. For instance, a lawyer deliberately tries to upset the expert witness ("Doctor, you are being paid for testimony," implying that the doctor is perjuring himself for money). Sports players will also call names and perform harassing actions during a game to undermine an opponent's confidence. But at the end of a day in court, the lawyer may ask his opponent, "How's your son?" and sports players will rush out on the field to congratulate the winning player.

Employ aggression to gain a goal. As we've noted previously, you fight to protect your rights—sometimes in a way that will hurt someone else.

In one instance, Rod D., a psychologist, won his Ph.D. and landed a good hospital job. He was about to marry. The hospital director agreed he could start on the job on August 1, following the honeymoon. When Rod returned from the Bahamas and went to the hospital to begin his stint, he found someone else in the job he needed desperately. His only recourse: to tear down the replacement. Ron showed how his own qualifications were superior; he even tried to prove that the other man couldn't do the job and possessed personality weaknesses. He had no qualms about hitting out in this way. Not only did he need the job, but it had been promised to him. And he got it!

Sometimes you must use aggression in self-defense. For example, an author felt the assigned copyeditor was ruining his book. Complaints to the editor got him nowhere. When the copyeditor changed a Mark Twain quote, the author resorted to aggressive action. To protect his book (on which he had worked for three years), he wrote a letter to the head of the publishing firm. He spelled out the copyeditor's ignorance, rudeness, carelessness, inflexibility. She was fired. A replacement came in. Finally, a competent job was done.

Constructive aggression works. An aggressive act does not mean you have to hurt someone. Even if your motive is to tear down the other person, you can carry it out in a creative, productive way. For example, a man attacks you at a charity board meeting with "That was a bad idea you had. You made a fool of yourself." You can shrug off the crack and later come up with a fund-raising plan that shows how wrong he was and how smart you are, then mail it off to all the board members. Part of your motivation may be to strike out at your victimizer, but you also prove your superiority through good thinking.

In using acceptable aggression, remember these cautions:

■ Beware of inadvertent aggression. You may have no aggressive intent but behave in such a loud, offensive way that you seem as if you do.

■ Don't confuse aggression with moving toward your goal. For example, you move out of a marriage where you're miserable. Your aim: to achieve your own freedom, not hurt the other person. (It's still possible, of course, that the other person may be hurt, but that's a side effect, not the objective of your action.)

■ Make sure you don't displace your aggression into the wrong context. For example, you may act aggressively in a situation when, in reality, something entirely different—say nervousness over an upcoming event—prompts your behavior.

■ Realize you may be unable to tolerate aggression in any form. You know that if you fail to perform an aggressive act, certain unwanted consequences may develop, but, for the sake of a higher value, you feel you must suffer them. In this case, go by what matters to you, but also realize that you may have to accept undesirable results for the sake of your core belief.

Think to Win

You have a great deal of control over whether or not you perform at your best in any situation. *Your performance does not just happen to you.* You can do things that produce the action you want. When you recognize you have that winning edge, then even if you become a victim, you can minimize and cope with the impact of victimization.

Athletes know that once they have reached a certain degree of proficiency in their sport, competitive performance becomes eighty percent psychological. For that reason, when an athlete prepares for an important event, he or she spends just as much time on the psychological as on the physical.

The sports psychology field has developed and tested a number of methods to enhance this psychological preparation, and I have used them in my work with the U.S. Olympic fencing team and also to help patients. The following three methods prove particularly effective in heightening the performance of ordinary people in real-life situations. They include developing the right attitude, psyching yourself up, and increasing "I am able to do it" behavior through coping rehearsal.

DEVELOPING THE RIGHT ATTITUDE

Our attitude to ourselves, others, and the situation we are in will influence not only the way we behave but the behavior of others toward us. If people go into a situation with the attitude that they have nothing to offer, do not merit respect, and are helpless to effect any change, they will act out of weakness and fail to mobilize the strengths they actually have. In addition, they probably will communicate this attitude to others and others will also act as if these self-judged weaklings have nothing to offer and do not deserve respect. Thus people get caught in a self-fulfilling prophecy. If you have the wrong attitude, you set yourself up to be the victim.

You must change this attitude. Experiments show that *if you have a negative attitude toward something but present as strong an argument as you can for the positive attitude (whether you believe it or not), your original attitude will shift.*

One of my fencers made this work. A certain rival had always beaten him at previous international tournaments. My fencer's problem was that he was in awe of his competitor and couldn't see himself standing up to him. Applying a sports psychology technique I had devised, the fencer made a two-minute tape saying positive things about himself that should make the opposing fencer stand in awe of him. He listened to it daily, once in the morning and once at night. This form of reinforcement worked "tremendously" (his word), and the fencer won his next important bout. The same attitude change can work for you.

ATTITUDE CHANGE EXERCISE

Goal: To switch your attitude about yourself and others in a situation so that your own confidence increases and you perform at your best

Step One: Identify the attitude you want to change and formulate the opposite attitude you want to develop.

Attitude: I don't really deserve to get that job.

Opposite attitude: I can learn to do that job and *deserve* to get the job.

Step Two: Muster up your strongest arguments to support your positive position. See how much boasting you can do legitimately, but keep it realistic. Avoid any qualifiers. Make your new attitude specific. For example, if you are going on a job interview, stress such points as "I have had three jobs in ten years and always have been successful in delivering for my employers" . . . "I am willing to work unusually hard and have always done so" . . . "I relate well to people" . . . "On my last job my boss told me how both superiors and peers enjoyed working with me and how much I contributed to morale." Write down notes. Research shows that the *act of writing out* your reasons for getting what you want has a very important reinforcing effect. Prepare to give a one- to two-minute speech on your new opposite attitude.

Step Three: Talk the speech into a tape machine with conviction. Listen to the tape. If what you plan to say needs major revision, do it over.

Step Four: Before the event, periodically relax yourself by any method that works for you (like thinking pleasant thoughts or doing exercises) and then listen to the tape two successive times. Try to stay relaxed while remaining attentive to what you say. Practice pushing away any doubtful thoughts.

Step Five: Just before you go into the situation where you need confidence, say the speech to yourself in your head. Strengthen that new confidence.

Do this exercise correctly and often enough, and not only will you act differently but you also will communicate the expectancy of positive rewards. You should have a strong chance for success.

PSYCH YOURSELF UP

As any athlete knows, for peak performance, you need to have the right energy level. Whether you want it for a speech, a meeting, an important date, or confrontation of a victimizer, you know in advance when you'll need this edge. If you feel good, up to it, "right," then you are more apt to be at your best. *You want that winning feeling.*

To achieve that feeling, you want enough tension to stimulate you but not enough to interfere with what you do. Professionals call this the "optimal performing state." Too little tension, and you don't have the edge of quick thought and action. Too much, and you may lose both mental and physical coordination.

I remember one of my fencers during the 1984 Olympics had finished his stretching and warm-up exercises. He sat down on a bench, eyes closed, getting himself into the right mood for his best fencing. He told me, "These psychological exercises are as important as the stretching ones."

Remember, the correct optimal state is highly individualistic. What works for your friend may prove too relaxed or too tense for you. Discover your own peak-inducing state. Following are three psyching-up exercises designed to help you find it. They are based on the outstanding work of my colleague and friend Dr. Richard M. Suinn, professor of psychology and head of the department of psychology at Colorado State University and member of the steering committee for sports psychology training for the Olympics teams.*

PSYCHING-UP EXERCISE ONE

Goal: To recognize your winning feeling

Step One: Recall an incident in which you were at your personal peak and had that winning feeling. Preferably, it would be in the same area as the situation you will be facing.

Step Two: Think back to how you felt the evening before the event and immediately prior to it. Concentrate on three areas:

    1.   *Your body.* How did it feel? Did it feel loose, heavy, full of goose bumps?

    2.   *Your thoughts.* What was going through your mind—problems that might occur during the upcoming event, people who might show up, winning, losing, purely irrelevant thoughts?

    3.   *Your mood.* Was it relaxed, excited, up, down?

Keep remembering that personal peak experience. In your mind go through it over and over. Recall the exact optimum level.

PSYCHING-UP EXERCISE TWO

Goal: To put that winning feeling under your control through a trigger word

Step One: Get that winning feeling fixed in your mind and try to find a word or phrase you can use that automatically brings about that sense of being unbeatable, at top form. You must find a phrase that suits your personal needs. While an athlete might use "personal best at nationals," you might try, "being on top," "ready to go," "I can do it," "I'm the best there is in the field."

---

*Richard M. Suinn, *Seven Steps to Peak Performance*, Toronto: Hans Huber Publishers, 1986.

Step Two: A number of times before the upcoming event, relax yourself and picture that winning feeling while repeating your phrase or sentence. Condition your winning feeling to those cue words so that your winning feeling will come on automatically when you say them. For example, in an important conference, you say your "I can do it" phrase silently to yourself and thus psych yourself up for your best performance.

Step Three: In the actual situation, if you feel a need to be psyched up, say that phrase to yourself and again recreate that winning feeling in your body.

PSYCHING-UP EXERCISE THREE

Goal: Last-minute psych-up

Step One: Just before the experience, compare your feelings with the way you felt during your optimal experience. Compare body feelings, thoughts, mood.

Step Two: Where your feeling differs from the winning feeling, take deliberate action to change it. If you feel your level is too low, do what you can to raise it up. For some, playing march music helps . . . or being with certain people . . . or thinking specific thoughts (exactly what you want to achieve). If you are too keyed up, try relaxation or meditation. Listen to relaxing music. Put yourself in a quiet place without such distractions as TV.

Remember, high tension feeds on itself. Slow down your actions and you will reduce undesirable tension. Always keep in mind that psyching yourself up will help you mobilize and use your strengths.

CONVINCING YOURSELF OF YOUR OWN CONFIDENCE

Many athletes, running the gamut from basketball forwards to skiers, have learned to deliberately increase and maintain their confidence in their own ability. You, too, can do this. You can build up your confidence by increasing your awareness of your own capability to cope with potential problems. Your ultimate goal: to feel deep inside, "I am able to do it."

In the journal *Psychological Review*, Dr. Albert Bandura of Stanford University writes, "The strength of people's conviction in their own effectiveness is likely to affect whether they will even try to cope with the given situation." The base of real inner confidence stems from knowing you can cope with whatever comes up. The technique: Do *not* emphasize winning. *Do* stress knowing what you have to do at each step of the way to *maximize* your chances of winning. For instance, concentrate on how you will talk to the V.P. at tomorrow's meeting and how you will make your presentation during that meeting rather than on your longer-term goal of getting the promotion you want. In this way you minimize or eliminate defeatist behavior.

You gain this sense of self-mastery from a three-pronged procedure.

1. Make certain your goal is clear. For instance, you may want to convince a colleague to take a certain course of action.

2. Figure out ways to cope with whatever difficulties may arise. Emphasize the problem and the solution; don't ruminate about what else might go wrong. Don't think, "If he says no, how helpless I will be." Instead change this to "If he says no, I can try to convince him to change his mind by showing what he has to gain by saying yes."

3. Using imagery, *rehearse* what you have to do.

To explain the use of imagery, I always give the example of the marathon runner faced with regaining his lost confidence before an important competition. A week before the competition, his sports psychologist instructed him to imagine specific problems that might come up during his run and to experiment with different methods of coping with them. The runner did that, using such problems as getting a cramp in his leg at the seven-mile mark, getting a painful stitch in his side at the twelve-mile mark, slugging through rain and puddles, being jostled by another runner, and anything else that could possibly happen. With each, he tried to visualize the different things he could do. Once he had decided what might be the best response to each situation, he mentally rehearsed his successful coping strategy over and over. By the day of the competition he felt certain he could cope with whatever might come up, and his confidence zoomed to its highest level. He ran the best race he could, and even though he wasn't good enough to win, he felt quite satisfied, knowing he had performed at his best. Vicarious performance through imagery has been proven to increase confidence.

Use of imagery as a problem-solving method works well in everyday life. For instance, I had a patient with a fear of driving in bad weather. She was terrified of having a bad accident. So I had her imagine going into a skid in a snowstorm and told her to rehearse in her head what she might do during the skid: correction with the steering wheel, easing up on the gas pedal, bringing the car into alignment, and not reacting with jerkiness. The confidence she gained through this sports psychology method removed most of her fear of bad weather driving.

You can also use images in a straightforward rehearsal method to practice doing something in the exact way you'd like to perform it in life. Athletes do this all the time. In *Golf My Way*, Jack Nicklaus describes how he programs himself for success: "I never hit a shot, not even to practice, without having a sharp, in-focus picture in my head."

INCREASE YOUR "I CAN DO IT" BEHAVIOR

Goal: To use imagery problem-solving and coping rehearsal to develop your inner sense of confidence

Step One: Take the situation that concerns you (you have to have a talk with your child's teacher . . . fire a lazy employee . . . end a victimizing relationship) and get some ideas of the problems that might arise when you try to cope.

Step Two: Relax yourself by whatever method you use. This helps because it counters anxieties that might arise.

Step Three: Solve the problem in imagery. As the marathon runner did, imagine the situation and running into the problems that you think may occur. In your mind, work out different ways to cope with the problem until your solution seems right (what to do if your victimizer lover turns the tables and attacks with what's wrong with you . . . your employee is abusive . . . the teacher is unfair to your child). For example, if you have terrible neighbors and a common hall plumbing problem, be concerned with the objectives. Will the neighbors respond to tears? To assertive insistence? To a typed list of estimates from three plumbers? *Focus on solutions that will lead to the outcome you desire.*

Step Four: Once you've found an acceptable solution, rehearse it over and over in your head. Imagine the upcoming problem. Rehearse your coping. Set the solution—or solutions.

Now, add a final part to this rehearsal—visualize some kind of successful outcome (you and the neighbors agree to go ahead with the second plumber bid and all of you behave politely). Experience shows that a *positive outcome in imagery* makes it more likely you will behave in an effective way in the real-life situation. Golfers who utilize this technique do not just imagine a putt; they also imagine the ball going into the cup. If you add this last part, you emulate the top sports figures who have a record of proven success with this combination of imagery problem-solving and rehearsal.

Always remember your basic aim: to know that you can cope.

Stop Thinking Like a Victim

Much of the anger, anguish, and helpless feelings we experience as victims stems from incorrect thinking. The distorted perceptions that make us victims when we're not or keep us from seeing we're being victimized also emanate from thinking errors. Whether we make the mistake of reasoning emotionally rather than factually or discounting our good points, it is essentially a matter of "dysfunctional thoughts." These break down into demands and/or delusions. In each case we interpret situations incorrectly and that leads to overreaction on our part.

If you don't think like a victim, you won't feel like a victim. You can break the habit of uncontrolled thinking.

GET RID OF YOUR "SHOULDS"

You may base your expectations on your fantasies rather than on the reality of the situation and the people involved. When what actually happens does not conform to these fantasy expectations, you overreact and feel the victim. For example, you ask your husband to get a picture framed. You think he *should* get it done pronto, as you would. A month later the picture remains buried in his desk pile. You feel victimized—your husband hasn't lived up to your expectations. But if the other person is not you, why should he do something in your style?

The words *should* and *shouldn't*, which often initiate or exaggerate victim feelings, can serve as red alerts to your victim feelings and the unrealistic expectations to which they lead. You have rules for yourself and rules for others but don't stop to ask yourself if they fit the situation well. For example, at work you feel, "A good supervisor should be helpful." But if you are a nurturing kind of supervisor and it doesn't work out, does it occur to you that a supervisor is hired to lead, not to be cozy with subordinate staff?

Catalog your shoulds to identify the false expectations that make you an emotional victim.

EXORCISING THE SHOULDS

Goal: To help you identify the unreasonable rules that exaggerate your victim reaction

Step One: Take a specific situation in which you had a strong reaction. It can be one involving a spouse, family, or friend ("He/she should have known what I wanted"), a coworker, or even an impersonal situation with a salesperson or airline host ("He/she should pay more attention to me").

Step Two: Search for the shoulds involved in the situation. The shoulds may be anything, but typical ones run the gamut from "Other people should never be rude to me" to "I should be a nice, all-giving person" and "I should always act like a lady/gentleman."

Step Three: Analyze the rules you follow that give rise to your particular shoulds. This varies from person to person. For instance, your friend criticizes you by saying, "You need a man—what a pity you don't have one." You become angry: "She should not talk to me that way." Behind the should lies the rule "Good friends never say anything critical."

Step Four: Write out the specific rule in your Behavioral Psychotherapy workbook. Then answer the following questions about it:

■ Is there anything wrong with this rule? (Answer: Yes. Friends have moods and perspectives of their own. Just because you act a certain way does not mean others should or will.)

■ Does it take reality into account? (No. The friend has marital difficulties and is projecting.)

■ Does seeing the rule clearly change your emotional reaction to the situation? You may have a right to feel angry with the remark, but seeing the unreasonable rule behind your response may take away the impression of unfairness. You may still be angry but no longer feel like a victim.

Always remember that many rules and shoulds stem from childhood. Forty-five-year-old Guy D. complained about the unreasonable demands from his wife, mother-in-law, and just about everyone else in his life. This included his four-year-old son, who insisted that his father sleep in his bed. Guy hated all the nighttime kicks and separation from his wife, but gave in and did it because he believed that was the way a good father acted. Finally, he was able to see how foolish he was to let himself be controlled by a four-year-old boy and returned to his marital bed. He also saw he was following an irrational should—"My needs don't count. I should always do what everyone in the family wants me to do," based on the childhood-acquired rule from mother: "Be obedient. If you are, I will love you."

PARANOID THINKING

People who behave in a paranoid style set themselves up for victimization. In psychiatric parlance, the paranoid believes "they" (people real or imaginary) are united in a "plot" to destroy his or her reputation in life. While few of us are true paranoids in the professional sense, we may possess tendencies that in many life instances make us victims of paranoid-style thinking. We make mountains out of molehills and use expressions like "*They* are out to get me" . . . "*He* picks on me" . . . "*She* looks at me in a funny way; I think she hates me."

A bent toward this kind of thinking may stem from childhood. If we couldn't trust our parents and felt frequent humiliation, we developed a sense that our environment is hostile. The result is that, as adults, we have the tendency to ruminate about imagined slights and are hypersensitive, magnifying insignificant events into intentional hurts. Another explanation: We feel hostility toward others but must repress it, and we accomplish this by projecting our hostility onto others.

Paranoid-style thinking can affect all ages and types. One patient said to me, "I want to be famous. Then no one would pick on me." A super-celebrity friend, who *is* famous, with a nationally syndicated column, confides that when she's left out of a party, she tells her husband, "Bill, I guess you're not invited because of me." The psychiatric term has penetrated everywhere. A recent national magazine referred to recluse writer J. D. Salinger as having "paranoid eyes." Shortly after the beginning of the London import musical *Chess,* a leading character sings a song entitled "I'm Not Paranoid."

Personality Traits of Paranoid Thinking Types
■ *Misinterpretation of the other person's motive*. What we see as actually happening may be correct. The other person did say a certain thing, perform a specific action. But we at-

tribute a wrong meaning to this comment or action. Because we feel so sure of our appraisal, *everything* the other person does is interpreted as confirming it. And we constantly watch for new examples of hostility.

For example, take the *paranoid pause*. A person makes a comment to someone. Before responding, the other individual pauses. There really *is* a pause, but paranoid types interpret the silence to mean "He didn't like what I said. He's out to get me." Then they take defensive action against attack in one of three ways.

    1. They suffer in silence or attempt to placate the other person. This reaction leaves them feeling the victim of the other's alleged malevolence.

    2. They perform a preemptive strike. During the pause the paranoid-type person hits out. No matter what the other person responds, the former becomes even more convinced of his false belief. Now both the attacker and the attacked feel they are victims.

    3. They practice the waiting game technique, letting the pause go on but always regarding it as an attack. Then the paranoid thinker counterattacks when an opportunity presents itself.

    ■ *Expectation of trickery.* For example, a young man likes a certain girl. She calls him and during the conversation reveals she's going skiing that weekend. The man assumes she's going off with another male whom she prefers and that the purpose of her call was a deliberate attempt to make him jealous and hurt. In actuality, she is going away with another female, and the intent of the call was to share, not to hurt.

    ■ *Overconcern with hidden motives.* We misinterpret the nicest of actions and remarks as being aimed at exploitation. For instance, a friend comes back from the Orient and gives a close friend a valuable antique silver box. The latter comments, "How beautiful," but inwardly is convinced, "She's doing this to manipulate me. She wants something from me."

    ■ *Oversensitivity, often stemming from a social phobia.* As with any phobia, some people are hypersensitive to the slightest sign or suggestion of the thing they fear. For example, if you have a phobia about criticism, you may very well see two people whisper to each other and think, "They are talking about me." And if they even glance your way, that confirms it. The paranoid-like sense of victimization burgeons.

■ *Paranoid contagion.* Like flu, we can catch the paranoid style from someone else and ape it until it becomes part of our style.

Escape from Paranoid Thinking

Whether your tendency toward paranoid thinking stems from lack of confidence, fears, or learned suspicions of the world, don't continue your subjective suffering. Start the shift to a "They/he/she like(s) me" style of thinking.

1. *Learn to spot your paranoid-type thinking.* Knowing that you engage in this kind of thinking serves as the most important point in stopping!

Some people can't or won't learn. For instance, a teacher, assigned to a new school, began to feel that the principal did not want her. When she asked for new equipment and was refused, she was sure the principal was going to fire her. The teacher requested a transfer. Another refusal. The principal wanted to keep her—she was good. But because of the teacher's incorrect interpretation, she started fighting with the principal and the relationship became more acrimonious. At the end of the year, the principal insisted on a transfer to a less desirable school. The teacher's unrealistic thinking got her caught in a self-fulfilling prophecy.

Recognize your own oversensitivity, misinterpretation, suspicion, and "They are ganging up on me" feelings. Listen when friends, coworkers, lovers, or your mate tell you, "You're paranoid." Use this as a clue for self-change.

2. *Recognize the reality.* Look for the positives in what people say to you. It's often behind the words if not in them. Your paranoid thinking may make you miss the genuine fondness contained in a comment. For example, one highly erudite man always teases a friend about her passion for nineteenth-century women novelists. She reacts with, "He picks on me." In actuality, by focusing so much on her literary interests, he shows respect for her intellect.

Sometimes it's true—the other person is out to get you. In that case, decide how best to cope with the reality. Sometimes you can drop the person. At other times that's not possible, and you must be watchful to see you control your own overreaction.

3. *Every time you have one of those "making mountains out of molehills" thoughts, try to seek some alternative explanation.* For instance, you feel jealous because A called B instead of you. Your interpretation: "Maybe A likes B more than me." In actuality, he or she may have called you first to tell good news and got a busy signal.

4. *Don't anticipate disaster. Wait and see.* You don't want to live in a constant state of anxiety and suspicion. And you don't need to. Most imagined disasters are just that— imagined.

THE CASE OF THE SUSPICIOUS OFFICE WORKER

One day Marge D.'s boss invited her to lunch for the first time. Marge had been working on a top-level project, and the boss had been terribly critical of her. Certain that the purpose of the lunch was to fire her for incompetence, Marge made a paranoid plan to fire the first shot. She prepared a detailed list of everything wrong with the company and the boss's management of the project.

Then, realizing the boss's own stress over the project, Marge decided she would let him speak first, even though she knew he would criticize her. He began, "I wanted to tell you in a personal setting what a good job you've done and that in a month you'll get a raise." He went on to reveal his own nervousness about the project and added further praise of Marge's creativity. By holding back, Marge not only saw how foolish she had been but felt much better about herself.

Paranoids have been proven to be very bright. If you find yourself engaging in paranoid-type thinking, use your brightness to stop. Realize that you are making yourself a self-thought, self-taught victim of your own paranoia. Once you recognize your tendency to paranoid thinking and test it, you may actually see people whispering and shift to nonparanoid thinking: "They *are* talking about me—so what?"

How to Acquire Self Smarts

Street smarts involve a certain shrewdness in dealing with tough situations. Self smarts go beyond that. They reflect a quality of advanced assertiveness. With self smarts we possess an enlightened perception of interpersonal relationships so that we don't set ourselves up for victimization. We can develop innovative thinking and coping capabilities, as well as creativity to solve the problem and get us what we want that's best for us. We can use abilities we may not even have known we have. In the process we make our lives feel right, not wrong.

DEALING WITH THE VICTIMIZER: A LEARNING PLAN

Actual and potential victimizers will always exist in your life. Your aim: to change your own ingrained attitudes toward them and their game plans.

1. Pay Attention to the Warning Signs
Often a victimizer masks possible cruelty with sweetness and a light facade. But usually he or she provides signs that victimization is the real motive. Learn to recognize such signs as inconsideration; thoughtlessness; demands; stories a person tells that reveal victimizing traits or attitudes—for example, dirty tricks he or she has played on others with great enjoyment.

Again, recall your past history. When did you fail to recognize a victimizer and fail to use self-preservation measures? Was a particular person out for your job from the minute he joined the firm and got it? Was a woman after your husband from the minute she shared ribs with him at your neighbor's barbecue—and she got him? Did you slough off the cues (luncheon dates à deux, extended private conversations at parties)?

Analyze people in your present life who might victimize you because of their power or popularity needs. Joan M., a young secretary, had a roommate who said, "Such nice men call you up. I wish one would call when you're not here." Then one evening the situation occurred. The roommate made a date with Joan's caller. Says Joan bitterly, "I knew she'd do that." But even with this perception, Joan had taken no precautions. She never talked with the roommate about what to do if the situation came up, never thought of a solution—like having her own phone with her own answering machine attached to it.

2.   Recognize That the Victimizer Has Many Motives

Actually, victimizers may do what they do with the best of intentions. For example, one woman invited her cousin and the cousin's daughter, who had been on the outs for years, to a Thanksgiving dinner. The hostess thought of it as a "patch-up opportunity" and told neither that the other was coming. The good intentions didn't work. Mother and daughter felt victimized. So did the well-meaning hostess.

3.   Be Aware When You're in a Position to Be a Victim

No matter how benevolent the company, a boss, peer, or subordinate can always threaten your job. You also risk victimization in any close relationship. To gain closeness, you must reveal yourself. When you do so, you must have a sense of trust in the other person, the feeling that if victimization does occur, you will have the opportunity to speak up about it, the other will listen, and both of you will try to work it through.

Caution: Watch out for victimization when you feel particularly good. That's when you make promises you repent and resent when the euphoria disappears. Salespeople know instinctively who will fall for a good pitch. So do fund-raisers.

4.   Find Out What You Do to Collaborate in Your Own Victimization

Challenge the ideas that lead you into collaboration. *You may have erroneous principles* that make you passively accept unnecessary victimization.

THE CASE OF THE
NO-FAULT EXECUTIVE

A successful merchandising executive, Boston-born Vickie T., grew up hearing, "Don't let others do for you. It only bothers them." Recently construction workers redid the penthouse floor above her newly decorated living room. The ceiling broke. Fresh cement cascaded through, ruining her new carpet. For three days Vickie cried. She managed to send a letter to her notoriously penurious landlord but got no help from him. Because she had internalized that erroneous rule "Don't bother people," she did not call on a lawyer, her decorator, or other experts to help resolve her problem. She should have!

You may seek help from the wrong sources or ignore good advice. Perhaps you insist on consulting losers. Or you set yourself up for confirmation of your own ill-advised actions. For example, you go to a friend for help with a victim problem but present it in such a way that the friend says, "You have no choice. Keep on doing what you're doing." You slough off any savvy questions the friend asks. You don't really crave counsel but reassurance.

You keep focusing on what the other person should do. For instance, an out-of-town relative visits continually and keeps tricking you into going to expensive restaurants. You expect to pay for the meal—but not such a costly one. You make no attempt to think in advance of a restaurant you want and say "Let's go there." You stay in the collaborative pattern because you accept or minimize rather than try to change.

5. *Know and Understand Your Goals*
This is essential if you hope to break up the collaborative pattern. Your goals may be simple or complex. To achieve them, you must:

- Know what you have to do
- Possess confidence in your ability to do it
- Realize that getting out of a victimization need not mean a fight

THE CASE OF THE
COLLABORATING COLUMNIST

Elsie J., a public relations executive who liked the dependency she had with her authoritarian female boss, created a column for her, sold it, and watched it grow into a booming success. Elsie fantasized that her boss would be so impressed with the achievement that she would pile kudos and promotions on her. Instead Elsie got neither a thank-you nor credit (said the boss, "I want a more philosophical column"). Realizing that bestowing any accolade ran counter to her boss's egotism and in danger of losing her job because she and the boss had changed from collaborators to combatants, Elsie's initial excitement changed to resentment. To get out of her victim position, she used self-smarts thinking. To keep her job on amicable terms, she prepared an excuse she knew the boss could accept: "Work on the column is interfering with my social life; better get another writer." Elsie never said one word about the lack of respect the boss had shown her, and then used the column to get herself a better job.

6. Put Victimization in Context

The existence of one problem area does not mean you must end a relationship. The victimizing aspect may be just one side of a person you otherwise value. For example, if someone fails to repay a debt, forget that one and vow never to lend that person money again.

You may find that different situations produce change in "using" patterns. Marilyn and Greta worked for the same firm. Fearing anyone who might threaten her own job, Marilyn grabbed every chance to knife Greta. Greta agonized. Subsequently both went on to other companies, and Greta had occasion to call Marilyn about a professional meeting. They lunched. They are now friends and exchange visits at their respective weekend homes. Neither mentions the past. Neither ever would work with the other again within the confines of the same company.

TRANSLATE SELF SMARTS INTO ACTION

If you want your life to be positive in your terms, you must not remain in an inaction rut. If you have an idea, don't let inhibition prevent you from following through. Look for openings. Initiate actions. This requires a willingness to risk. You may fail. But many times thinking through *creative* solutions to situations that require coping will get you just where you want.

Example One: Soon after college David B. landed a job as a training specialist with a major airline company. He heard the rumor that some twenty employees were under consideration for the position of regional personnel manager. The local VP would select two or three to go to company headquarters in Buffalo for the final interview. After David researched all the facts and analyzed his own strengths, he went to the VP, enumerated his strong points, and said, "If you don't select me as a candidate, I'd like to write to the executive who will do the final choosing." The VP liked David's approach and sent him to Buffalo. David got the job.

Example Two. At a midwestern conglomerate, Mary D. held a very mediocre $15,000 job. Then a friend told her about a vacant $30,000 job with a retailing chain. Never revealing her previous salary and masking her inexperience, Mary got the job—but for only $22,000. A demon worker, she made a great success of the post and six months later demanded a raise, with her sights set on $30,000. "You'll find it in your next paycheck," smiled her manager. It was there, but for $27,000.

Mary felt the $30,000 was due her but realized the boss might not be able to give it to her. So she devised an alternate solution. When she confronted him again, her boss admitted he could go no further. "How about a three-thousand-dollar a year clothing allowance?" asked Mary. The boss liked her thinking. "You do have to meet the public a lot," he observed. "Send me a bill."

David and Mary might have become victims. Instead, each took creative action.

We may say, "I'd never come up with the idea of that clothing allowance," but all of us can learn coping self smarts. The important thing: *"I can do it."*

Go back to past problem events. What *could* you have done? Clip stories involving others' creativity in real-life situations. Use the research as a trigger for creative planning. Also, follow role models. Ask yourself how someone you know and respect might handle a certain situation. Realize that self smarts impose no restrictions or stereotyped solutions. They can be simple. One woman nearly didn't get a top job because the company powers didn't want a peer to know she'd be making more than he. She suggested, "Let the check come to me from headquarters." Sometimes, like Gregg, in the following story, you can even use self smarts to change the heartbreak of a lifetime.

THE CASE OF THE
FATHERLESS FIFTY-YEAR-OLD

Gregg M. had always thought his father died when Gregg was two years old. That's what his mother had told him. When Gregg reached his early teens, his mother remarried, and he called his stepfather "Dad." Years later, as a middle-aged man, Gregg felt bored at his advertising job and lonely without his grown children, who had left the nest. Irritated with Gregg's irascibility, his wife had also fled home. Depressed, Gregg yearned for a "real father." When he told this to his mother, she confessed she had lied. Gregg's father had not died. They had had a messy divorce, and she had used what she thought was the simplest way of handling things. She suggested, "Maybe he's alive somewhere."

With only the clue "Your dad worked in show business" to go on, Gregg decided to track down his father. Gregg had two things going for him: (1) the talent that had made him creative director at his ad agency; (2) *the knowledge that he had the know-how to find his father if his father was still alive.* His search technique: He behaved as if he were looking for a long-vanished celebrity to feature in an advertising campaign. He contacted the Lambs and Friars clubs, wrote two hundred letters to comedians, actors, network heads, ASCAP officials, lyricists, and playwrights he could think of, plus retired *Variety* columnists. Ten answers came back. One was from a former network official, who wrote, "A few years ago your father was living in Tampa with his second wife."

More research. Then Gregg found his father. Two days later

a Florida reunion took place. Gregg felt so good about his success in finding his father that he took action in a whole series of life areas. He quit his job, sold his suburban house, and went to live in Arizona, where he built a new house and acquired a challenging job. His wife returned and went with him. She liked the new Gregg.

As Gregg did, *you* can change your life.

Try one of the acceptable aggression methods you have always shunned. You may surprise yourself how much easier it is to be the doer rather than the done-in.

As athletes do, change your psychology of thinking. The techniques they use work.

Figure out the self smarts at your disposal and use them.

Become a victor instead of a victim. The choice is yours.

6 □ When Is a Friend a Friend?

We are social beings. When trouble occurs, we want to know that there is someone to whom we can plead, "Come! Help! I need you," with the assurance that that person will come. Even more important, we need to share our feelings, thoughts, pleasures, triumphs with another person. We all possess that inner desire to be with someone else, to feel bonds and warmth rather than simply exist on our lonely own, whether physically or psychologically. However, we may hold erroneous ideas and perform actions that prevent satisfying friendships, whether temporary or lifelong, and thus shortchange ourselves.

Friendship Fundamentals

■ *Different kinds of friendship exist.*

There is the *friendly connection* (the kind of relationship we have with our next-door neighbor or the person in the adjoining office with whom we chat at water cooler meetings). There is the *acquaintance*, the *friend*, and the *close friend* (an intimate who is not a lover or family member).

Within these four categories, many variations exist. We may have a rarely seen acquaintance—for example, a fashion authority who accompanies us every year on a day-long expedition to choose that season's important dress or an ex-college roommate with whom we still play tennis every week, but that's it. One young woman, about to quit her job and attend graduate school defines her circle as "for-the-time-being" friends. She says, "I'll be leaving town soon and won't see them anymore."

There are fair-weather friends for fun and foul-weather friends who come through for us when need occurs. A dentist comments, "One friend appears only when he can do for me. When things are good, he disappears." We may also have special friends who are aware of our vulnerabilities and weaknesses but would never use them against us. Most important, friends exist who, despite any inconvenience, are always there for us.

Our friendship needs vary. Some of us want only a few close friends and deep relations with each. One lawyer says, "I don't want too many good friends. I'm too vulnerable. I'd have to give too much. I have three close friends, and I'd do anything for them. I have a multitude of acquaintances." Others want the excitement of many friends but with more superficial relationships. *Difficulty arises when we try to force ourselves into a style incompatible with our needs, and thus victimize ourselves.*

■ *Use of the wrong model for friendship means trouble.*
In the present, we may still cling to our idea of the immature *chumship* of our childhood. For instance, during your preteen years or early adolescence, you had a "first best friend" or "second best friend" with whom you spent hours talking, doing, sharing every feeling. When the friend and his or her family went off for the summer, unless they took you along, you felt, "Something is missing." If the friend talked animatedly with someone else, you felt hurt. The two of you were inseparable.

Sometimes we may have an adult relationship that resembles a childhood friendship. For example, Amy and Janet, two thirtyish career women talk daily and lunch weekly. When Amy was between marriages and dating all the time, Janet would call and pretend to be a suitor so that a date sitting in Amy's living room would be impressed by Amy's popularity. But Janet and Amy aren't inseparable. Each is an independent human being and accepts the fact that the other possesses areas of interest that cannot be shared.

Trouble occurs if we continue to use the chumship model for all friendly relations. We make friends too quickly, expect too much, become too vulnerable, and get clobbered because adult friendships don't flourish that quickly. We may also try to achieve the same degree of intimacy with everyone. If we don't get it, we feel there's not really a friendship and thus experience deep feelings of pain and disappointment.

■ *Wishful thinking produces false expectations.*

Some people believe a new acquaintance will become an immediate helpful friend. Others want qualities the friend lacks and won't face the reality of that friend's personality deficits.

A person may lack the talent to distinguish between true and pseudo friendships. Pseudo friendships often exist for convenience but lack the commitment of true friendship. For example, two thirtyish bachelors may hang around together, using one another to relieve loneliness. They go to parties and neighborhood bars as a duo. But when one finds a good friend of the opposite sex, he drops the other. This often happens with single, divorced, or widowed people who lean on one another to fill time.

Some people lack a sense of balance. They just set their needs aside. They want others to mind-read what they want. Asking for anything would spoil this. Their shoulds operate—"Friends *should* do for me without my asking, just as I do for them." Others may be unable to speak up. One woman, recovering from surgery, was appalled when a close friend said, "Let me know if you need anything. I have a staff." The sick woman could not bring herself to respond, "I don't want the staff. I want *you* to come and see me." Often this form of wishful thinking leads to constant testing. Does the friend meet our criterion of what a friend should be? Does she or he act "the same way I would?" And many of us make a continual mistake that results in our viewing ourselves as the perpetual victim. To paraphrase Dorothy Parker, we often try to please those who can't please us!

With illusory friendships we may find we have imagined a degree of friendship that never existed—except in our heads.

THE CASE OF THE
IMAGINED FRIENDSHIP

Since their childhood in suburban St. Louis, Lillian and Sarah had been friends. Sarah gave. Lillian took. Somehow this satisfied their respective needs. Years passed and they both moved away. Recently, a local women's club invited successful Sarah to return and give a lecture. Fantasizing that everyone would talk about the reappearance of our "wonderful hometown girl," Sarah obliged. The lecture was a fizzle. The ladies were too busy celebrating some ancient member's birthday to listen. That night Sarah called Lillian for sympathy, thinking she would understand her emotional disappointment. Instead Lillian commented curtly, "You can't go home again." She could not provide the sympathy Sarah needed. But then she never had been able to. It took Sarah twenty years to realize this.

■ *Friendships change.*

Like anything else, friendships change within the context of a changing social and family life. A friend may move far away and we replace him or her with a new friend. Years later the old friend returns and the friendship picks up where it was. Or newly acquired spouses of mutual friends don't like one another, and the once close friendship decreases to an occasional luncheon or seeing the Harvard–Yale game as couples and attending the annual New Year's Eve gala thrown by a mutual friend.

With a particular friend, a friendship cost analysis may prove the rewards too low and costs too high. Sometimes stocktaking may result in a heartbreaking housecleaning. A friendship either grows, matures and changes as we do, or it dwindles. In contrast, an acquaintanceship may remain unchanged for years.

■ *An active orientation to friendship will produce a social network.*

If we have a "let happen what will happen" attitude, usually nothing will. Some of us don't know how to find the friends we want. To ourselves, we say, "I'm just as good-looking as they are. Why do they move with such interesting people?" We never wonder, "What do they *do* to develop such an interesting friendship network? What *don't* I do?" A person may not even recognize the pluses of friendship and thus lose out on those. One executive claims, "Friends are God's apologies for giving us relatives." Another may say simply, "My friends are my family."

Ask yourself these questions to determine your friendship path:

What kind of people do I want as friends? What do I do to seek them out?

When did I last think of the kind of friend I myself would like to be? Of what I want to give in a friendship?

When I don't get what I need from a friendship, what is it that sometimes makes me feel disappointed or victimized and, on occasion, turns me into a true victim?

When I am the victim, how do I feel and what do I do about it—sulk, fight, act vindictive, communicate, or decide to swallow the "betrayal" and thereby keep the friendship.

Picking the Right Friends for the Right Reasons

Because of our own needs, beliefs, habits, too often we fail to realize that while a special chemistry between us and a friend may be complementary and fulfilling, often it leads to some form of victimization. To avoid falling into a victim trap, there are a number of cautions to observe when choosing friends.

■ *Keep away from users.*

For some of us, relationship with a user provides a sort of reassurance. We feel that if others use us, we're not completely worthless. Usually we tend to rationalize this kind of need. For example, one well-to-do woman continually called upon a friend to type her letters. Rationalizing that being used in that way served her conception of true friendship, the friend did it. She could not allow herself to recognize her true motives in going along with the demands made of her—to bury her own deep feelings of unimportance. The user rationalized her exercising power and dominance over her friend with a *quid pro quo* attitude: "I find blind dates for her; I have the right to expect her to do things for me."

If you feel yourself in a relationship with a user, answer this question: *Are you collaborating in the victim process?*

THE CASE OF THE WOMAN WHO WANTED TO BE USED

For a long time Sybil and Mary had been close friends. Sybil had looks, popularity and the better job. She supplied Mary with dates, took her to parties, and really created a social life for her unattractive but intellectual friend. Mary eagerly accepted the nice gestures but then criticized, "You're frivolous." One night Sybil asked, "What do I get from you?" Answered Mary, "I listen to you." Sybil realized she had had it. She retorted, "That isn't enough."

Sybil decided to end the friendship but still wishes she could "do" for Mary. In the Behavioral Psychotherapy formulation, Sybil unconsciously feels that if she could win Mary over to be sweet, kind, and loving to her, it would be like winning over the mother who never liked her and died when Sybil was twenty-two.

To achieve their ends, users take, exploit, and manipulate. They have an "I'm entitled" attitude and make requests but don't repay in kind. They are commonly self-centered energy exploiters who want others to provide the liveliness, companionship, and originality they feel missing in themselves. Often they want two things: to increase their feelings of superiority and your feelings of insecurity.

The fault may be yours. Through ignorance you fail to realize that the person you consider a friend has an ulterior objective: your signature on a club application, nomination for an office, an introduction, a deal. Mission accomplished, the friend may drop you or do you in.

For example, Danny J., then living in San Francisco, landed a big star for a friend who was putting together a film. Danny also provided the friend with the creative ideas that became the script's pivot point. However, at the film's premiere, Danny's name was conspicuously missing from the credits. Danny comments, "My friend was insecure. He wanted only *his* name to appear. This experience taught me a lesson. Now if I work with friends, I choose them more carefully or set up a contract."

If people repeatedly use you, something in you may want to be used. Dig back into preconscious memory. Has this been a pattern since childhood? Through these "using" friends, do you fulfill an unconscious fantasy of being servile, punished, pushed?

■ *Don't choose hostile friends.*

Often these are people who use attack and criticism to achieve a sense of superiority. Their comments can run the gamut from caustic remarks beginning "There's something I feel I should tell you" to continual put-downs like "You wouldn't understand; there's no point discussing it." They only want you around to provide themselves a fall guy.

Or they lash out to cover their feelings of inadequacy about themselves. For example, on four occasions, Tom D., a public relations executive, came up with professional introductions for Al A., a frequent job loser. Because of Tom's good name, companies created jobs for Al. Years later, Tom happened to mention the favors. Al's hostile response: "You never forget, do you?"

Why do people ally themselves with these hostile types? For many reasons. They may reinforce our low opinion of ourselves or may give us a reasonable excuse to strike back. They supply the chance to let us view ourselves as defenseless victims, an image many of us irrationally crave.

■ *Avoid people who play neurotic head games where a person has to end up the victim.*

People get into a pattern of playing head games for a variety of reasons. In some cases, the problem may stem from *a friend's own sibling rivalry,* which carries over into the relationship with another friend.

THE CASE OF THE GOLDEN GIRL

Connie and Josie had been friends ever since childhood. Connie was the Golden Girl—tall, good-looking, smart, and much richer than Josie. Connie married young, had two children, and then her husband developed a fatal illness. As always, devoted Josie came through as an after-work unpaid babysitter while Connie's younger sister, a well-known actress, was conspicuous by her absence. Connie rewarded Josie for her help with a patronizing, "If you marry, I'll give you the wedding."

Time passed. Josie, by then a banker, became engaged to a prominent doctor. Connie, now widowed, made no offer of a wedding. In fact, she dropped Josie. A few years ago, the always loyal Josie suggested a reunion lunch. Connie broke the date three times. This ended the friendship. From a mutual friend Josie heard about Connie's remarriage. Josie received no announcement of Connie's wedding. There is no contact.

The psychological explanation here is that Connie, extremely jealous of her younger sister, who had achieved the fame Connie thought she should have, acted out a displaced sibling rivalry with Josie. As long as Connie felt superior to Josie (a husband, more money), the friendship worked. Unlike Connie's real sister, Josie served as the "sister" to whom Connie could feel superior. When Josie's status changed so that she became well known and well married, and Connie's husband's death left her in financial difficulties, Josie no longer fulfilled Connie's sibling rivalry needs.

We may let an overly dependent friend turn us into a parent. Because he or she can't make any decisions without us, we assume the responsibility for the other person's life. Resenting it, we become victims, sometimes without knowing it.

In one case, a free-lance writer with a book contract telephoned a friend constantly over every comma, revisions, and editorial fight. Finally, publication day came and the book received a prominent review in the Sunday book section of the *New York Times* (the put-upon friend had arranged for an important public figure to review it). The writer immediately telephoned her constant consultant, but not with thanks or to share her excitement. Instead, she complained, "I've got severe stomach pains."

"Call a doctor," the friend responded.

Replied the writer, "But I had to call you first!"

At that point the friend decided he'd had enough of the dependency.

Realize that the friend who turns you into a parent does this because of transference problems. We can't fulfill this person's unconscious needs for a mother or father, so, despite our efforts, he or she will feel disappointed, let down by us—and a victim. We *do*. Our so-called friend *takes*. Both are victims.

Conversely, sometimes *we turn a friend into a parent*. Because of his or her problems the friend collaborates and permits us to do so. For instance, you seek a friend who will succor you, provide warmth, permit dependency. Every night you check in to report trivia, just as you did with your parents at the end of a school day. You become the victim because people see you as a weak, dependent person; you can't take action without discussion with your guide; you rob yourself of initiative and are unaware of your potential strength.

This kind of situation can have a series of possible impacts on your friendship. The friend may begin to feel burdened and victimized. That person's choices: to resign from the parent role or strike back with anger. Then you feel you are the victim. Or because it fulfills some neurotic need on the friend's part, he or she accepts the role. Of course, this leads to a distorted unequal relationship and both of you eventually suffer. Two tips: (1) Before you ask for help, try to solve problems on your own; (2) recognize your friend's limitations.

A Personal Devictimization Program for Friendships

When things go wrong in our social life, we tend to blame circumstances. But often things go wrong because there's something wrong with us or what we do. Blaming others leads to feelings of helplessness; it distracts us from what we can do to improve our social relationships so that we don't wake up Sunday morning and say, "I'm so lonely I could eat worms." Here are some tips on overcoming fear, knowing whom to trust, and friendship guidelines. Follow them and you don't have to eat worms.

PUTTING WHAT MATTERS OVER MIND FEAR

John is just as shy as you are. How does he make himself buy tickets for cultural events and invite a guest? Doesn't he worry that the other person won't accept?

Where did depressed Doreen, who has just had two successive relationships end badly, get the guts to call back her friend and ask, "Is that nice lawyer you mentioned to me still available? I decided I was making myself a victim by saying no"?

Fran barely knows how to open a can and fears strangers. And yet she carries out the idea of combining with three friends, making up a list of personality types and sending out an invitation to a party for which each person is asked to bring a friend of the opposite sex: "We're inviting the best and the brightest. From what we hear you fill the bill. Will you come on _____ at _____?" Everyone who was invited came and brought a friend. How did Fran do it?

Like many of us, John, Doreen, and Fran feel deep social fears and anxieties. Unlike many of us, *they put what matters over mind fears.* They get out and do. In the process of moving through the fears, they lessen them. Sometimes, like old soldiers, fears just fade away.

You *can* learn to control your fearful thinking and increase confidence, whether you obsess about wrong moves in the past or think of low-probability catastrophe possibilities as if they were certain and imminent. Most people find the following exercises fun. And they get results!

■ *Switch the put-down thought.* Change your "I will be a flop" thought to "I will act in a friendly way and see what happens." Here you must be careful to switch your thinking to something within your own control, not to something uncontrollable—"I will be the most popular person at the party."

■ *Stop that defeatist thought.* As soon as you become aware of a foreboding thought, calmly and firmly tell yourself, "Relax," and push the thought away. Then briefly relax—you might concentrate on relaxing a specific set of muscles, say your shoulder muscles. Deliberately divert your thinking to something, anything else (like a movie you want to see, a gift you want to buy). Use this technique every time the negative thought returns.

■ *Challenge that thought.* Often fear and anxiety provoke an illogical thought, an overextension of the consequences if something should really go wrong. To change this pattern, first identify the illogical thought and challenge it. Will people really hold you in contempt if they see you're anxious? If you say something silly or behave in an awkward way, does that really make you an "entirely worthless person"?

Use just one method or whatever combination of them that seems best for you when you need thought control.

Also, *put yourself in the right frame of mind.* Do as athletes do; try to reach your optimum performance level. You want to get in the right mood to do what works for you before the social event. Rehearsing success will help. (Use the "I Can Do It" exercise given on page 84.)

However, your fear may be such that you need a coping model to help you get to the event. Here, concentrate on your *feelings* first.

1. Pinpoint the situation. Example: You're walking over to start a conversation and you feel anxious.

2. In imagery, cope with the anxiety. Use any of the thought changing methods just discussed; tell yourself how terrific you are, try diaphragm breathing, yoga.

3. When you've reduced the anxiety even a bit, concentrate on the action. Imagine starting the conversation just the way you'd like to start it. Keep rehearsing until you come up with something that satisfies you.

For many people these behavioral methods of changing social thoughts and actions will work. For others, like Mark S., they won't. You must try to catch your *unconscious* feelings.

THE CASE OF THE
FEARFUL DATER

Mark S., a personable twenty-eight-year-old securities analyst, tried hard to change his victim behavior with the opposite sex. Nothing succeeded. He was always afraid to call a girl for a date. The more he liked a girl, the more he feared rejection with excuses like "I'm busy" . . . "I'm going on vacation." Mark assumed that the fear of rejection represented his core problem and that he was stuck at Level Two (blocks). A smart man, he knew he must change levels, so he went on to Behavioral Psychotherapy Level Three—the unconscious.

Looking into himself, Mark realized that anger lay at the root of his problem. Using his preconscious, he went back to his early teens and understood how furious he had been whenever a girl said, "No, I can't go out with you." For many years, this "unfairness" had churned within him: "Why should women have the position of power? Why do I have to be the supplicant? They shouldn't have the veto power over me. I want to be the one who does the rejecting."

Once Mark understood that the real reason that kept him from calling his current female interest was his own desire to do the rejecting, he got the courage to call the woman and ask, "Does it pay to keep calling you?" (she had turned him down twice). Her response: "Look, I'm getting involved with someone else. At this time, going out with you isn't a good idea."

The girl did reject him. Mark's fear had been correct. However, because he had thought it through, although he still felt the situation "unfair," he did not feel emotionally victimized.

TRUSTING: WHEN, HOW MUCH, AND WITH WHOM

The ephemeral quality of trust pervades, affects, and often ends friendships. Some friends pretend concern for other friends, but their sweet words lack a sense of truth. Others make promises but fail to fulfill them. Still others will act like friends in one area but fall short in another. To avoid victimization, we must know whom we can trust with what—and how. Trusting the wrong person in the wrong area will surely lead to feelings of betrayal.

AREAS OF TRUST QUIZ

Goal: Evaluation of whom to trust with what

Step One: In your workbook, write down the name of the friend whom you're evaluating.

Step Two: Think about how much you can trust your friend in the following areas:

- Money
- Help in minor practical problems
- Help in trivial emotional problems
- Help in important emotional problems
- To keep business secrets
- To share family problems
- To share sexual problems
- To keep promises

Take into account not only your past and recent experiences with your friend, but also his or her actions with others. Show the extent of your trust by putting the appropriate number from a scale of 1 to 5 next to each area cited.

          0—No trust whatever
          1—Moderate distrust
          2—More distrust than trust
          3—More trust than distrust
          4—Moderate trust
          5—Absolute trust

You may want to add additional items to the areas of trust.

By considering other areas, you begin to recognize the areas of trust limitations.

Usually, the more personal the areas of trust, the closer the friendship. However, even that closeness may possess limits. You may have a very good friend with whom you can share the most personal things and yet that person has a problem keeping promises. His or her "Cross my heart" means little. If you go on trusting that person to commit to what he or she says, you may end up the victim.

The trust problem can stem from many causes.

Example One: Sometimes it's *upbringing.* For instance, his mother always told Glenn A., "If you do good things, good will come to you." So Glenn became the good, trusting boy who grew into the good, trusting adult. Mother had no influence on his professional life, where he became marketing head of an advertising agency. Outside the job, he misjudged goodness. For his wife, he chose a "beautiful bitch" who left him. When Glenn inherited $50,000 from an uncle, he turned it over to a friend, supposedly a money management expert. Six months later the money had gone the way of bad stocks. Always trying to "do right," Glenn opens his home for various public events, then finds valuable objects missing. He won't learn. Comments his sister succinctly, "He just trusts the wrong people."

Example Two: *We may want trust from the wrong person.* As a sophomore at the University of Chicago, Bob M. had a professor whom he venerated, thinking they were friends, not just teacher and student. Then Bob switched majors. He received poor grades in his new course of study and returned to his former mentor for an objective point of view and "help." Says Bob, "I trusted him to be interested in me as a person, not just a student to mold. He had no interest. When I was no longer his student, he was finished with me. I feel he betrayed me."

Example Three: *Life can provide surprises; no guarantees exist.* You're always learning about trust in every friendship.

Kitty T., a young TV commercial maker, had a married best friend. One day Kitty lunched with the friend's husband, Larry. They fell in love over the chicken Marengo, and Kitty and Larry went home to bed. Larry divorced his wife and married Kitty. They became friendly with another professional couple. Larry died young. The couple befriended Kitty and her two fatherless children. Then Kitty took this husband away from his wife. Moral: When Kitty has a husband, she sticks. When she's single, she steals. Her friends must decide whether they can accept this trust limitation.

FRIENDSHIP GUIDELINES

Set Behavior Guidelines for Others

■ *Don't let others show lack of respect for you.* Sometimes they don't realize what they're doing. In longstanding friendships, a friend may treat you as if you're exactly as you were as a teenage chum, and that's no longer what you want. Or you permit rudeness, last-minute backouts from dates, unacceptable aggressiveness. Do this and you collaborate in your own victimization.

For example, Sylvia and Cathy decided to give a singles party. Because Sylvia lived in the suburbs, where edibles are cheaper, she took a vacation day off from work, purchased all the essentials, made the food, and drove down in a packed car, only to find Cathy still washing her hair and cat hairs all over the floor. Says Sylvia, "I only wanted to be nice, but she didn't know how to be nice."

■ *Understand that others may do the wrong things with the best intentions.* One couple constantly criticized the man their close friend was dating. She comments wryly, "They were right, but they had no right." The problem: They nagged. She became the victim because the friends never thought through how to discuss in a tactful way what they saw as the problem.

■ *Realize that behavioral standards vary from person to person.* Setting behavior guidelines for others includes taking their individuality into account. What a friend may accept, you may not. Then you feel manipulated because people follow their guidelines, not yours. One wife became upset when, after she and her husband had given a party for twenty people, a couple took the telephone number of each guest and called them all to invite them to *their* party, leaving out the host couple. The first hostess thought this pushiness reflected on her. Actually, both host and hostess knew what the couple was like. The mistake: inviting them.

■ *Decide whether you'll accept little—but perhaps meaningful—slights.* Two women had been close friends for years. Then Joan heard that Gloria was going around asking people, "Do you think Fred [Joan's spouse] is a good therapist?"

Annoyed, Joan told her, "We don't like your going around asking that question." Gloria did not stop. After hearing of three similar incidents, Joan put an end to the friendship.

■ *Inform others of your guidelines.* If they know how you feel, they may not like the rules, but the matter is out in the open. Say, "Look, if you meet at my house and like each other and make a luncheon date, that's great. But *include me,* the first time. After that, you're on your own." To others this nuance of behavior may not matter. That's why you have to explain.

Teasing offers a good example of when to speak up. Even though you know a friend's continual teasing remarks are only loving jests, representing a certain conversational style, the cracks still make you feel defenseless and exposed and you can't figure out a way to respond that makes you feel right. Tell the friend, "Please don't tease. It upsets me."

Set Behavior Guidelines for Yourself

If you want to make new friends and not feel a martyr because you do nothing to make anything happen, you must take action. There are two basics:

■ *Do what you feel is you.* You will feel less of a victim if you tailor your socializing to your personality. One man found personal columns did not work for him ("I resented taking out women I didn't like for expensive dinners"), so he joined a classical-concerts-for-singles group. Another eschews the personals columns in *New York* magazine but finds that *Harvard* magazine produces just the personality type she wants.

■ *Recognize your own strengths so you don't ask too much of others.* For example, Mike, a lonely young man, kept begging a friend to take him to parties. For a while the friend obliged. Then he told him, "This is a burden. Do things on your own." So Mike joined a computer dating service. He told his popular friend about it, no longer asked the friend for help, and was delighted by the new people he met. His action had a double effect. Relieved of the pressure of serving as Mike's only social contact, the friend took Mike to a New Year's Eve party where Mike met new friends minus computer. But the computer dating had given him the confidence to cope.

The Friendship Compromise Quotient

There comes a time when we must decide, "Is this friendship worth it?"

Sometimes the burden may be too much. For example, Marlene F. had a married friend with "separation anxiety" who called constantly, leaving numerous messages on Marlene's answering machine and instilling guilt whenever Marlene failed to return a call. Recalls Marlene, "Our relationship had a hidden contract. For her the contract meant I was always supposed to be there for her calls and to listen to her dinner menu. The more things I had going, the clingier she got." When Marlene begged her to call just once a week, the friend had a temper tantrum. Marlene ended the friendship saying, "I saw in her what wasn't there."

A person sometimes drops a friendship for what seems a value reason—and then changes his or her mind. For instance, Pete S. and Joe J. both worked in Denver as stockbrokers. Joe was going through a painful divorce and decided to return to New York, where he had grown up. Pete told him, "You're running away. Stay here and work out your problems." Acrimony developed. Joe did move. The long-term friendship seemed finished. Two years later, Pete came to Manhattan and called Joe; they had a happy reunion. Claims Joe, "You have to let bygones be bygones."

At other times we decide the positives outweigh the negatives. For instance: Susan L. felt put upon when she spent a day mopping up the debris of a friend's apartment, which had been flooded. The friend, out of town, but alerted by the super, had called, screaming "Help." Susan never received a thank-you. She felt exploited but reminded herself of their warm talks and shared dates and decided to keep the friendship. Months later the friend introduced Susan to her boyfriend, who got Susan a terrific job. "She does things in a different way from me," admits Susan. "But she does them!"

In determining *your* friendship compromise quotient, keep several points in mind:

■ Are the particular actions that turn you off central, peripheral, or trivial to the relationship? If a long-time friend is supposed to drop over, doesn't show up, and then explains, "It was raining," but you learn she went to a matinee that day even though you changed your plans to accommodate her, do you really want to end the friendship even though she victimized you? She may be completely unaware of how important her lack of courtesy is to you.

■ Don't think in black and white terms of friendship or no friendship. When a friend lacks qualities you want, you can move to a more superficial relationship. You don't have to drop the relationship altogether.

■ Evaluate whether the relationship's good points outweigh the bad. Are you going along with a friendship that means nothing to you? Would you be better off establishing a new social circle?

■ If you want to enjoy a fulfilling friendship, be clear about what you want to receive—and give. Then ask yourself, "Can I achieve what I want with this particular friend, or will I end up the victim again?"

Remember, finding, having, and keeping the right kind of friends will make you feel right about yourself—and lead to positive self-feelings in others.

7 □ Super Strategies for Emotional Problems on the Job

Janet L. grew up in a tiny tenement apartment where she shared a room with her brother. From the age of eleven, she worked at part-time jobs. She put herself through college as a nightclub hat check girl, joined the Peace Corps, and eventually went to work as a secretary at a buying office.

Consciousness of her early background always made her feel "deprived." She recalls, "I blamed my parents, felt lonely, cried a lot. All my friends and acquaintances seemed to have had economic, educational, and social advantages that I had not."

At age thirty, Janet stopped crying and learned "not to be a victim." Passed over for a promotion, she made several *deliberate* decisions: "Not to be poor any more, to work and fight for success." The chance for betterment came quickly when, through a former coworker, she got an interview for a job as fashion director for a major company, a job that was several steps up the ladder for her professionally. Sick with nerves but knowing her future depended on getting the job, she researched every aspect of the job involved, enlisted mentors, practiced for the interview, and bought a special ensemble to wear to it. She got the job ("I felt like another person").

Through the job she became involved with an advertising tycoon (married). For almost four years they were lovers, and he introduced her into a world of sophisticated business projects. From him, she gained the courage to start her own fashion marketing business, which boomed. The tycoon returned to his wife, but Janet got herself a series of long-lasting clients. She regards herself as a successful professional with a happy life that she controls.

Says Janet, now sure of herself, even glamorous, "When I decided not to be a victim—with the help of therapy—I understood how one allows, even invites, other people to make one unhappy and insecure. I learned not to be seduced into uncomfortable or destructive situations. I like my major client because his home base is thirteen hundred miles away. He can't look over my shoulder. When people complain to me about being stymied and never able to get ahead, I tend to believe it's their fault. I now feel confident. I feel I have earned the right to my opinions and my life."

Confident serves as the key word that describes Janet. She set her goals, achieved them, and is not in the least bothered by remaining single. She is thoroughly satisfied with what she has.

Can we do the same—feel satisfied with what we have—even if we possess different aims? Our ability to exist and progress in the business world, to prevent victimization of ourselves by ourselves and others, depends on one word, *confidence*.

A Behavioral Psychotherapy Guide to Job Happiness: Practical and Emotional

KNOW THE KEY FACTS OF WORK LIFE

■ *A difference exists between job relations and close relationships.*

In family, friendships, and love, at least the myth exists that we will take care of each other. We have a right to expect care and support. If victimization in these relationships occurs, we feel we have the right to regard it as betrayal. But by regarding our job as a family situation, we transfer deep, primitive feelings about love and acceptance to our business life, and there is danger in that. We must depersonalize the job situation and handle it as an aspect of reality that is not governed by emotional considerations. If we do not, we surely set ourselves up to be victims.

The personality traits our families tolerate (lateness, sarcasm, "I told you so" behavior) because they love us, can cause serious interference at work. For example, at the office you and your unit must produce. In your family, you've played the role of the "responsible one" who gets things done. But this trait that works in family life often makes you impatiently step on toes at the office. Result: You lose the job or get bypassed because you disrupt things by becoming impatient and overcritical, disrespectfully taking over others' work without giving them a chance.

■ *Good interpersonal relations on the job will reduce emotional victimization.*

A person's style (haughty or friendly), ego (too strong, too weak), and perhaps a personality that lacks compatibility with others, will prove strong factors in creating a possible job victim. Claims management consultant David McLaughlin in reference to difficulties on the job, "The human problems stand in the way more than the technical." Evaluate your strengths in dealing with peers, subordinates, superiors. What are you good at? Are you best at one-to-one situations, groups, formal meetings? It's important to know. For example, if you have a suggestion for your firm, decide in which of the three situations just cited it would be best for you to present it. Capitalize on *your* special strength. In my practice, I have found that almost everyone *knows* his or her situational strength. The problems come in putting it to use.

We must also evaluate the need-fit factor. In marriage, we want our mutual needs to fit so that we spur closeness. In work, we have different objectives: to keep relations with the boss, coworkers, and subordinates smooth so that we can handle the practicalities and overcome the problems. We must put our emphasis on *doing* so that possible hurt feelings don't turn us into emotional victims.

■ *Don't view the work world as a loving one.*

Certain paternalistic companies still exist, but for most it's the bottom line and good performance that count. Says one executive who lost his job after twenty years, "You *know* it won't happen to you. You say, 'They can't get rid of me.' But they do." Even though your work is good, you may get fired because the new CEO wants to cut costs, there's a merger or takeover (five floors of bodies may be wiped out through one memo), or because you don't fit a company's image (like the secretary in a very visible position who chewed gum, was reprimanded, didn't listen, and lost her job).

Like personal victimization in relationships, professional victimization works two ways: We can exaggerate the disaster and give up or use the enforced change in our life as an opportunity to learn and change for the better.

SELF-MADE VICTIMS AT WORK

Comments veteran personnel agency director Lillian Roberts, "Most people allow themselves to be victims." Is that true of you at work? Do you identify with any of the following common job victim situations, based on our four victim types?

The "Kick Me" Person

The "kick me" person, you'll recall, is one who sets him- or herself up for victimization.

Problem: Insecurity. Carol J. reveals, "By feeling I wasn't enough of an experienced business person, I made myself a victim with management. I had no M.B.A., wasn't an accountant or lawyer. I took the role of being pupil to the big boss. He considered me his favorite daughter, but when the business got in trouble, he thought of me as weak—because I thought of myself that way. I should have told myself, 'I've earned it. I'm smart.' Instead I lost the job." Despite women's liberation, many women, like Carol, make themselves victims because they feel gratitude for being given any halfway decent job and fail to realize their professional and psychological potential. The same dynamic can come into play in men who lack confidence in their abilities.

Problem: Self-destruction. This may take the form of everything from procrastination to too many personal phone calls. Management takes on-the-job behavior seriously. One executive comments, "Not showing up has become an increasing problem." For example, a minor executive who fears losing her job nevertheless will allow herself to procrastinate—coming to work late and arriving late for meetings. The failure-to-show problem can happen even with people who need work. One stylist invited an out-of-work photographer to a large press conference. He neither called nor came. Regretfully, she notes, "I would have told everyone, 'This is Jimmy, the terrific photographer I told you about.'" But Jimmy didn't see the conference as a chance for job leads and instead forgot and made a lunch date with a friend.

The lack of taking responsibility for yourself serves as one of the most common forms of self-destruction. This kind of self-destructive pattern can cause people a lot of trouble. Not only must individuals who follow this pattern recognize that they're on a professional suicidal merry-go-round, but they must get off it. If the problem gets severe, they should seek professional help.

Problem: Failure to do homework. One day a leader in an allied field called Tom B. and asked him to join the firm. Happy where he was, Tom refused, but the other persisted with "Let's have dinner at my club." Curious, Tom agreed and received an offer of double his salary. Unable to refuse, Tom agreed. He joined the company and performed miracles. Six months later, the boss fired him. Stunned, Tom asked, "Why?" Responded the boss, "You did for me what I wanted." Tom had not investigated the company, its policies, or the boss's reputation and had not insisted on an employment contract. By failing to do his homework, Tom set himself up for victimization.

The Know-Not Victim

The know-not victim isn't aware of being a victim but suffers just the same.

Problem: We blindly assume roles picked for us by others. Mel T. grew up in a success-oriented family. His brother joined the family business. Mel went into another business with more intellectual overtones but still a bottom-line situation. Now forty-two, he comments, "Until recently, I never found out that I had been programmed to think that business was the place where I belonged. Now I know this is foreign to what I am naturally. I should have been a professor."

Problem: We unwittingly ascribe emotional roles to others. Because of past influences or lacks, we may fit others into a role that turns out to be dangerous for ourselves. One motherless woman came to a company as a young business school graduate and viewed the boss as the mother she lacked. She always refused advancement opportunities because she could not leave "mother." When "mother" retired, "daughter" was let go with minimal severance pay and benefits. She had confused her business life with her emotional life.

Problem: Self-sabotage. Lawyer Joe M. would find all sorts of ways *not* to do his best job. For example, if he had two clients, one major, one minor, he'd find some justification for concentrating on the less important client at the expense of losing the larger. To colleagues he would denigrate any triumph ("Anyone could have done that"). Actually, Joe feared recognition of his own competence. His very competent father had died unexpectedly young. In Joe's distorted thinking, if he allowed himself to become a competent adult, he, too, would die. As a result, he felt compelled to deny his ability. He had no idea that by so doing he was victimizing himself.

We can sabotage ourselves by talking about things better left unsaid. Joy B., a thirty-three-year-old top salesperson at a good store, had a history of childhood diabetes and talked incessantly about her symptoms, diet, and monthly tests for glaucoma. At a store event, her boss commented to Joy's coworker, "She sure is one sick girl." Repeating this to Joy, who did a superb job, the astute colleague told her. "You're well enough to work very well. Keep quiet about your health." As a result of this well-meant critical comment, Joy learned enough to nip any self-victimization by shutting up about her health.

The Misperceiver

Misperception can result in self-victimization in all kinds of circumstances and situations.

Problem: Failure to recognize what is needed. One man ghosted his boss's speeches, boasted about his work, and got fired. The personnel director told him he was not right for the job. Recalls Marve D., "The boss wanted everyone to think he wrote his own talks. I didn't make that same mistake on my next job."

Problem: Blaming the boss when the fault lies in oneself. In private life, Jill J., a decorator's assistant, was trying to become more assertive. Jill made a serious mistake with a client. Over the next weekend the client phoned Jill's boss, who straightened the matter out. Furious because the boss had not referred the matter to her, at her next Assertiveness Training group, Jill explained her rage at her "thoughtless boss." In reality, through her own poor performance, she had made a victim out of her boss and herself.

Problem: Misperceived unfairness. Here the difficulty lies in viewing a situation as unfair when it's really not that unfair. This happens all too frequently.

THE CASE OF THE EMPLOYEE WHO SLEPT WITH THE BOSS

When the compassionate man who headed a medium-size company retired, the conglomerate powers appointed a handsome lawyer from another division in his place. Dick M. promptly started an affair with Betty J., a smart junior executive. Betty's boss disliked the set-up and quit. Betty acquired her boss's job and a much higher salary than she had been earning. The entire staff felt this unfair: "She sleeps with the boss!" Even though talented Betty brought off a series of triumphs, other staff members felt victimized by her promotion. Eventually Dick lost his job. Because she was so good at her work, Betty kept hers and has gone on and up with the organization. The "unfairness" assessment represented an employee exaggeration. Regardless of her sexual activities, Betty would have made it on the basis of brains in any company.

The Exaggerator

Sometimes an on-the-job victim problem exists, but we distort it rather than make an attempt to resolve it. For example, Kevin C. loved his job in his company's marketing division. Suddenly, without explanation, he was transferred to employee relations, which he viewed as a dead end. Seeing the shift as "ostracism without explanation," he got himself a job with another company, moving laterally. When he said good-bye, his superior told him, "It's a shame you're going. Didn't you realize we transferred you to move you up? We wanted you to know every part of our operation so you'd be able to move on to other things." He had been so preoccupied with what he thought was a job insult that he never thought to ask why he had been shifted.

RECOGNIZE THE VICTIMIZERS AT WORK

Victimizers exist in every job area. Some bully; others receive pleasure from tricky dealing—like telling two employees to work on the same project without informing either about the other's assignment. The demands and impersonal nature of the job often encourage a person (usually a superior but sometimes a peer or subordinate) to victimize. The job pressures imposed by the victimizer often interact with our own style and emotional needs.

Here are some suggestions for effectively dealing with typical victimizers at Behavioral Psychotherapy Level One behavior.

The New Manager: An Impersonal Victimizer

Upon entering the firm the new manager's mission is to cut, fire, reorganize, reassign. The actions taken may be unfair because he or she lacks detailed knowledge and the situation ("get rid of ten bodies") forces unfairness upon the manager. There may be a directive to select on the basis of team compatibility rather than past work performance. The manager may feel the need to solidify his or her own power and eliminate potential competition. He or she may be completely unfair and make the selection on the basis of personal preferences and insecurities (for example, the manager never went to college and you have a Harvard M.B.A.—out you go).

You can fail to cope or try to conquer the problems.

Example One: Phil D., the psychologist for a major company, felt threatened when the president brought in a woman with "less experience" as his boss. He recalls, "I did things that if someone else had done them, I would have said 'How stupid.' I let my resentment overcome my brains." Because he didn't know what to do, Phil chose the flippant route to failure. Typical of his faux pas, at one meeting, the new manager boasted of the department's $10,000 cost-cutting in six months. Quipped the psychologist, "Only ten thousand dollars in six months." Soon after he was out.

Example Two: Suddenly a huge conglomerate bought the store where Sandy M. was divisional merchandising manager of sportswear. Wanting to keep his job, Sandy effected a series of strategies that would increase his chances of remaining. He allied himself with no element in the store. That meant no lunches or cocktails with fellow workers. Then, knowing the new bosses cared only about bottom-line figures, he called his buyers together and informed them that they must make a good showing for the new regime—bins cleaned each morning, stock out ahead, customers taken care of immediately, no chitchat among themselves. In every contact with his bosses, he emphasized his strengths. He had an ability to create fashion promotions that could utilize everything from windows to advertising to make a sales impact. He submitted a new promotional idea, backed up by records of his past successes, to his new boss. Sandy kept his job because he did what had to be done and knew must be done in the best way he could.

The Power Player

In the case of the power player, business behavior takes a back seat to a need to victimize associates. Sometimes this is done out of ignorance. The power player can do his or her own work but lacks the knowledge to supervise others. When they fail to fulfill the unfair demands made of them, he or she turns victimizer. Or the power player may need to humiliate, to find an Achilles heel, to protect himself with mediocre underlings. This *sadist* likes to demean and belittle. Some may be as ruthless as J. R. Ewing in TV's "Dallas." Some even go as far as to keep dossiers on employee gossip for use as possible weapons.

THE CASE OF THE WOMAN WHO
SAW HER BOSS AS A SADIST

Karen J., the brilliant creative chief at a top western advertising agency, was continually persecuted, criticized, and called unpleasant names by Norman C., the agency president. Finally, though knowing her job was at stake, she told him, "I won't give you permission to treat me like that." Norman did not stop his persecution. She protested again, saying, "I won't work under these conditions." Nevertheless Norman continued as before.

Because Norman acted like a sadist, Karen saw him as one and decided to fight back instead of being a helpless victim. She told her tale to the company board chairman, who requested her permission to reprimand Norman. The next day Norman yelled at Karen, "How could you do this to me?" Karen reiterated, "I can't work your way. In my family if my brothers and I fought, we weren't allowed at the table." Taken aback, Norman confessed with just a touch of humility, "My brothers and I would fight, but then we would all sit down for dinner and forget it."

Now there's a temporary truce. Seeing that Norman grew up using an offensive, sadistic style and doesn't see fighting as more than incidental, Karen explains, "If he screams, I shrug. My speaking up did something for me." She also got counsel from a lawyer on just how to protect her job if Norman ever again becomes too offensive.

When you work with power players, it helps you avoid job victimization if you have a mentor or friends in various departments and are in on "the company grapevine." One middle management executive comments, "There are lots of things you can't put in the company bulletin. There's always someone who will spread lies about you. You want the truth about you on the grapevine. I get friends to do it for me."

There's also a special kind of power player victimizer: the entrepreneur who builds up his business until it becomes a spectacular success and then acquires an "emperor" complex. However, the new "emperor"—formerly so nice and well meaning—just does not have the skills to run the newly expanded business. With growth he needs greater discipline and financial tightening. He can't manage it, however. Things get out of hand and he thinks he has no choice but to fire a worker who contributed to the company growth. So "off with his head," he says. If you get caught in this trap, don't sit around weeping. Keep your head. Start looking before it happens—via friends, agencies, any means at your disposal.

The Boss with Personal Problems That Prompt Victimizing Behavior

■ *The ego victimizer.* Ego victimizers characteristically claim and get credit for everything. Because of their own insecurity, they use others to do their work, provide no support and only part of the information needed, and try to get a victim to accept the blame for their mistakes.

When your boss or a colleague criticizes you, recognize the motivation. Does it spring from insecurity or jealousy or from a sincere desire to help you? If it comes from insecurity or jealousy, you are dealing with an ego victimizer, but not all criticism is victimization. There are people who will try to put you wise to a mistake you're making—for example, not delegating or not running a tight enough ship. In response, you can try something like "What do you think I should do? I'd like to come back in two weeks and talk about it." Thus you demonstrate your goal orientation.

Sometimes we can cope with an ego victimizer by deliberately doing nothing. Tim R. worked for a "mean dummy." In a pleasant way, Tim would suggest, "This way might be better," but the boss would throw a tantrum and yell, "Let me do things my way." Vowing to "let him sink" but feeling very much the temporary victim, Tim quietly followed orders. Eventually the boss blew the job. Tim got it.

■ *The indecisive boss.* This person believes it is always possible to change his or her mind and still be right. At first he or she tells a subordinate, "That's all wrong." Three days later, the comment is, "Just what we want." In the interim, the indecisive behavior of the boss has completely intimidated the employee, who now also feels unable to make any decision. Then the boss rages, "Why can't you make a decision? What am I paying you for?"

■ *The addict.* The addiction can be to alcohol, sex, drugs, or gambling. The addict spends time that should be spent in working at a bar, sniffing coke, in a daytime liaison, or at the races. The consequence: The addict's associate becomes victimized because he or she inevitably carries out more and more of the boss's job without getting paid for it and lacks the backup and power to do the job well.

■ *The workaholic.* Because workaholics fail to consider the limitations or agendas of others, they recognize no difference between work and play and feel everyone should feel about work as they do. They tyrannize their coworkers and subordinates. They victimize not only workers who want some play time, but also the workers' wives and children. For example, one CEO never permitted his assistant to take a vacation.

You cannot let a workaholic boss make a victim out of you. You must at least try to create a workable balance between job and home life.

Molly A. figured out a strategy to cope with a workaholic boss. A secretary and recently married, Molly had two bosses. One, a workaholic, ignored the clock. The second hated his family and always worked late. As a result of the office atmosphere, Molly worked later and later, and her new husband resented this more and more. Feeling she might lose her job if she failed to keep the lengthy hours, Molly found herself losing the balance between work and marriage. After much thought, she decided she would offer to work two nights a week—no more. Her two managers responded to her reasonable presentation of her feelings and agreed—"provided there was no exceptional situation." Thereafter, they were more respectful to Molly.

BASIC BUSINESS
BEHAVIOR STRATEGIES

■ *Watch your back.* Remember that all victimization won't come from the boss. It can come from subordinates, as in the case of defensive criticism through which others try to blame their failure on you ("I only did what you told me to do"). Or at a meeting a peer announces, "Joe has misjudged the situation." You must respond to the criticism as a job problem. The subordinate or peer may want your job or stab at you from insecurity. Here is where it is helpful to have a mentor, someone who can help guide you through the maze of interoffice relations.

Sometimes victimization can go far beyond a hastily tossed off crack. It may come from a *competitive victimizer* who excels in dirty tricks—often to draw attention to a professional objective or project rather than just to gain glory for him- or herself. For instance, John M., a researcher at a chemical institute, asked another lab for the formula for a particular chemical compound. The lab provided directions, but after four months of exhaustive labor, John realized the formula he had been given was incorrect. Because the other lab had wanted to submit for research grants before John's lab, the head of the other lab had deliberately given an incorrect formula.

■ *Build up the skills to achieve your goals,* whether your goal is to stay where you are or advance. Doing what you do well will preclude much victimization. If you want advancement, evaluate your abilities not in terms of "Can I do it?" but "How well can I do it?" If you can do it seventy-five percent well and want to do better, ask yourself, "How can I do it eighty percent well?" Remember, different goals motivate people in different ways. Management consultant David McLaughlin points out, "Marriage, financial change, will propel some. Sometimes the rockets and slow learners meet later at the same place."

■ *Prepare.* Just as sitting at home will not get an emotionally insecure person started on a social network, passively sitting back in the business world will get the ambitious person nothing but the feeling of emotional hurt. Prepare for what you want, whether with special courses, through gaining an advanced degree, or simply by asking for what you want. Be prepared to ask for a raise—even from a victimizer boss. You may hear a surprise reaction, "I've been waiting for you to ask." A public relations executive asked her company to double her already high retainer. She got the increase because she proved that every three and a half weeks she delivered in media credits and stories space worth the value of the firm's total yearly retainer plus what they gave her for expenses.

■ *Don't make decisions prematurely.* One secretary felt terribly victimized because she worked for a physician who dictated at "nine hundred words a minute." She was about to

quit when he interrupted with "I'm sorry—I dictate too fast. I
can't seem to get out of the habit." Encouraged to stay by her
boss's admission, she eventually got used to his fast pace and
then liked her job.

■ *Don't permit victimization when the company doesn't
take care of you.* Use your self smarts. You may find you succeed
in remedying a situation that otherwise puts you in the position
of a victim.

THE CASE OF THE WOMAN WHO FOUGHT BACK AND WON

Recently, because of changes in management, company heads
wanted to force Lynn W., fifty-six, into early retirement. They
realized that Lynn was in a position to contest this and make
things difficult, so they decided to offer her a special induce-
ment. They (mainly the "bastard business manager") assigned
her a series of self-help booklets to be done on a free-lance basis
with a generous budget. It would be a three-year project, with
Lynn in charge. Lynn accepted and agreed to early retirement.

The company had no intention of proceeding. The minute
Lynn left the office premises to begin the project at home, the
bosses cancelled the booklet plan, which they had used as a
force-out device.

Determined to get back at her former firm, Lynn bypassed an
attorney and the company's business manager. Instead, she
wrote a letter explaining her outlay of time and the commitments for which she felt responsible to the chairman of the
company board, a multimillionaire who was extremely conscious of his good reputation. Two days later a subordinate
telephoned Lynn, "Mr. _____ is sorry for the inconvenience.
We are sending a check for twenty-five thousand dollars."

In this example, Lynn's successful use of self smarts stemmed
from her realization that the force-out maneuver was the manager's fault and that the chairman possessed a certain amount
of decency along with a fear of adverse publicity. With a different kind of company, her strategy might have failed. Comments Lillian Roberts, "You haven't a chance against a company
with a staff of lawyers on retainer." Nevertheless, in this case,

Lynn took a chance—she applied business self smarts and won.

You aren't born with business self smarts. You have to learn them and use them.

STOP RUNNING BUSINESS SCARED

It's all too common for people on the job to victimize themselves without any thought to the consequences they expose themselves *and others* to as a result.

Example One: Len J. worked for a conglomerate as a senior vice-president reporting to an executive vice-president. When Len made his monthly report to his boss about his unit's work, if anything had gone badly, he took full responsibility. If things had gone well, he made sure his most responsible subordinate got full credit. Len would not reveal to his superior how much he had organized, shaped, and supervised the subordinate's work. The result: Because he played down his own abilities he got a low bonus and felt victimized.

Example Two: One employee always came in late. Boss Guy L. protected him by saying nothing. However, the company top boss heard about the lateness behavior; ordered, "Fire him"; and chastised Guy.

Example Three: In the middle of the night, Martha L., a university housing officer, woke up and realized that she had totally forgotten to see that the trunk room was staffed on the college's opening day, a Sunday. Thousands of freshmen would find their luggage totally inaccessible. She sat and sobbed and did nothing.

In the examples above, Len suffers from the fear of being the authority; Guy suffers from the fear of being disliked—he wants to be seen as "the good boss" so everyone will love him. And Martha suffers from a paralyzing fear of punishment for making a mistake.

Remember, whatever the job and situation and how the situation changes, to prevent emotional victimization you must have confidence in yourself and your ability to do what *you* want to do. That requires another must: You must understand and do something about your job fears. These, operating on Behavioral Psychotherapy Level Two, can be fairly simple, like fear of responsibility, or more complex, like fear of failure. Underlying the fear of failure lies the wish to fail. You reason that if you fail, you will be safer because (a) you won't have to fend off attacks from others and (b) you won't have to worry about maintaining success.

Fear may dominate our behavior under either (or both) of two conditions:

In the first case, *we don't know we have the fear.* Sometimes we have such an excellent avoidance pattern that we manage not to expose ourselves to the situation we fear. We can disguise this even from ourselves. For example, one man wanted time off to attend his sister's wedding. Afraid his supervisor would refuse, he never asked. Hiding his fear, he saw himself only as a procrastinator. He just told his sister, "I can't get time off."

Or, we may be unaware of a fear because we automatically rationalize it to ourselves. For instance, a manager asked his assistant to take over an important project involving extensive travel. The assistant refused—"Time with my family matters more." While often this is a valid concept, this particular employee feared responsibility, avoided it, and rationalized his avoidance with the reasonable-sounding excuse of family needs.

In the second set of circumstances, *we know the fear and automatically assume that the dreadful consequences we imagine surely will happen.* We assume things like "People will make fun of me if I'm nervous during my speech" or "He will not only refuse my request for a raise, but he'll sneer at me for asking." Because we avoid the situation, we never put ourselves in a position to see that even if the worst happens, the worst may not be as bad as we think.

Fear-Fighting Actions

■ *Use remedial assertion.* You can correct mistakes and thus overcome the fear. For example, the university housing officer could have stopped crying and made arrangements to have each trunk delivered to the room of its owner during the following week. Don't make the self-demand, "I should never make a mistake." That leads to a paralyzing kind of fear.

Instead, recognize that mistakes will happen—but you can remedy them if they do.

■ *Take action to build your confidence.* Go back to the exercises for Getting That Winning Feeling and Convincing Yourself of Your Own Confidence in chapter 5. Adapt them to the business situation you fear (taking more responsibility, moving up within the company, asking for more money) and rehearse in imagery. Then make yourself do the feared act.

■ *Realize that fear can be good.* Psyching yourself up to overcome your fear and deliver your best performance can result in perfect performance. Actors use this technique all the time. Theatrical luminary Kevin Kline acknowledges, "I agonize at every step along the way. If we're in casting, I worry about the first read-through. . . . People who don't worry, worry me."

DELVE INTO YOUR UNCONSCIOUS

Our unconscious may work overtime just as often in the job situation as with friends and lovers. We may have distorted reactions to others so that we respond to them *not as they are,* but in some very personalized manner. We *project* onto them some of our childhood experiences. A person may see a coworker whom everyone else terms a "nice guy" as an angry person (like his father). Or we may see the boss as a kindly father figure when all our work friends warn, "Be on guard." The late psychiatrist Dr. Harry Stack Sullivan called this way of thinking "parataxical distortion" (indicating that emotion distorts thinking and perception). Seeing qualities in others that do not exist means *we* have unresolved problems. These create problems on the job because they lead into victim-provoking behavior that affects interactions with others and interferes with our whole work performance.

What are some of the unresolved problems at Behavioral Psychotherapy Level Three (the unconscious) that affect our work?

Self-effacement

Because of unconscious feelings of self-denigration (or as Karen Horney says, "self-despising"), we concentrate on others' approval rather than on getting the job done. Eager to have clients think he's superman, one accountant gives them the advice they want to hear, not what's best.

A person may not ask for a special project because should he or she get it, peers may be envious or jealous. When our boss fails to provide the signs of love we crave for reassurance (lunches or invitations to his or her home), we feel upset. Thus, because we want love in a professional situation where it is unlikely to be forthcoming, we continually victimize ourselves.

Masochism

We may feel a need to be punished. On the job we show this in two ways:

1.   So we can feel persecuted, we take on unrewarding tasks.

2.   We want to reinforce our low self-image by bad performance. Unconsciously, we make errors, fail to follow through on important things, use bad judgment when, in actuality, we are capable of very good judgment.

In charge of a contest in which three award winners would arrive from their various states at different times on a national holiday, department head Elaine M., in charge of a staff of ten underlings, assumed the chore of meeting the contestants. All the way to the airport, she felt abused, but she had never asked any of the assistants to take on any of the chore. She sought out victimization by taking on an unrewarding task.

Seth M. acquired a new boss brought in to reduce costs. Ignoring the reality, Seth started a new performance appraisal project, using college students. His boss told him, "I can get this done with existing staff." Annoyed and disliking his new superior intensely, Seth began arriving at 11:00 A.M. The new boss said, "Good-bye." Seth got his punishment (firing) and reinforced his self-image of being a "terrible" person.

Naïve Dependency

This involves a need to gain care from others. On the job this pattern makes for failure. For example, with the fantasy demand that help be offered gratuitously, a person doesn't ask for it, so doesn't get it or do his job right. If you need files from another department, you don't request them. "They should know—they heard what I said at the meeting," you tell yourself. Or your firm is breaking up but you do no job scouting. Instead you hope that someone will emerge from the blue and offer help gratuitously.

The Abel Syndrome

As we observed previously, some individuals suffer guilt over their capabilities or successes. This involves more than a simple fear of achieving or maintaining success. In this pattern, because of guilt about our success, we set ourselves up for destruction. We have a drive for success but can't live with it—we don't think we deserve it.

A boss and his top assistant conducted a very successful client presentation. The assistant had done practically all the work. Riding back to the office, his boss congratulated him heartily, but instead of accepting the praise the assistant reverted back to his lifetime pattern—reacting to success with guilt and subsequent moves to self-destruction. He started a fight with the boss over something the boss had said during the presentation, got the boss mad, and thereby set himself up to be a victim of the boss's counterattack. Because the assistant couldn't take the credit the boss offered, he managed to annoy him.

FREEING YOUR UNCONSCIOUS AT WORK: AN EXERCISE IN RECALL

Goal: To understand how early life patterns have affected your lifetime job pattern

Reflect on your reactions to problems or situations that confronted you in earlier years of your life. As an example, examine your relationship with responsibility, which may influence many behaviors. Recall as best you can the way you viewed responsibility for tasks you were given.

As a child. Were you afraid of being judged when you did tasks? Did your parents compliment or did they find fault? Were you punished if you failed to perform assigned duties? Did you fear your parents' reactions? Even as a youngster, did you begin to avoid responsibility? Why? Were you afraid that no matter how well you did a chore, your mother would criticize you?

As a teenager. Did you have a chance to serve as monitor or class officer—and refuse it? Did the thought of such responsibility make you feel so frightened that you knew you could not do it? When you did do it, did you have a feeling of power and like it? Did you take your position seriously or lightly? How do these reactions compare to those that you have in your present job?

As a senior in college. Did you take on any responsible position? How did you feel if you competed with someone else for a post—and lost? Won? Did your college career inhibit your present job choice? For example, you wanted to be a lawyer, but didn't think you were smart enough—even though you may have been. Again, evaluate whether there is a carryover of these feelings into the present.

As a job beginner. How did you react when your superior assigned you a task involving responsibility . . . when you turned in a piece of complicated work for evaluation? Did you seek opportunities to take on additional responsibilities? Did you envy friends who landed better jobs? Would you willingly have taken on the work of these jobs?

These preconscious reminiscences should offer clues as to why your unconscious needs may have kept you from going as far as you can professionally. See what you can do to change them.

Although we commonly think of problems on the job as those affecting our performance and relations with bosses, co-workers, and subordinates, there is another dimension to consider as well. We may function perfectly well in our job—relate effectively to bosses, coworkers, and subordinates and carry out our responsibilities in an exemplary manner, thereby winning promotions and all the trappings of success—and still feel a victim. Inner pressures with their roots in hidden feelings and expectations have pushed us into a career of work environment that cannot satisfy us, no matter how well we *appear* to succeed. Here, too, a change from being a victim requires getting in touch with feelings and expectations that block us from pursuing what we really want.

THE CASE OF THE VETERAN PRO WHO SWITCHED FIELDS

After graduation from the Wharton School, Mark Z. joined a major Wall Street firm and zoomed up the financial ladder. Happy in his marriage but miserable with the "money types," he thought back to his childhood dreams and realized he had always fantasized about living in exotic places, learning new customs. Because he had feared being different from his peers, he had buried the dreams, focused on financial success. After talking with his wife, an artist who could work anywhere, Mark made the decision to move to the Far East. He studied Japanese for two years, and got a good job with an import-export firm in Tokyo. He had the courage to remember and conquer the suppressed fear of challenge. He was able to take charge of himself, change and take action.

As mentioned, dreams can provide helpful clues to what is holding us back—keeping us a victim. *Use your dreams.* Some people like to write them down. But whether you write, remember, or use whatever method of dream recall that works for you, *pay attention to the feelings* you had in the dream.

Think of the problem most on your mind in the work area—for instance, the way your boss has been blaming you. Ask yourself, "What does the dream tell me about that situation that I don't really know?" Don't look for a specific answer. Let your mind daydream. You're looking for clues to your unconscious feelings rather than a narrowly specific answer. The feelings may help you find the real answer.

Job Situation One: Dale G. had a deadline, and for weeks his supervisor had been on his back. Dale felt irritated, pushed, pressured.

The dream: Dale was in his kitchen, where the pipes had burst and flooded the room. Garbage had spilled over from the can. Dale was trying to turn valves when the phone rang. It was his cousin Carolyn, with whom he'd grown up—her baby was sick, her husband had a headache, etc.—an endless refrain of complaints. Dale tried to interrupt with *his* troubles, but *she* wouldn't listen. He felt angry and frustrated.

After the dream: Letting his mind roam, Dale thought, "I've done so much for Carolyn and she's done so little for me." Then he asked himself, "What does the dream show about what's going on at the job?" He realized that a good part of his irritation was not just because of the fatigue and work pressures, but because his boss, also caught up in the stresses, didn't seem to appreciate the sacrifices Dale was making. Just as he had grown up with his cousin, he had been with his boss a long time. Because Dale had a good relationship with his boss, he told him his feelings. That gave Dale the feeling he was being heard and he felt better.

Job Situation Two: At work, Charlotte M. constantly felt picked on, especially by her boss. "They don't like me; they're trying to force me out," she told herself.

The dream: A crowd from the local church moved toward her, appearing angry and threatening. Their faces resembled assorted Satans. Charlotte felt frightened. Half of her thought of escape; the other half tried to figure how to fight the mob. She felt the group possessed power and that she was helpless. As the crowd neared, gradually her perception changed and she realized the group was pleading for help, not threatening her. The Satan-like faces softened and took on a scared, pleading look. Speaking up, the members explained that aliens from outer space had arrived in town and were committing terrible crimes. "We need you to help stop them," they chorused. When she heard this, Charlotte's fear disappeared, and she felt both sympathetic and part of the group.

After the dream: Charlotte daydreamed and then asked herself, "What does the dream show me about my job problems?" She suddenly realized that her coworkers (represented by the church congregation) and her boss (the minister) were upset by the corporate system and some new things that were happening at the office—*not* by her.

Using dreams in this way won't always work. Your dreams may not concern the job at all. But often enough this kind of dream use will start you thinking in different ways about your problem situation.

The Victim Strikes Back

In the business world, some job situations evoke all the power and love needs found among siblings. When these situations lead to our being victimized, we may have the same vindictive fantasies we had as children.

Sometimes we can cope without hitting back in any vindictive way. For example, one woman deliberately halted *jealous action* from a male peer with assertive "sweet talk." He repeatedly told fellow workers that the woman's performance was "not serious" and spread rumors about her personal life. Refusing to become a victim, she retaliated, not with fire but with friendliness. Every time she saw him, she gave him a compliment. She acted so friendly that he finally gave up his campaign to discredit her.

In the business world are many "killers" who will employ all sorts of underhanded tricks to save or advance themselves and eliminate others. To protect ourselves from being victimized by such people, sometimes we must use acceptable aggression. *To change an intolerable situation, we may have to alter our normal personality pattern and become aggressive.*

Gail M., a usually easygoing retailing executive, had a secretary "who didn't like me because I made her work. The secretary had managed to keep her job in a hierarchical corporation because she had 'things' on her two previous male bosses. One drank; the other, a married man, had a girl friend. The secretary was always on the phone. I'd come in. She'd put the call on hold, and then return to it. I had to get her fired, so I collected a dossier of her misdoings and my many warnings, and I got her out. I felt justified. I knew she was not doing her job adequately, and I needed strong secretarial support to get my own work done."

We may have to overcome our own fear and insecurity to defend ourselves. After many years Mary B. finally made it to the presidency of a medium-size company. To keep her job, in which she felt inexperienced, Mary knew she must get rid of a hostile board member who kept "accusing me of changing my mind about things." Knowing she had the support of the company lawyer and actuary, she forced herself to talk to the other board members, described her enemy's drive for power, and saw to it that as a result of the trail she established he was not reappointed to the board. "In fact," she recalls, "everyone got to dislike him as much as I did."

Firing may not be possible. *We may have to settle* for less than total victory—even a stand-off. Linda L. found herself the victim of her company's sales manager, who linked up with the comptroller in an attempt to get Linda fired for "incompetency." The comptroller refused Linda information she needed to do her job. So Linda wrote a memo to the company president requesting that the sales manager be fired. Management met, told Linda they were on her side, but said she "would have to work things out." She had achieved a partial victory but proved her *competence and authority*. The feud with the comptroller continued on and off, but Linda kept her job without feeling additionally victimized by inaction on her own part.

Be alert to the reality that *a rival may set you up*. Joan R. and Stan B., her boss, wanted the same job. A meeting was scheduled to be held in the board room, located in another building where Joan had never been. Pretending friendliness, Stan warned, "Dress warmly. It's always cold in that room," so Joan wore a tweed suit with a fur-trimmed jacket. When the board room turned out to be stifling, Joan told the assembled group, "Forgive me, but I have to take off my jacket. Stan said it would be like ice." She commented afterward, "I exposed him." By revealing part of Stan's "black side," Joan sensitized board members to other snide things Stan had done. She got the job.

Maintaining Your Confidence on the Job

Confidence grows from confidence. With it, you experience less anxiety. You have an awareness of goals, realize that you possess skills and knowledge, have the sense that "I can do it." With more confidence, you have less chance of victimization. Here are some job confidence basics:

■ *When a new situation arises that frightens you, determine what you must do to conquer it.* Again, apply the confidence-building techniques introduced in chapter 5.

THE CASE OF THE
FRIGHTENED SOCIAL WORKER

Kay D. had always had a problem with public speaking, but in her present administrative job, she did not have to confront her terror. When a significant promotion came her way that involved speaking, she accepted it but couldn't sleep for thinking about it; she almost called to refuse the job.

Determined to take the most prestigious position, Kay joined one of my Assertiveness Training groups. At the initial session, I told her to prepare a three- to four-minute case presentation for the next week. She did it well, with body and voice confidence. How? She answered, "I knew I would not be asked any questions." Her assignment for the next week: Prepare a case and the group would ask questions. Again Kay did well. How? "I knew they were not professionals and would not ask questions I couldn't answer." Third assignment: She was to prepare professional questions on cards. Again, no anxiety. "I had the questions and knew the answers."

At this point Kay came to an understanding of the mistake that had caused her lack of confidence. She had always concentrated just on her *written* case reports. When she thought through possible questions and answers in advance for an oral presentation and was completely prepared, she heightened her sense of "I can do it." In her professional life, Kay had victimized herself by not taking steps to maximize her confidence.

■ *Grow from failure.* In two years Ron W. switched jobs three times. Each job turned out to be a misrepresentation and a horror. Rather than let himself feel victimized, he feels, "Every change made me better able to master a new task and assess a job description. Now I have a job I want—because of those three terrible jobs."

■ *See reality. Feel confident about the qualities you do have. You don't have to see yourself as a victim.* You may want to go further, be unable to, yet still like yourself.

For example, famous stage, screen, and TV star Anne Jackson frankly admits to "limitations" that might make others feel a life victim. In no way does she see herself as a victim. She is confident.

Born in poverty ("Being poor gave me an understanding of what the world is all about"), daughter of a Croatian immigrant father and an Irish Catholic mother from a coal mining family who had a nervous breakdown during Anne's youth, Anne says succinctly:

"I'm not crippled by my past."

"I'm still working on my mother."

"I'm still working on myself."

Born the baby of her family ("It has been a battle to grow up"), she married star Eli Wallach ("I try hard to hold on to my own identity"). She is the mother of three. Anne frankly admits she cries a lot, hates criticism, has a fear of taking chances. She engagingly reveals, "I don't have a good sense of self-worth. I know I can be a director, but I find it difficult to deal with men and tell them what to do. It's a fear of failure. It's not having a realistic sense of self. I let my agent do it all. I shouldn't. Eli goes after things."

Jackson, even though a celebrity, has survived situations many ordinary persons could not have coped with—a difficult childhood, religious intermarriage, being wife to a star, being a star herself, and an inability to say yes to opportunities outside of acting. But the woman you meet personifies charm and confidence ("As an actress, I'll take chances"), and demonstrates the ability to keep moving despite limitations of which she is fully aware. How? She keeps herself aware of her strengths and the good things in her life and sees anything bad in perspective. The word *victim* seems not to exist in her vocabulary. It is this approach that keeps her growing and expanding her self-knowledge—and perhaps what makes her a star, not only in the theater but as a wife and mother.

■ *Do the right thing for you.* You allow yourself to be a victim if the career choices you make reflect what others feel to be right or appropriate but not what feels right for you. The same is true if your behavior on the job reflects only others' priorities without reflecting your own standards.

THE CASE OF THE WOMAN WHO DEFIED AUTHORITY TO BE TRUE TO HER OWN PROFESSIONAL STANDARDS

Marge O. worked for the community relations department of an internationally known company. She had set up a series of goodwill appearances at local events, but her boss got the axe. In came a new boss, an inexperienced wealthy woman, sister of the company's owner. The new boss summoned Marge and ordered, "Cancel those appearances you set up for Mimi _____." Dark-tinted glasses veiled the boss's eyes. Beside her sat a yes-man executive, a friend of the powerful brother.

Gathering her courage, Marge answered, "I can tell the people involved what has happened, but they will have to make the decision. What you ask me to do is professionally wrong." The woman stared coolly at her. The executive shrugged, "You are making a mistake."

Marge returned to her office and began packing. The next morning she received a royal summons. The glasses were off. The yes-man executive was not in residence. The new boss said simply, "I called my brother, and he said you were a brave young woman. Thank you for telling me how wrong I was. Now I know I can trust you." By taking a chance on being the boss's victim by refusing to victimize herself through denying her own standards of professional conduct, Marge had won a good start with the new regime.

All of us have less chance of being an emotional victim on the job if we aren't emotional on the job.

8 □ A Patient's Guide to Doctors and Therapists: How to Ask, Learn, Decide—and Quit When Necessary

In contrast to the job situation, in which economic realities predominate (the boss has power; we need that paycheck), we view doctors and therapists with emotionally tinged fantasies, often endowing them with magical powers they don't have. By setting them up as archetypal authority figures, we make ourselves helpless, dependent, victim-prone.

However, these archetypal figures are human beings with both strengths and weaknesses. With them we must be strong, not powerless. When dealing with doctors and therapists, we have the right to know, question, complain, and shift.

Dealing with Doctors

Unconscious factors may affect our attitudes toward doctors. Because doctors do to some degree have the power to "make it better," even to make sickness disappear, many people project onto them an all-knowingness and powerfulness ("It is in *his* power to make me well"), regarding them in the same way they regarded their parents as children. Even though the public perception of doctors is changing (witness the use of informed consent and recourse to second opinions), many of us still feel a need to act passively and placate our doctor. We fear to offend.

Doctors are human. Don't make them into parents. Don't be a victim of passivity or timidity in your dealings with them. Too much is at stake—your health and your peace of mind.

THE PATIENT'S BILL OF RIGHTS

■ *You have the right to ask the fee,* whether for an office visit, consultation, or surgery. It *is* possible to ask, "Can we do anything about the fee?" In some cases the query may produce results, in others it won't. A graduate student had a circulation problem but couldn't afford the fee of the eminent surgeon she wanted to treat her. When she raised the matter, the doctor agreed to accept the standard Blue Cross/Blue Shield payment, provided one of his residents could handle the follow-up.

■ *You have the right to ask questions and receive answers* given in terms a layperson can understand. People should know the side effects of any medications prescribed, the after-effects of surgery, the length of recovery time—or the chance of nonrecovery. Suggestion: Write out your questions in advance, ask them one at a time, and write down the answers. Because of stress and fear, selective memory often operates to confuse things in this area. One woman thought her doctor had told her, "You have five years to live." In reality, he had stated. "In five years you'll have forgotten you ever had this condition."

■ *You have the right to be treated decently.* A lawyer became so enraged at being kept waiting for two hours by a doctor that he sent a bill for his time. Some doctors will always make us wait, and we must decide whether we will put up with it. Liking your personal doctor helps, but mainly we must feel his or her competency. This also includes the doctor's secretary. Some doctors deliberately keep a "bulldog" to keep people off their backs. In other cases, the doctor may be willing to help in many ways; it's the secretary who tells us when we have the flu, "He can't see you for three weeks." In that case, just respond, "I'm sick now. Shall I call another doctor?" You'll probably get an appointment.

■ *You have the right to call a doctor.* We do not have to feel we are intruding on God.

■ *You have the right to quit a doctor.* Don't be afraid no other doctor will take you. Lately, according to a prominent internist, "Doctors are more competitive."

You don't have to defend your reasons for wanting to change doctors. Your reason may be simply, "I don't like him. We're not on the same wavelength," and have nothing to do with his or her ability. However, as with all professions, unfortunately, bad or unknowledgeable doctors do exist. A young doctor simply may be unfamiliar with certain diseases (one internist had never seen a mastoid case and diagnosed it as "boils on the neck"). Or the doctor may be money-oriented and malevolent. One young woman discovered a breast lump on a Saturday when her regular doctor was out of town. Panic-stricken, she went to an unknown neighborhood practitioner who wanted to cut off the breast that day. Luckily she was smart enough to wait until Monday, when her regular doctor diagnosed the lump as a benign cyst, which he aspirated.

The doctor is supposed to take care of us, but sometimes we must take assertive action for ourselves. For example, a diabetic woman had surgery on her finger. When the doctor wanted to send her home with an open drain, she refused, knowing that an open drain would increase the chance of infection, especially for a diabetic. Luckily her husband, a physician, removed the drain. Feeling she had been the doctor's dupe, the woman paid for the surgery but not for the period following, when she had the problem with the drain. She wrote the doctor a letter telling him he had been unprofessional and her reasons for refusing to pay in full.

THE DOCTOR'S SIDE

Sometimes you and your doctor become *mutual victims*. Just as you feel a medical professional's victim when you don't get better, that person feels victimized by your blame. Feelings run much higher than when you are negotiating with a salesperson or airline representative. That's to be expected. Your health, your life, are at stake. You know it. The doctor knows it.

Just the same, we must not let our anxiety and concern with self—sometimes legitimate, at other times exaggerated—combine with unreal expectations to turn the doctor into our victim.

■ *Don't make it difficult for the doctor to do his or her job.* Some patients just don't think. For example, you don't take the prescribed medicine and then tell friends, "The doctor didn't help me." Or you leave word with his answering service of an "emergency" and then tie up your phone for hours. When the physician finally reaches you the next morning, you scream, "You didn't return my call."

■ *Guard against unrealistic expectations.* Your unrealistic expectations may victimize your doctor. Perhaps your cure wasn't as complete as you expected, the discomfort greater. Blaming the doctor for the failure to do something not achievable, you support your accusations with stories about other patients who got cured. You may expect the doctor to be a medical magician, to perform an instant miracle. One investment banker felt depressed after surgery and criticized her doctor because "my head doesn't work sharply." The doctor had warned her it would take her three months to feel at her professional peak.

■ *Understand the doctor's fear of being victimized by malpractice suits.* In some cases a physician's negligence may justify a lawsuit. However, many avaricious or angry people, justifiably or unjustifiably, think they will gain money in an easy way and bring lawsuits. As a result, many doctors now practice defensive medicine; they *don't* do the very things they may feel would help the patient most. Thus the patient becomes the victim of the system, and the same system may make the doctor order unnecessary, costly tests to protect himself.

You don't want to be a victim of your doctor. Don't make a victim of the doctor.

Dealing with Therapists

Because the relationship with a therapist is so intimate—personal and emotional—we often experience intense feelings of victimization. Often these feelings occur because we chose the *wrong practitioner*. The one who did such a great job for a friend may not be right for us. And, as with doctors, there are bad, medium good, good, and great therapists. (The top ones—because they take the most difficult cases—are especially vulnerable to malpractice suits.)

A person may unconsciously select a therapist who will help him or her maintain a neurosis while going through the motions of trying to change it. A person may stick with a particular therapist because of an unconscious fear that if an attempt is made to leave, the therapist will inflict some punishment. We may not recognize the danger that a therapist, because of an emotional reaction to a patient, will get involved sexually with the patient without considering whether the patient is in a position to give informed consent.

Therapy can succeed completely, partially, or not at all. A person can undergo treatment and not know if it has worked. For instance, a few years ago, thirty-year-old Alice D. started treatment with a well-known psychologist who leaned toward the Freudian approach. At the end of two years, she felt dissatisfied ("He keeps wanting to talk about my past, and I want things to happen now") and left him. However, a year later Alice got a job promotion, subsequently moved to a vice-presidential slot at another company, and formed a serious relationship. She feels she did it all herself and gives no credit to her treatment.

SOME STEPS TO MINIMIZE PSYCHOTHERAPEUTIC VICTIMIZATION

■ *Remember that you have a right to choose your own form of treatment.* Select from Behavioral Psychotherapy, strict Behavior Therapy, Gestalt Therapy, Psychoanalytic Therapy or traditional psychoanalysis (the last two include Sullivanian, Freudian, Horneyan, and many other respected variations). Read books and select a form that seems compatible with your needs and personality. You might go for a series of consultations with masters of different approaches. You might not be able to afford their fees on a regular basis, but you may be able to swing one or two consultations. Ask questions and get a clear understanding of what the approach involves. Then go by your gut response.

■ *Check out the therapist you select.* Look up the therapist in professional directories to learn about his or her background, training, and academic affiliations. In some states, anyone can hang out a sign and call him- or herself a psychotherapist. Formal qualifications have limitations and shouldn't be used exclusively as criteria for selection, but they're a good guide.

■ *Understand financial arrangements at the beginning.* This means not only the session fee but whether the therapist charges for cancelled visits (even when you're in the hospital) and when he or she is off on vacation. Then you can accept or not accept. There are therapists who change these rules in midstream, and you want to be able to speak up to them.

■ *To ensure progress, be assertive with your therapist.* You must say what you feel and think. If you believe you are a victim of inconsideration, say so ("You take too many calls during my session" . . . "I feel abused when you keep me waiting"). If you feel your therapist does not understand you, say so.

There are therapists who manipulate patients emotionally to satisfy their own power needs. There are also therapists who don't exploit but carry over feelings from their own pasts. One patient claims, "My analyst had a countertransference—she kept talking about her own unresolved emotional problems." The patient was afraid that if she expressed her annoyance, the therapist might tell her to leave. She couldn't bring herself to say, "Why are we talking about *your* life? *I'm* paying you." Because she maintained that hold-back attitude, she acted out a victim pattern in the therapy situation. If she had talked freely, she would have helped herself more.

If you feel your treatment is on a wrong track, say so.

THE CASE OF THE DEPRESSED WOMAN

Vickie M., married and a part-time working mother in her midthirties, became increasingly depressed and retreated more and more from life. When she came to me for Behavioral Psychotherapy, I tried to get her to engage in various social activities, whether she enjoyed them or not. Vickie performed the assignments but complained that I wasn't helping and that the therapy did not work. I encouraged her to speak up about what was wrong. Immediately two factors became evident: (1) She wanted change to come about from me, not from what *she* did; (2) she wanted improvement to be sudden and magical. Small lifts in the depression didn't count.

As Vickie finally spoke up, she herself began to realize the depression had decreased. She was able to see that rather than recognizing her own strength and ability to bring about change, she had a need to see herself as a victim of inadequate treatment. This produced a new revelation. She saw a life-long pattern of depression, stemming from her need to view herself as a victim of the inadequacy of others. With her new knowledge, she became able to change in many ways.

■ *Take the responsibility for your own life decisions.* One man comments, "My therapist told me to get a divorce and I listened to him and did. It was a mistake." The therapist has enough trouble running his or her own life and can't possibly run yours. If he or she suggests a change in job, life-style, or relationship, that suggestion may be right, wrong, or just a matter of trying to stir up feelings and associations that could be helpful in therapy. Don't assume it to be a directive you must follow. A few therapists may pressure you to do or not do something, but remember, *you* must live with the consequences, and *the decision must be yours.* Listen carefully, but do what is best for you.

■ *Remember that there are times to get outside advice.* If, after discussion, you still believe your treatment is going nowhere, you may be right. Again, get an outside consultation from a master. You can ask your therapist to recommend someone for consultation, but keep in mind that he or she may suggest a former teacher whose personal loyalties may make an objective assessment difficult or impossible. Do your own research. Understand that you are questioning not only whether your therapist is right for you but the correctness of the treatment form.

The following questions, adapted from *I Can If I Want To** by doctors Arnold Lazarus and Allen Fay, should help you determine your satisfaction with your therapist relationship:

*I Can If I Want To, by Arnold Lazarus, Ph.D., and Allen Fay, M.D., New York: Warner Books Inc., 1975.

Are you comfortable with your therapist?

Is he or she flexible and open to new ideas rather than insistent on pursuing one point of view?

Does the therapist admit to limitation and not pretend to know things he or she doesn't know.

Does the therapist acknowledge being wrong or inconsiderate instead of justifying this kind of behavior?

Does the therapist act as if he or she is the consultant rather than the manager of your life?

Does the therapist encourage differences of opinion rather than telling you you are resisting if you disagree with him or her?

In general, do your contacts with the therapist lead to your feeling more hopeful and having higher self-esteem?

If you find yourself answering no to any of these questions, reevaluate your relations with your therapist. You may be risking victimization. Discuss your feelings with the therapist.

In therapy, whatever the kind of treatment or personality of the practitioner, always remember your goal: to feel more and more right about yourself and your life.

☐ Part III

Relationships

9 □ Moving Toward Closeness: Risks and Rewards

Evaluation of a relationship in the early stages can mean the difference between heartache and happiness.

The Basics of Getting to the Close Relationship

Writing on "A Triangular Theory of Love" in the journal *Psychological Review,* Dr. Robert J. Sternberg of Yale University points out that love possesses three components:

1. The intimacy component
2. The passion component
3. The decison/commitment component

The intimacy component (the "warm" component) refers to those feelings that promote closeness, bondedness, and connectedness. More specifically, these feelings include the desire to experience happiness with the loved one, a sense of high regard and desire to promote the welfare of the other, sharing of self, being able to count on the other, receiving and giving of emotional support, and intimate communication. We may experience these feelings as one overall sense rather than separate entities.

The passion component (the "hot" component) involves physical attraction and sexual consummation. In a loving relationship, sexual needs may predominate. However, other needs—such as needs for self-esteem, dominance, submission, nurturance, and self-actualization—may also contribute to the experience of passion.

The decision/commitment component (the "cold" component). First, we make the decision we love someone and then we commit ourselves to maintain that love in the long term. Many people neglect this factor because it lacks the "heat" of the intimacy or passion components.

In short-term romantic involvements, the passion component plays a large part. It develops the quickest and dissipates the quickest. For example, one twenty-five-year-old woman wasn't satisfied with her lover sexually, felt she hadn't "come to grips with her own humanity," and craved more relationships before settling down. Once she lost sexual interest, the whole relationship fell apart. She became thoughtless and just wanted out. In a long-term relationship, the intimacy components and decision/commitment components play large parts, but the passion must also be there or you have friendship, not romantic love.

TAKE STOCK AT THE BEGINNING OF GETTING CLOSER

We want to recognize the availability and commitment potential of the person with whom we *think* we may have a romantic future. The following four cases may help us see why we have made wrong choices in the past so that we often end up a victim or victimizer.

Case One: Attractive and rich, at thirty-nine Steve P. seems like everyone's dream man. Married briefly once, he now heads many hostesses' list of eligible bachelors. With women he has one-night stands and short-term affairs. A friend told him, "You've spent your adult life creating a structure of work and friends to support your unmarried state. There's no reason to change. If you leave New York for a place where you have no structure, you'll be married in a year." Steve admits this. He says, "Recently I met the perfect woman. She lived in California but yearned to live in New York. Here I didn't need her."

Analysis: A relationship is not for Steve. His strength: He knows it. Experiencing pressure from societal conventions and friends, many people feel they must have relationships. If you don't want to accept the limits of a relationship, accept this fact about yourself. Steve can be a victimizer, not a victim. Through passion and intimacy in brief dalliances, he satisfies his needs, but he has no desire for long-term commitment. Any woman who gets involved with him without realizing this will end up the victim.

Case Two: Popular Lorraine F., a twenty-four-year-old architect, often has a date for dinner, another date later that same night for disco dancing. But Lorraine admits she never really becomes involved—"I'm afraid of relationships."

Blaming both her parents and herself, she remarks, "My parents hardly talk to each other. Because of that I learned negative things—I try to get what I want by playing the silent game, as my parents do with each other. Because I think that's how people in love get what they want, I manipulate that way in a relationship, too. I'm always afraid a relationship won't work out, so I pretend it's fine when it's not. When it's fifty percent good, I pretend it's one hundred percent good.

"My mother is a housewife who immersed herself in her husband so much that she never had her own identity. I'm afraid of doing that, too. I'm also afraid I'll get involved with the wrong person and won't be able to get out. The fault is mine. I don't know how to change."

Analysis: Lorraine exhibits two common relationship fears: fear of failure and fear of loss of identity. Like Steve P., she has a problem in making a commitment, but hers differs from his. She yearns for closeness, but fears it so that she plays head games with herself. Hiding the real extent of commitment in the relationship, she turns it into something it isn't ("One hundred percent good"). When the reality of the bad relationship hits her (one man left her because "I did everything for him"), she feels she is a victim.

Case Three: Allan M., an oncologist, has a bad track record with two failed, fairly long-term relationships. The first broke up because he was a workaholic and ignored his loving friend, who finally walked out. He recalls, "Then, because I thought no one would want me, I got involved with a bitch whom my family hated. They were right. This time *I* walked out. For the last five years I have dated many women, always making sure each was unsuitable for marriage.

"A year and a half ago I grew up. I no longer want an inappropriate woman or someone to whom I can give my kid-along treatment. My work makes me like a monk, and I'm almost never free, but in my head I'm being reborn. Today I could make a relationship succeed. Now I'd make the effort. The word is *commitment.* I'm going looking—I just don't know how to start."

Analysis: With experience, Allan has changed, but the change is probably not complete. He knows what he wants from a mate—warmth, understanding, elbow room to do his work without hassling demands that might interfere. But he thinks only of his needs and convenience, not what he wants to *give,* so he limits his concept of intimacy. Even with his admitted new attitude, he makes his demanding work situation worse than it is. Other hard-working professionals meet appropriate women. Perhaps he's not as ready for a committed relationship as he thinks he is.

Case Four: Seymour D. and Sarah S. both live in Indianapolis; each is divorced with no children. They met two years ago. His ex-wife "was too much of a free spirit," too unconventional, too "nonwork-oriented." Sarah divorced at twenty-eight: "I just hadn't figured out who I was. Because I was afraid I'd make another mistake, I've waited ever since."

Sarah now feels more secure and that she can make a go of marriage. She also accepts what some people might regard as faults in Seymour. He, a free-lancer, likes the fact that she has savings, a weekend house, a desirable job, and the ability to be a charming, popular hostess.

Seymour also feels happy in the relationship. He notes, "I've changed. I'm less selfish. I take more responsibility for our lives together." He adds, "With her, I can make it. She's a blend of nurturing and fun and has a sense of herself—despite the track record of a brief marriage and an affair that made her less secure than she is."

Analysis: They've gone through the pain of previous failures and have really changed. They see one another's weaknesses, appreciate the strengths. Sarah and Seymour are concerned not only with their own needs but with their partner's and, above all, with the relationship. Their failures have proved to be growth experiences. Now they're ready. All three components—intimacy, passion, and commitment—are working.

EVALUATING INITIAL RELATIONSHIP STAGES

Goal: To know where your relationship is at and where it is going

Step One: Ask yourself the following questions and grade yourself on a scale of 0 to 100:

- How much passion is there in your relationship?
- How much intimacy?
- How much commitment to the long term?

Step Two: Evaluate where you see the relationship headed:

- Backward
- Staying status quo
- Progressing forward

Step Three: Ask yourself two more questions:

- Is your partner willing to do what she or he has to do to improve the relationship (anything from controlling an annoying roving eye to spending more pleasure time with you)?
- Are you willing to do what you have to do to improve the relationship?

Openness to change is essential to making a relationship work. For example, Lila P. realized her self-centeredness early enough in the relationship to take action. She and Jack F. had enrolled in a costly weekend photo workshop. Then some friends invited Lila to the christening of their newly adopted baby to take place that same weekend. She automatically accepted. Furious, Jack asked, "What's wrong with you?" She realized, "I had to be the good girl—still pleasing mother or whoever—by proving my friendship. I forgot that my relationship with Jack mattered more, that somebody cares enough about me to be hurt when I choose something else over him."

Breaking Up

Breaking up will hurt, but do not magnify the hurt into permanent emotional damage.

People break up for many reasons. A person may have the inner feeling that it was good while it lasted, but the time has come for other things. Or the chemistry fails to grow, leaving an emptiness, a lack of fulfillment and satisfaction. Maybe the other person passively goes along; in drifting, both become victims. Often each collaborates to make the relationship fail. Though one crystallizes the breakup, both agree to end it. With the disappointment, you may experience relief. You also experience feelings of doubts and your own inadequacy. These emotions make it necessary for you to show yourself the victim.

With almost any breakup, a person pays a price. *The more we concentrate on the bad and our victimization, the less chance we have of a new relationship.* Our failures may create such fears that we don't want to try for closeness again.

IF YOU'RE THE DUMPER

Your head has its reasons. For example, you made it clear to your friend some time ago that when you had saved enough money, you wanted to live abroad for a number of years, but he or she did not listen or refused to hear it. Or you may have gone along with the relationship because of the lack of an alternative. Then your situation changes and you act. Recently a businessman walked out on Tina J., a special friend, because at a business party he fell in love at first sight with a woman in his same field. Everyone commiserated "How could he do that to Tina?" But the man involved felt he had been bored and just waiting for the right person to come along.

Or, perhaps your partner remains satisfied, but you realize the relationship will not provide what *you* want over the long term. Your life-style and values may differ too much and you say, "This isn't for me." For instance, Elaine G., a party girl, was dating a serious-minded chemist. He told her, "Look, I want marriage and a home. You want fun. We've met at the wrong time in our lives."

THE CASE OF THE INSECURE WOMAN

Paula A. had everything going for her. At twenty-eight, she ran her own successful catering firm, had good looks, a lively sense of fun. But Paula lacked confidence. Through a work project, she became involved with a personable married man. She knew he would never leave his wife, but she had hopes. Anytime Paula thought of ending the affair, Les realized it and became so loving that she gave up the idea.

Paula came to me for Behavioral Psychotherapy. Her question was, "I have no future with him. Why can't I leave him?" We tried working at Level One to change her behavior. She tried hard to plan activities with other men. She couldn't do it. Yet, for her own self-esteem, she knew she must give up Les.

Working at Level Two (blocks), we found that despite all business triumphs, Paula was completely convinced that no other man would want her, much less marry her. She was so caught up in this mistaken belief that she virtually wore a "keep off" sign. Her belief became truth. Other men rarely looked at her. I pointed out to Paula that her mistaken belief led to fear and the kind of actions that made her fear come true. I gave her the attitude change exercise from chapter 5 and had her make up reasons "Why Men Should Be Interested in Me" (some reasons: "I'm smart. I'm pretty. I make money"). Then, in imagery, she rehearsed successful performances with men in various social situations.

The treatment worked. Paula got different vibes from men she met in daily life. A few called for dates. This made a dent in her mistaken belief that no one would be interested. Thus she was able to end the relationship with the married man with whom she really had got involved out of loneliness rather than love.

You simply may not want permanent commitment. You dump someone because you have come to see—or been helped to see—that the relationship plays into a problem that lies deep within you.

Danger trap: The dumper may become the victim of his or her own guilt. Seeking absolution, he or she may point to the other's wrongdoing, keeping the feelings of guilt buried in the unconscious while building up his or her self-concept as a victim. Or the converse may happen: The dumper may magnify his or her own faults, thus building up a false sense of power and an exaggerated self-image as a victim. With either mode, you mask the give and take that you did have in the relationship, thus losing the chance to learn from the experience.

IF YOU'RE THE DUMPEE

In your innocence, even stupidity, you've never acknowledged that your relationship is headed for the rocks. Probably you ignored any signs and idealized the relationship as something it never was.

Maybe you saw signs but kept hoping. You wanted the partner so badly that you put up with any slights (for example, your partner romancing someone else at a party at your house). Your ever optimistic (and unrealistic) assumption: "This will work out."

You may have a need to fail so that you can accuse yourself— "I'm inadequate as a person . . . as a sexual partner . . . as a man (or woman). What's wrong with me?" Your subconscious demands that you show yourself as the victim of a cruel partner.

You exaggerate what's happened, as well as your own alleged unworthiness.

You may actually be the victimizer. You sabotage and set up a situation so that your friend neglects you. Through your criticizing, sharpness, and manipulation, you make things so unpleasant that to sustain his or her self-respect your lover must exit. Or you may expect the impossible. One woman had the idea that her partner should never become angry at her. Of course, he failed to meet this false standard, and as insistence on it proved grating, eventually walked out.

SOME HELPFUL REMINDERS WHEN YOU'RE THINKING OF BREAKING IT OFF

■ *If you really care about the relationship, try hard to better it before breaking up.* You might attempt to change your own behaviors or have a discussion or confrontation. Try to improve the conditions ("Jane, these last-minute date cancellations have to stop"). Be frank ("Gerry, this relationship is going nowhere. Do you want any relationship at all?"). You want it clear to both of you that a breakup may offer the only answer to your troubles if no other alternative can be devised or made to work.

■ *Either of you has the right to break it off, especially in the early stages.* Even though the breakup may be unfair and you may emerge the victim, the truth is that these early stages represent a testing phase.

■ *When you know your partnership has not worked, don't cling.* In my Behavioral Psychotherapy work, I see life dropouts who wait for the call that never comes. Hurt once, they're afraid of being hurt again and thus paralyze themselves, holding on to fantasies about a relationship that has failed. Others break off, but guilt makes them cling to part of a relationship. Barbara D. finally said those four fateful words, "You'll have to leave." Even then, she went out the next day and found an apartment for her lover and stocked the kitchen.

■ *Don't dwell on the breakup once it's happened. Stop magnifying.* Don't keep obsessing, "If I had stuck with it, it would have worked." It wouldn't have.

Whatever happens with the relationship, keep in mind that *good can come of failure*. You learn about yourself, what you did wrong, whom you can trust, risks you should have taken and did not (or vice versa), what you might do better in terms of future relationships.

Example One: The businessman described earlier, who walked out on his "special friend," found he was much more bored with his new flame. The first woman didn't blame; she welcomed him back and married him. She says, "I love him. I forgave him." Each had learned greater appreciation of the other.

Example Two: Carolyn J. met Bill T., an internist at a hospital, and immediately fell for him. Recently divorced, he had a different girl for every night in the week except Saturday when he was usually on call. He warned Carolyn, "I have a whole series of girl friends." She became the Friday night girl. She never pushed him ("I'd be giving him a reason to leave") but always made herself available. One Monday night Bill called at 9:30 P.M. and said, "I'm with the Monday night woman. Can you make it at ten?" Carolyn agreed. That night Bill came through: "Give me two weeks to wind down the girls and we'll live together." They did, then married.

Knowing just what she was getting into, Carolyn deliberately took a relationship risk—but limited it. Knowing the danger of just drifting, she set herself a six-month limit. If in that period no change took place and the girl friends were still there, she knew she would have to break up with Bill, even though she loved him. This knowledge gave her the courage to go through with her plan, and in this case, it worked out.

For your own happiness, with any breakup, you must *orient yourself to the immediate future*. Accept that:

> It hurts.
> You've done the best you could at this point.
> It's finished.

Now ask yourself, "What steps do I take next?"

And tell yourself, "I'm at a new emotional threshold with the chance to make a new relationship that's right, not wrong for me."

10□Emotional Victims in Love: The Reasons

From coast to coast, men and women find they have become emotional victims in marriage or a close relationship, despite a union supposedly based on mutual love. The cause may stem from past or present circumstances, but the result is the same: Love dwindles or disappears, often to be replaced by disappointment, distance, mistrust, and the desire to end it.

In this and the following chapter, we will show how Behavioral Psychotherapy techniques can help people understand why they do things that hurt themselves as well as those they love most, how to repair the damage, and how to achieve emotional closeness through a combination of showing love and constant change within the relationship.

In *Ardèle*, playwright Jean Anouilh points out two romantic truths that apply to all relationships. Love, he writes, "has one archenemy—and that is life." He also notes, "Love is, above all, the gift of oneself."

Some Close Relationship Basics

Every close relationship contains a mixture of *defensive intimacy* and *expansive intimacy*. Your goals should be to recognize each component, be aware of the ratio between the two in your own union, and to *strive to develop expansive intimacy* so that you, your partner, and the relationship itself grow and mature.

In *Toward a Psychology of Being*, the late Dr. Abraham H. Maslow wrote of the difference between D-Love, a selfish, needy, deficiency love, and B-Love, an unneeding, unselfish love.

Defensive intimacy, or D-Love, stems from weakness. Self-protectiveness characterizes our role in the relationship. We may use it to keep away fears like loneliness or to hide parts of ourselves such as our feelings of being unlovable or inadequate. A woman says, "I married him not because I loved him but because he loved me and made me feel worthy as a person." Sometimes a person's partner gives enough love and protection so that our need for self-protection lessens. More often, we need a greater amount of love and acceptance than we feel we are receiving.

If we possess very little self-love, we may expect the greater love in our relationship to come from our partner. But we can't control another's outer or inner expression of feelings. Regardless of our own behavior and our partner's problems, we will test his or her love constantly. Any criticism, irritability, or hint that our partner may love us less than we require proves our worthlessness to ourselves and threatens the relationship.

Defensive intimacy influences our entire perception of our partner. We do not see the partner as a whole person but primarily as a giver or withholder of love, acceptance, or security. Thus we limit the achievement of true closeness and intimacy. Possible victimization always lurks in the background.

In *expansive intimacy*, or B-Love, we function from strength. Our strength expands that part of us that seeks growth and fulfillment in closeness with another. Because this kind of love represents a creative rather than a defensive process, the very act of loving is pleasurable and satisfying. We emphasize giving rather than taking. Because B-Lovers are less needy, such individuals require love only in steady, small maintenance doses and can even do without it for long periods of time. Along with your lesser need to receive love, you are more able to give it. Because you are less dependent, you are not constantly testing your partner. You feel a minimum of the anxiety, resentment, and hostility found in defensive intimacy. You are simultaneously more autonomous and individualistic and yet more altruistic and generous. Furthermore, not only does the relationship grow, but both of you grow.

Despite these positive traits, you may become the victim of your own strength. As you expand into new areas of intimacy, this strength leads to more openness, and thus you make yourself more vulnerable. You may have misjudged the importance of some weakness in your partner. Your partner may turn out to have some limitations you didn't know. Or *you* have the limitations, and your partner draws away from you. Because of your commitment, this may hurt deep down. You may really be a victim.

In a close love relationship, everyone has a mixture of defensive and expansive intimacies. The more we recognize the defensive ones, the less hold they have on us. Also, then we can more deliberately face the risks of expansive intimacy. This all-out giving may frighten you. You may end up hurt and victimized. Just remember that the goal may be worth any price you have to pay.

When viewing the goal of a close relationship, we must be careful to avoid an expectation that once established it will never change. *A close relationship must be a growing, changing process rather than static.* Trying to keep things the same will only work to stifle love. Successful relationships develop and mature.

Dr. Robert J. Sternberg, a psychologist at Yale University, did a preliminary study of eighty adults, ranging from seventeen to sixty-nine years of age, with the hypothesis that so many intimate relationships fail because the people select partners on the basis of what matters early on in an intimate relationship (physical attraction, having good times) but *not* on the basis of what matters over the long run (willingness to change in response to the other, supportiveness of each other).

The initial attraction between couples is based on more superficial aspects such as similarity of backgrounds and interests.

The professional word is *homogamy*. The concept is expressed in the adage "Like marries like." Usually this applies to sociological variables such as race, religion, the same kind of upbringing. For instance, a twenty-five-year-old Wharton M.B.A. will shortly marry the law student with whom she has been living since undergraduate days. She claims, "I care about a man's pedigree."

For some, homogamy is enough. Others need more than shared interests and similar backgrounds. The first time around, Peter and Mary O. made homogamous marriages with other partners. Both failed. Their second marriage—to each other—is much more satisfying. Says Peter, "Mary had more in common with her first husband. She likes reading, music, cooking. I run from all that. But we have a passionate marriage."

In their second marriage, Peter and Mary are examples of people who get involved on a deeper level. Even though they don't read the same books or possess the same political affiliations, they have the same general attitudes and values. They may share the same concern for the needy, want to spend money in the same way (conservatively or extravagantly), have the same ideas on child care.

Such a partnership becomes a filtering process in which both work on "need-fit." One partner may want a complementary mate who has the qualities he or she lacks. Perhaps one is shy, the mate demonstrative. My wife always claims she married me because I was the first man who saw her as she *really* was, the first to recognize her need to be taken care of in emotional areas even though she's extraordinarily efficient about practical things.

Are you fulfilling one another's needs?

Sometimes need-fit relationships work well. Sometimes they don't—because the fit isn't right or fails at some later point.

Example One: During a summer vacation in Provincetown, two young people met. Donald S., twenty-eight, proposed. He thought he would be marrying a bright, upwardly mobile woman whom he could mold into a super hostess to help him in his management career. Because her father had been a business failure, Pat, twenty-two, craved economic security. Donald fulfilled his part of the implicit bargain and became the highly successful CEO of a *Fortune* 500 company. Pat didn't keep hers.

She had two children, refused to join a country club or entertain in any way, and insisted on buying an extremely unpretentious house to which Donald felt unable to invite his tycoon friends. Twenty years later, with their two children off at college, the empty nest is silent. Donald and Pat rarely speak to one another. Their need-fit factor did not work out. And each became the victim.

Example Two: Roger and Leslie T. have a marvelous complementary marriage. He's weak. She's strong. Though they would never admit it even to themselves, this difference is what drew them together. Roger had been a dyslexic child, despised by his father because he "got left back in kindergarten." As an adult, he was fired from several selling jobs. At age thirty, at a Club Med resort, he met Leslie, then a grade school teacher. Roger explained to his sister, "I want to marry her because she'll push me." And Leslie did push. With her behind-the-scenes help, Roger established a thriving business. She gives him strength. He gives her care and comfort. They love each other and their life-style. They have fulfilled each others' needs.

MEN AND WOMEN: DIFFERENT PERSPECTIVES

Men and women have different reactions to emotions. According to Dr. Kathleen White, a psychologist at Boston University, women seem to be uncomfortable with separateness while men are wary of intimacy. Dr. White's research has shown that the more comfortable a man is with intimacy, the more satisfied his wife is apt to be. The reverse is not as true.

According to Dr. John Gottman, a psychologist at the University of Illinois, wives are generally more willing to complain about problems in marriage and to confront them than men. A woman wants to resolve an argument so that she can feel closer to her husband and be respected by him. A husband doesn't see disagreement as an opportunity for closeness, but as trouble. He wants to avoid a blow-up.

Marriage makes a woman draw closer to her parents while a man often becomes more distant from his. Wives even place more emphasis on preserving ties with both sets of parents, not just their own. Sometimes women turn to their mothers for intimate involvement they don't get from their mates. They set aside earlier, childhood rebellion.

Dr. Sternberg (along with many other authorities) has also found that the double standard still exists. His study shows wives feel exclusive fidelity to be very important for both spouses; men feel it is more important for wives than husbands.

What Causes People to Make Wrong Choices?

INCORRECT PERCEPTIONS AND EXPECTATIONS

Merely because we feel that a partner is a certain kind of person doesn't mean he or she is. In the early stages of a close relationship, feelings often warp our perception of reality. If we *feel* that a person possesses kindness, understanding, and sympathy, we assume that this must be true. In later stages, when these rose-tinted impressions turn out to be false and we find cruelty instead of kindness, we feel the victim of our own lack of perception.

We may also delude ourselves by imagining nonexistent values or character traits. One dedicated social worker married a newspaperman six years her senior, believing "all those interviews with famous personalities must make him fascinating company." Instead, she discovered that as a life companion he was a bore.

People may have a fairy tale idea of married life. They have no idea that any "work" is involved. They may feel their partner should desire the same things they do, whether that be hi-tech decor or constant eating out, or that whatever the mate's problem or temporary concern, he or she should do what the other wants at the time it is wanted. We may also expect an interest the partner doesn't have—the husband is a people person but the wife won't socialize, or the wife is ambitious while the husband stays content with a dead-end job.

Today's economic realities can keep a person from seeing the other person's true self. Rita, a Seattle social worker, moved into her lover's huge apartment, where his two best male friends also lived to save money, with the lover's permission. Seemingly much in love, Rita and her man set a wedding date. Then Rita discovered her fiancé had been unfaithful; she broke the engagement. She blames the roommates: "They were always there. We didn't spend enough time alone together. I couldn't get to know him. I just couldn't compete with baseball scores."

Love may blind us to what can be a serious problem. For example, one member of the couple may turn out to be psychologically disturbed. During the period of courtship and early marriage, we fail to recognize any warning signals.

In one instance, twenty-nine-year-old David M. did note that his attractive fiancée had few friends. He ascribed this to "her shyness." He completely disregarded her only two real friends, who told him, "She's a weirdo," thinking the term was being used in an affectionate sense. The marriage turned out to be a tragedy. A series of therapists diagnosed David's wife as psychotic and she went in and out of institutions. David comments, "I should have picked up on one cue early on. When she was five, her mother used to take her to double features three and four times a week. She grew up with a false sense of reality. At the beginning I couldn't see this. I knew only that I was in love."

GETTING INTO THE RELATIONSHIP FOR THE WRONG REASONS

Sometimes people get into a relationship not to maximize the good but to minimize the bad. For example, despite the new liberation, many women believe they must marry. To minimize loneliness and conform to societal expectations, they feel they must have a man of their own.

THE CASE OF THE
DESPERATE OFFICE MANAGER

At thirty-five, Emily M., an office manager, felt extremely lonely. For her, a man of her own represented the only way she could belong, but her affairs didn't work out. The men disappointed her. For their part, they found her demanding.

Through a personals ad, Emily met a telephone company employee, who, at thirty-eight, lived with his mother. From the beginning Emily realized his disadvantages—stinginess, a highly critical attitude, little interest in doing things for pleasure. But two pluses existed: He wanted to marry her and he, too, wanted a child immediately. And so they walked down the aisle, and within a year had the child.

The marriage has lasted, but not happily. Sex is poor. The family lives in virtual isolation, with little fun inside or outside the marriage. But Emily has her daughter. When she begins to doubt the marriage, she recalls her unhappiness as a single. For her, marriage serves as the lesser of two evils. She and her husband go their separate ways. She has what she wanted, preferring it to what was.

For a woman, danger lies ahead when she chooses a spouse out of desperation, thinking there's no one else left. And if you're a woman, you may feel that later is likely to mean never. According to a recent controversial survey by two Yale sociologists and a Harvard economist, just twenty percent of the women who reach the age of thirty without marrying can be expected to marry, only five percent who reach the age of thirty-five without marrying will marry, and for those beyond forty, "perhaps one percent will marry." While some successful women will develop their own life-style and feel content minus a partner, others look for a mate who is their equal, and when they can't find one will "settle" for someone inferior in every way.

For bachelors, another danger may exist. Mother dies. They need another caretaker pronto. They pick a woman who seems tender and mothering—and belatedly discover she is not.

Some people marry too young—their identity has not crystallized and they make the wrong choice. At other times people marry not because of the love relationship but to solve another problem—such as getting away from home.

THE CASE OF THE RESTLESS TEENAGER

Sally W. grew up in a sophisticated household in a Boston suburb with an economically comfortable but emotionally difficult home life. Her mother was the "other woman," waiting for her lover to divorce his wife of many years. Knowing this, and feeling uncomfortable, Sally wanted "out of the house." At fifteen, she met a handsome man seven years her senior. At eighteen, she married him—at the same time that her mother's long-time lover finally divorced his wife and married her.

Sally says frankly, "I was a child. My husband was nice but limited. I was bored, but I did grow up. I just married too young because I didn't want to interfere with my mother's new life." Sally became a decorator ("I saw I could change"), joined the local women's business league ("I saw I could mingle with educated women"), and then decided her marriage could not work ("He didn't deal with anything. Even though I was younger, I had turned into his mother"). She asked for a divorce, which her husband granted unwillingly. Now she comments, "I want an adult to live with. I broke our marriage contract. I grew up. He didn't."

Researchers at the University of Chicago conducted an eighteen-year study that points out the importance of knowing your own identity. If a man does not possess a well-formed identity in his early twenties, he is apt to be unmarried at forty. A woman with the same unformed identity may be married and divorced at forty.

Some people look to fulfill a deficit in themselves. This differs from "need-fit." Whether in character or appearance, *these people feel a definite lack that their mate must supplement, not merely complement.* For instance, a man who has doubts about his masculinity, selects a very feminine woman for a mate, hoping she will bring out his own innate manliness. She may. However, sometimes her seeming seductiveness may serve as a cover-up for her own lack of womanliness.

Insecurity can lead people into an incompatible marriage of this type. An unsure man often craves a beautiful woman. He wants to hear others say, "He must be quite a man to land such a beautiful wife." All goes well until her looks go. Or his insecurity causes him to be jealous, fearing her attractiveness to other men.

People change. A homely insecure woman attended college in a small New England town where she met and married a handsome "town boy." Despite his lack of education, she felt lucky to get the attractive youth as a spouse. Now she has become a corporate success. He's a failure, so uninformed and unsophisticated that she can't let him escort her to business parties. And his looks have gone.

USE OF THE RELATION-SHIP TO WORK OUT COMPLEX AND UNRESOLVED UNCONSCIOUS PROBLEMS

These usually center upon the parent of the opposite sex. Men often have such problems with their mothers, women with their fathers.

Some people, aware of their difficulty, try to master the situation. For instance, when you were a little girl, daddy was married to mummy and unattainable. Repeating the childhood pattern, you seek unavailable men. Singer Carly Simon has said about her father, "I was never sure of his interest in me and his love, and then he died of a heart attack in the early sixties and I was left with this unresolved dilemma. I've tried to win the love of those who were unobtainable. It's a mental trap I've had to release myself from."

Some of us may marry a fantasy of what our mother or father *should* have been like. When mother or father (now represented by wife or husband) departs from the fantasy, we feel victimized. For example, a woman had the fantasy of a strong, self-reliant father who always took care of her. One summer, she and her husband were bound for a Maine vacation. He was driving. They got lost and had to stop and ask for directions. She reasoned that if he were really self-reliant, he would have

turned to the map and figured out the correct route. Because
he couldn't handle their situation—and by extension, take care
of her—in a way that fitted her fantasy, she felt threatened and
responded with anger. In turn, he felt victimized by this anger.

On the other hand, because of these same unresolved parental conflicts, *we may want to marry someone different.* Our reason:
If we marry someone too similar to the parent who failed us or
whom we failed in some way, we arouse fears and guilts in
ourselves. Our solution is to move in the opposite direction.

For example, Mark L., a young architect, met a charming
dental technician who, after their second date, asked him in for
coffee. She told him, "My place is a mess." It certainly was—
complete with unmade bed and a week's supply of dirty dishes
in the sink. However, Mark's compulsively neat mother had
forced him to be orderly, and he thought the mess "charming."
To him it symbolized "freedom." But after marriage he realized
it was not freedom but compulsive disorder. He had got caught
in a trap that was the same but looked different. His wife was
just as compulsive as his mother, but in the reverse way. Again,
he was the victim.

We may want to resolve the pervading parent-relationship
problem by a *defensive self-orientation* that carries over into our
adult relationships. Because we always felt unacceptable to our
parents, we continually test "acceptability" in many different
relationships. Any rejection—actual or imagined—stirs up feelings of unacceptability. To protect ourselves from these feelings, we tell ourself, "My partner's sadistic and I'm the victim of
that sadism."

Not realizing that it serves as camouflage for other problems,
a woman may proudly admit to a father fixation. One former
glamour girl blames her aversion to marrying by explaining,
"No one could measure up to my father." She does not realize
that it is her basic abrasive personality, not a father fixation, that
turns off possible suitors and friends of both sexes. She has
made her father the scapegoat.

Marrying a person similar to a parent of the opposite sex
does not have to be bad. We may marry the comfortably familiar. We like strong, silent men who act and look like our father
or a lively, caring woman who achieves the same home atmosphere as did our affectionate, caring mother. If these

characteristics are recreated in the mate, the association with love, affection, and closeness can be very good. One happy woman says, "We have a marvelous marriage. He's very similar to my father. They even have the same birthdays."

THINKING OUR SPECIAL- NESS WILL OVERCOME ANY DEFICIENCIES IN A MATE

This kind of grandiosity often makes people select a person with whom the relationship can't work. The person with this conviction is not really trying to help the other so much as take the spotlight. His or her attitude is, "I'm unique. Where all others fail, *I* can succeed." With that kind of attitude, instead of ending a doomed relationship in the early stages, ego makes you chase and sometimes land the mate with whom the relationship must fail.

A female academic, yearning for an exciting life, linked up with a businessman. She recognized his thoughtlessness but admired his worldliness and felt she could make him more caring. She couldn't. She admits sadly, "My selfishness meter wasn't working." Recently she had a miscarriage. He went out that day, telling her, "It's your problem. I have to play tennis."

DELUDING OURSELVES ABOUT THE LEVEL OF INTIMACY

Convincing ourselves that real intimacy and depth of feeling exist in our union, we accept pseudocloseness. Past fears linger on in the present. We hide these fears from ourselves. We tell ourselves, "I'm okay"—when we're not. The relationship fears interfering with real intimacy have three bases:

1. Because we never saw true closeness in our own home, we don't know what it is or can be.

2. We have a need to avoid the anxieties of self-exposure that true closeness causes.

3. We must protect ourselves from the unresolved fantasies and feelings that closeness may cause to jump from our unconscious to our conscious.

To maintain pseudocloseness, both partners must play the game. As soon as one of them stops playing the game of pretend, the relationship experiences severe strain. Over time, one partner may acquire the potential for real intimacy feelings and no longer want the mate who lacks them. One woman who initially had this fear of closeness married a man who played the role of attentive husband but never shared intimate feelings with her. After two children, she decided she wanted more than a man acting a part. She divorced her husband. Two years later they remarried. She thought, "This time it will work." But it didn't. While she had conquered her fear of closeness, he still had not.

Victim Situations in Relationships

We may become a love relationship victim because of the role we play, because of the role we are prevented from playing, or because of certain interactions with our partner. Unfortunately, what succeeds in a social relationship does not always work in a love relationship.

THE ROLES WE PLAY

Because of a need to gain a certain kind of emotional satisfaction or because a specific type of behavior has served our ends in the past, we enact a relationship role. This varies. You may be a placator, a spendthrift, a baby (looking for care, avoiding responsibility), a protector, an encourager (pushing your partner to do the very things that will make you a victim—for example, you encourage him to criticize you because that is the only way you receive your partner's attention).

In the love relationship, many men and women make the mistake of assuming the savior role. Because of a tremendous caring quality (not because of any grandiose desire to be seen as a superior being capable of molding others' lives), some people take on an emotionally handicapped person—someone who is depressive, hypochondriac, alcoholic. Somehow they feel they can effect change. Often this desire to rescue the victim from the problem meets no complementary urge on the other's part. The partner lacks a true desire to change.

THE CASE OF THE MAN WHO NEEDED TO BE A SAVIOR

When Claire and John met on a cruise, the attraction was immediate. She had a life-long pattern. When stresses occurred, she would become nervous, agonize over possible catastrophes, and end up in a state of depressed anxiety. During the courtship period, John and Claire talked for hours about her problem. In the middle of his harassed business day, she would call, interrupting his work, and he would provide soothing support. His never-failing support lessened her anxiety, and he felt wonderful and powerful. To fulfill his need to feel strong, he unknowingly trained Claire to complain more and more.

After they married, John began to resent the burden of Claire's endless tirades about her miseries. Now they included not only her boss and friends but him. "How terrible you are . . . If you cared enough, you'd _____," she accused. As he began to withdraw emotionally, she complained more and more, *just as he had trained her to do*. She thought that behavior would regain her the loving support he used to give. One day John exploded and walked out. They made one more attempt to live together, but that failed. Both were victims of John's need to be the savior.

Are you an emotional victim because you play a role?

WHEN WE CAN'T PLAY THE ROLES WE WANT

Sometimes the bad relationship of our parents serves as a model that affects our marriage. For example, as a child one man hated his domineering mother, who never praised him. Now, at age forty, he loves his wife but constantly puts her down in private. Comments his sister, "He loves Mom but hates her. He's transferred this to his wife—and really all women. He needs help but won't get it."

In some cases the effect of parental divorce lingers. In the case of Jim D., his father left his mother when Jim was two. Now thirty-five, Jim has had a series of happy, lengthy, sexually compatible relationships. Understanding himself very well, he explains, "I'm so afraid of divorce happening to me that I hang on to everything, even old sneaker laces. I hang on until a woman wants marriage."

We may carry over the burden of a *responsible role in childhood* into marriage. For example, if your partner carries out his or her agreed-upon share of responsibilities, you may feel he or she doesn't do them well enough or in a way you can accept. Or because you have such a sense of responsibility, you may never give your spouse a chance to do anything. Then you feel burdened and victimized.

We may be the victim of *interfering parents*. We marry and expect to assume a junior but equal role with our parents as adults. But it doesn't work out that way. Feeling a desire to be helpful, a parent may assume he or she knows what's best for you and the kind of life-style you should have. This lack of respect for you as an individual—a refusal to let you take on an adult role—can wreak marital havoc.

THE CASE OF THE AMBITIOUS MOTHER

Lally L. grew up in Los Angeles, where her mother has a powerful job at a Hollywood talent agency. At thirty, Lally married a man from a blue-collar background. Tom is not what his mother-in-law Martha wants. She makes relentless efforts to end the marriage.

People in the business regard Martha as a "great lady." But Lally grew up feeling neglected. She recalls, "I went to Europe a lot but didn't feel loved. I wanted somebody there for me besides a maid. When I met Tom, he had a job as a salesman in the men's section of a department store. I wrote my mother that I'd be marrying him. She sent back a letter that said, 'What am I going to tell my friends—that he stands behind a counter all day?' Mother wanted me to have a husband who makes a lot of money. She hates Tom and won't let him in her house. She tells me, 'How can you be my daughter and not want the things you're used to?' But I don't want what she wants."

In her effort to break up the "unsuitable" match, Martha has taken Lally out of her will, leaving her only the family home.

Lally claims, "I want this marriage to work, so I've stopped seeing Mom. Our marriage is better. On a scale of ten, we're at eight now, not one. Tom may not be educated or classy enough for her, but I love him. We're struggling, but we have each other. To make it work, I have to give up Mom."

INTERACTING RELATION-SHIPS THAT VICTIMIZE

Relationships between very different types of people can turn out well if the need-fit factor works. Each adds to the other's life. For instance, a busy doctor marries a busy magazine editor. She likes her freedom to achieve. He enjoys the stimulating people she brings into his world of the sick and pained. They *complement* each other.

Other couples make victims of one another.

The Isolated Couple

Here the husband and wife exist in isolation from the rest of the world. Each partner is expected to fulfill *all* the needs of the other spouse. But, by sharing everything, each smothers the other to death—or divorce. Your aim should be to remain interesting individuals within the marriage, participating not only in shared activities, but in individual activities (whether going to ball games or becoming active in politics). If you can't do this, too much "we"-ness exists and the relationship is in trouble.

The Litigious Couple

As differences become apparent and difficulties arise, each partner builds up the case against the other with the attitude "I have no problem. If my partner acted differently, I'd be okay." In actuality, both protect themselves from any thoughts about what they do wrong. Neither wonders, "What could *I* do differently?" *Of all victim situations among partners, this emerges as the most common.* Because you blame your partner and never examine yourself, you build up a case of blame and more and more goes wrong. It's as a result of this focus of blame that many initial sessions in marital therapy turn the therapist's office into a virtual courtroom.

Even a little thing can trigger such a situation. One couple took their two-year-old, who was undergoing toilet training, for a weekend visit to family. She was a finicky child, so they brought along her own special potty. Going home they forgot it. The dialogue started: "You were the last to use it" . . . "You always have to blame someone." By the time they arrived home, the blaming had progressed from potty to "You don't earn enough money" . . . "You leave everything to me." Neither partner has ever said, "It's somewhat my fault. What can I do to change?"

The Suppressed Couple

In this relationship, one partner may have a stake in the other's suffering. By concentrating on the partner's fears and pains, the other mate avoids his or her own anxiety areas. A procrastinating man has an argumentative wife. He tells himself, "How can I do any work when I'm so upset by her anger?" He tells her, "If it weren't for you, I'd get things done." Failing to see his own problem, he also fails to see his stake in her anger: By focusing on that he does not have to face his own work inhibitions.

A common match-up of this type is *the no-confidence woman with the macho male.* Sometimes a woman uses a man's apparent sexuality to overcome her own doubts about herself. But the man may have his own doubts and pretend to a machoism that is only camouflage. Or the woman may see it when it isn't there.

THE CASE OF THE COUPLE
WITH DIFFERENT GOALS

Ivy M. and her three sisters grew up in an overprotected atmosphere of servants, fancy schools, and an eminent, professional father. Somehow Ivy emerged from this cocoon as an attractive woman, completely lacking confidence in her own sexuality. On a blind date, she met Fred, a highly masculine, blustery physicist who loved to take charge. She idealized him as her macho dream man. They married. She had the idea that through his strength she would be turned into a "real woman," competent and sure of her femininity.

She failed to consider an important psychological component: She did not perceive how much of Fred's macho behavior served as bluster to cover his own insecurity. Because he wanted Ivy to remain incompetent and unsure, in subtle ways he tried to weaken any development of confidence. His aim: to remain the strong teacher. Whenever Ivy tried to do anything—even cook a gourmet meal—Fred took over. Thus Ivy's confidence decreased even more. They split. The reason: They had different goals in the marriage. Hers: to gain confidence. His: to keep her down and maintain his macho facade.

Another common linkage of suppressed couples is that of *the overemotional partner with the withdrawn spouse.*

In this common victimizing situation, one of the couple, more often the woman, has an expressive personality. She is vivacious, emotional, empathic, and spontaneous. The man is more contained, intellectual, and detached. He would like to show more emotion. She's attracted by his logical, problem-solving kind of thinking. Sometimes this kind of relationship can become complementary. The man becomes more sensitive to his own feelings and able to express them. The woman learns to control her emotions and acquires a more logical approach to living and problem solving. Both grow.

But sometimes this situation results in a victimization spiral. Beneath the surface, the woman's emotionality threatens her mate. To protect himself from his own feelings, he becomes increasingly detached. She says to him, "Talk to me. I'm here." He continues to read. Because she feels more and more frustrated by his lack of emotional contact, she begins to express her feelings with greater intensity. The problem of withdrawn detachment in the face of emotional explosions grows. He sees intimacy and tenderness as risks he cannot afford.

Writing in the journal *Family Process*, Dr. Joseph Barnett, a New York psychiatrist, notes that the man may view these emotional outbursts as a threat to his neurotic self-image, an act against him, diminishing him as a person. Under his mate's emotionality lies a strong need for dependence. When he withdraws and behaves in a self-protecting but detached way, to his wife this behavior means, "I refuse to take care of you." So she tries harder—with more emotional outbursts—to elicit an expression of the love she craves but cannot get.

Sometimes a couple will collaborate in heightening the neurotic needs of the opposite partner.

THE CASE OF THE HUSBAND WHO NEEDED TO BE THE STRONG MAN

When recently married Wendy T., an executive secretary, and Lester J., a sportswear manufacturer, came to me for Behavioral Psychotherapy, they both saw the reason for treatment as *his* extraordinary jealousy. Lester would go into a green-eyed-monster frenzy whenever Wendy met with male coworkers from the past, male friends from college days, and particularly ex-lovers who had turned into "just friends." The simple act of sending a male friend a Christmas card would result in Lester's ranting for hours. Wendy began to feel confined and resentful. The more she cried, the louder he'd yell.

Realizing he was being unreasonable, Lester also knew Wendy deliberately provoked him. It was obvious he should stop being so hard on her, but he could not stop. Wendy felt more and more trapped.

Delving into his preconscious, Lester remembered how his father had always placated Lester's shrewish, critical mother. As a child Lester felt that when his mother yelled, she was telling his father, "You're not man enough." When his mother criticized young Lester with "You're no good," he felt she was also telling him, "You're not man enough." Now, in his marriage, when Wendy got in touch with her old boy friends, he felt she was telling him, "You're not enough of a man for me." So Lester did what his father did *not* do: He yelled. By doing this, he was proving his manliness to Wendy.

In therapy, Wendy also came to some realizations. Growing up as the youngest of six, no one paid any attention to her. She felt this strongly, particularly in relation to her father. All through childhood she had fantasies of a strong man caring for her. In her distorted thinking, Lester's anger came to symbolize his strength, and this strength fulfilled her childhood fantasy.

For Wendy and Lester, their relationship was a neurotic need-fit. As this came out into the open, both became aware of how they played into each other. She understood that his anger at her contact with other men meant, "Hey, I'm threatened." He saw that his having the power to make her stop contacting men provided him with a sense of manliness. He also understood her need for attention and that he could satisfy it in other ways than anger. Both partners needed him to assume the role of strong man. Both misread anger as strength.

Now Wendy and Lester have a greatly improved relationship. He no longer yells. She no longer deliberately provokes him with stories of her meeting male friends. They have agreed to one limit: She does not meet any ex-lover alone, even though they are now "just friends."

Caution: Always remember that in close relationships the need-fit factors may change. The change may happen with one partner and not the other. For example, the two-paycheck marriage can see a change in the power base of the relationship. If the woman suddenly becomes financially independent, she has new and different needs. The shift may undercut sex role stereotypes that the male has held. Partners can change in terms of power needs and dependency needs. As people grow and mature, their different needs may increase at different rates. Then they may have to establish new need-fit standards.

11□Emotional Victims in Love: The Solutions

Many couples who feel like relationship victims have recognized that walking out and slamming doors does not provide the solution. While some unhappy couples regard conflict as a way of life, others view dissatisfactions as problems to be resolved in an otherwise good marriage. They work the problems out and don't become victims.

How can we be relationship winners (those whose union survives, improves, and grows through problems) instead of losers (part of a marriage in which both partners constantly feel victimized)?

Give Up Those Marital Myths

Myths are our expectations of how reality should be as opposed to how it is. We believe things will work out the way the myths say they *should* and then act accordingly. However, myths do not reflect reality and thus the shoulds to which they lead do not work in real life. When as a result of applying expectations based on myths we cannot fulfill our self-demand or are led to do the wrong thing, we emerge as victims. To free ourselves of victimization, we must identify and then reject the myths that mislead us.

SEVEN MAJOR MARITAL MYTHS

MYTH:	And they lived happily ever after.
FACT:	Happiness doesn't just happen. We *make it* happen.
PRICE YOU PAY:	If you don't do what you have to do to make marriage work, you end up as the victim.

MYTH:	My spouse will always stay the same.
FACT:	People inevitably change.
PRICE YOU PAY:	If you expect the relationship to remain the same, you will refuse to adapt to change. The result: You develop false expectations and feel yourself the victim.

MYTH:	If we fight, it will result in the destruction of the marriage.
FACT:	In the close relationship, you *must* air disagreements, but with your objective being to clarify misunderstandings and clear the air, not to win.
PRICE YOU PAY:	If you don't fight, you may bury a series of grievances until one mate has a terrible outburst—or develop the other alternative: a shallow union.

MYTH:	We can get exactly what we want in a marriage.
FACT:	Each partner has different needs. Each must respect the other's needs. This means working out compromises.
PRICE YOU PAY:	If you always insist on getting your own way, you pay a twofold price: (1) You deny the individuality of your partner and make the relationship superficial; (2) as you can't possibly satisfy your fantasies, you are bound to end up the victim.

MYTH: Outside forces won't affect a good relationship.

FACT: Outside pressures *can* lead to a transitory or perma-
               nent disruption of the relationship. Sickness,
               money problems, family stress, etc., can cause ma-
               jor dissension and destruction—even separation.

PRICE YOU PAY: You may let temporary tension built up as a result of
               outside pressures destroy a basically good rela-
               tionship.

MYTH: A good relationship always proceeds smoothly.

FACT: In any long-term relationship, we experience peri-
               ods of dissatisfaction. Typically, such periods of dis-
               satisfaction occur about the seventh and fifteenth
               year of marriage when tremendous dissension and
               reevaluation often occur between partners. If we can
               recognize such a period for what it is, there's a
               chance we'll emerge with a far better relationship. If
               we avoid the problem, the marriage will not grow
               and deepen.

PRICE YOU PAY: If partners can't adopt the perspective that dissatis-
               factions naturally arise from time to time—but can
               be worked through—the marriage may end.

MYTH: Doing our own thing is incompatible with making
               the marriage work.

FACT: Each partner needs his or her space.

PRICE YOU PAY: The partner prevented from pursuing personal inter-
               ests will feel trapped, smothered, limited. To escape,
               he or she may find a life that does not include you.

Build Your Sense of Trust in One Another

Think of trust as the cornerstone in marriage and
the intimate relationship. Constant everyday contact means we
have more of a life investment in our partner than with friends.
However, each partner possesses trust limitations. If we recog-

nize the limit of how much each partner can trust the other with what, we accomplish two things:

    1.   We can be more trustful in the areas where the partner merits trust.

    2.   Both can either accept the limitations or work together to increase trust in doubtful areas.

RELATIONSHIP TRUST EXERCISE

Goal: To pinpoint areas of trust weaknesses and strengths in your partner

   Step One: Make two lists in your notebook. In making the following lists, use this rating table:

        0 — not one bit
        1 — very slightly
        2 — more distrust than trust
        3 — more trust than distrust
        4 — very much
        5 — completely without reservation

   Actions: How much do you trust your partner in the following areas?

- Making money decisions
- Doing necessary things around the house
- Handling money
- Doing optional things around the house
- Transportation—including driving and car care
- Grooming—appearance and clothes selection
- Taking care of the children
- Taking care of you when you are ill
- Outside social behavior
-

   Feelings: How much do you trust your partner not to misuse the feelings you share with him or her? Evaluate in the following areas:

- About your own family
- About your partner's family
- About friends
- About the children

- About work-related areas
- With good feelings having nothing to do with your partner (e.g., your chance at a great new job or the wonderful time you had at a baseball game)
- With bad feelings having nothing to do with your partner (e.g., you had a fight with a friend)
- With good feelings (love and affection) about your partner
- With bad or critical feelings about your partner
- With your reactions to the feelings your partner expresses
- With your needs and fears during adversity

Step Two: Have your partner make out the same lists and rate his or her answers.

Step Three: Exchange lists and answers. Allow time for each of you to think about what the other feels. Discuss what you've learned about yourselves.

In evaluating your trust relationship, you may find some areas of trust that don't matter at all in the marriage. A woman comments, "He's the one who remembers my mother's and his mother's birthdays. It doesn't matter to me, but he cares about things like that." You may discover neither trusts the other with money and decide to hire a money manager. Or you may find you've recently grown in trust. For example, your mate had a serious illness and you came through in a way that surprised even you. You may learn that in an emergency, you can automatically count on your partner. When Roy F.'s partner stole "thousands from him," his wife, Jill, cut down on expenses drastically. In turn, when at forty she felt "out of the mainstream," Roy found her her first job.

You may find that any mistrust you have isn't realistic—you're dealing with your own possibly unconscious fears of betrayal rather than a problem with your mate.

You may also uncover or rediscover feelings you thought were lost forever. For example, one couple, who stayed together solely because of their young only child, found trust in each other through dealing with other people's distrust in the husband. Haunted by debt, a liking for gambling, and demons from the past in the form of a mother who urged, "Get rich," Dwight L. embezzled money from the bank where he worked. He got caught and faced a possible jail sentence. Wife Betty said, "I married him for better or worse. This is the worst. And it made me realize how much I loved him." Dwight avoided jail. He's in therapy. Both are working to pay back the bank. Betty comments frankly, "After years of not talking to each other, we talk now. Because we talk, I trust him."

Bind the Bonds Tighter

CONCENTRATE ON THE PLUSES

Center on actions, feelings, and qualities that will bind the good in your union. If you concentrate only on annoying trivialities, you will feel the victim.

Don't get upset about small things that possess little relationship importance. For example, a fun-loving woman reports, "My husband has high blood pressure and never drinks during the week. However, when we occasionally go to a big party, he'll drink too much. I don't fuss. The next day I'll tease him because he has a rare hangover. On the other hand, I'm a compulsive straightener-upper. That's when he teases back." This couple has learned not to let minor idiosyncracies become a source of tension.

REVEAL THAT YOU CARE

Without expressions of tenderness, your partner feels the victim and wonders, "Does my mate really love me?"

Caring couples display continual affection. A twelve-year marital veteran says, "We're always kissing, holding hands in the house, touching if we are next to each other. We talk on the phone two or three times during the day." A Philadelphia district attorney comments, "We touch a lot at home and in public. My ex-wife refused to touch me." One wife leaves "I've missed you all day" notes on her husband's dresser. Before he leaves for work, another husband leaves a note under his wife's pillow, reading, "I can't wait to see you."

Advises one man, "Think of your partner as someone you're dating—even having a relationship with outside of the marital situation. Marriage makes it so serious."

Some Caring Basics

■ *When your partner expresses tenderness, accept it.* If he or she comments, "You're so sweet to me," do not turn him or her off with "I know, and I also know you don't deserve it," or, "Yes, but you're never sweet to me." Do this and you set yourself up for a return crack and discourage further tenderness attempts.

■ *Keep in mind that your mate's and your wants may differ.* You may think your expression of tenderness is what your mate wants, when in reality that kind of tenderness is what *you* want, *not* what your mate craves. For example, you spend hours on a gourmet dinner. Your mate prefers a plain meal, because that won't tire you and you'll be more pleasant. He has told you this. You think you're being nice, but you're not. He wants pleasantness. You provide a fancy meal and some crankiness.

■ *Accept your partner's evaluation of whether or not you express tenderness and whether it gets through.* Also, let your mate know if he or she is getting through to you.

Here's a simple caring exercise: Each day make a written note of one time your partner has expressed tenderness and got through to you that day. Then *tell* your partner. For example, you might say, "I know how harassed you were today and so your phone call in the middle of all those meetings made me feel so good!" In this way you reinforce your mate's behavior.

BUILD UP YOUR SENSE OF INTIMACY

In *The Journal of Personality and Social Psychology,* Dr. Kathleen M. White and her associates explore intimacy maturity and its correlates in young married couples. The same factors come into play in almost all relationships.

Some Marital Intimacy Factors

■ *Orientation to the other and the relationship.* Again, your goal is to understand your mate's point of view and see your partner as an autonomous person with complex motives. Avoid slotting your partner into a role, such as "He's a good father"—that's a label, not a person. You want to know the individual qualities, not just the reciprocal qualities that exist between you—for example, "He's so adventurous. I love his love of fishing."

■ *Concern and caring.* This means the extent of expression of affection and other feelings and the provision of emotional support when needed. And we are speaking here of the extent and how you say and do *specific* things when needed—for instance, "I try to be there when my partner is most upset"—not vague generalizations like "I try to be there."

■ *Sexuality.* Naturally, you want to feel comfortable with and enjoy your own sexuality in your sex life together. But within the context of a satisfactory relationship, sex beomes an *exchange* of feeling and excitement, not a test performance. When occasional frustration occurs, it's not of major importance. Higher forms of intimacy include the ability to be playful and to talk freely about your sexual relationship.

■ *Commitment.* You intend to stay in the marriage. Rather than commitment to the marriage as an institution, your commitment, affection, and loyalty are to your partner. As well as demonstrating appreciation for your mate's individuality, you often show this by such emotional investments as buying a home together and having children.

■ *Communication.* It's important that you reveal your thoughts and feelings not only about concrete things external to the relationship (what your boss said today), but also about the relationship itself and what goes on inside you. You listen, respond, confide, confess, and show yourself completely: "This is me. This is what I am."

INTIMACY QUIZ

Goal: To help you understand how you rate in overall intimacy with your mate and what you can do to strengthen the relationship

Ask yourself:

■ *To what extent am I self-centered?* Evaluate how much you focus on your own feelings, problems, plans. At the same time, consider how much you take your partner's needs into consideration. Frequent judgmental reactions characterizing your partner as wrong or deficient in some respect reveal that you think a lot about yourself. If you're judging your partner to his or her detriment, consider this as an expression of your own problem with intimacy.

■ *To what extent do I see my mate in terms of a societal role rather than as a person?* Evaluate the extent to which you think of your partner in the husband/wife role or father/mother context rather than as an individual.

■ *To what extent do I relate to my partner as a person?* Can you deal with frustration and conflicting needs and still value your mate for his or her unique qualities? You don't always have to accept all behavior, but you must show respect for your mate and your mate's qualities as a person in his or her own right.

■ *In which of the five marital intimacy qualities (discussed above) am I the strongest?*

■ *In which of the same five areas am I the weakest?*

After doing this self-quiz, you may want to start work on improving your relationship with your partner. *Begin with the weakest area.* Perhaps you share in all areas of intimacy except communication. When one middle management employee and his teacher wife discovered this to be true of themselves, they immediately set aside 10 P.M. as "our talk time." They close the door, ban the children, and inform friends, "Call anytime except after ten."

Another couple spotted trouble in the concern and caring area. Instead of expressing feeling reactions, each constantly criticized the other, and both experienced never-ending victim feelings. Their solution: to deliberately stop emphasizing what the other did wrong and instead *stress feelings* about what the other did. For example: "I feel deserted when you sit and watch TV all evening long" . . . "I feel harassed and pressured when you object to my watching the football game" . . . "I feel helpless and unwanted when, even in our most intimate moments, you complain about things going wrong at work."

By telling your partner the feelings that arise as a result of what he or she does, you avoid the courtroom battle of who's right. At the same time, you open the way for emotional—not litigious—discussion. Your partner may challenge. You explain. Perhaps your mate's feeling response will change *your* feelings.

How to Change Your Love Pattern for the Better

■ *Clarify the problem and try to solve it.*

Ken D., a thirty-four-year-old businessman, recalls, "The problem was between my wife and my mother. They fought over who would get me." In his mother's eyes, Ken was perfect. His wife tried to keep the peace, but his mother always started a battle ("I told you to bring me iceberg lettuce and you brought romaine"). When the blowups became more and more serious, and the wife felt more and more victimized, Ken called a summit meeting, insisting his father also be present. Putting first things first, he firmly stated, "I am married to my wife for the rest of my life." Because Ken openly declared his loyalty, his wife felt very close to him and no longer cared what his mother thought.

Another instance: Tom P. was a daydreaming school psychologist, Kathy a goal-oriented mother of their two young children who couldn't wait to return to work. Tom continually mused aloud about "When I get my doctorate . . . where we'll live . . . someday . . . someday . . . someday." The couple resided in a Cleveland suburb, but Tom had vague dreams of joining a Boston hospital. Unable to stand Tom's focus on fantasies rather than on practical facts, Kathy bluntly pointed out that the bulk of Tom's income potential lay in private practice and not a job, and that his referral sources lay in the Cleveland area. Tom recalls, "I realized that all my talking out loud and lack of focus was making her suffer. Now we plan to move to another Cleveland suburb near the hospital where I can affiliate."

Both of the stories above illustrate the need for involvement of both partners in identifying and dealing with problems that affect the relationship.

■ *Know what problems to work through and what to ignore.*

Trying to resolve some conflicts may create so much disruption that you threaten your main goal of maintaining the relationship. It may be best to disregard issues that revolve about individual differences when these do not of themselves threaten the relationship. Make a judgment of when to stand up and clarify the issue and when to just live with it.

Example One: Susan regrets all the hours her spouse jogs alone but makes no complaint. She feels that "jogging separates us, and I hate it, but it's necessary for him. Because of it, we are a happier couple."

Example Two: When Mary N., a native of London, visited Washington, D.C., she met and married Matt C., a government official. She stayed a subject of the United Kingdom. For nineteen years of marriage her husband stayed silent over this issue, which mattered very much to him. She notes, "All those years he let me struggle with my decision alone. Even though I knew what it meant to him, I just wasn't ready. Last year I told him I'd become an American citizen. He never tried to force me."

■ *Instead of just seeing yourself as the victim of a problem, learn to give and take help in resolving it.* Frictions and crises will occur. Rather than withdraw as a reaction, work to overcome your feelings of victimization. Again, give priority to the relationship.

Example One: When Millie B., a single working woman with a very demanding job that included bringing work home nights and weekends married Al D., she also became a weekend step-mother. An extremely devoted father, Al had his two young teenage children every Friday through Sunday. Millie did all the extra housework willingly, but when each child wanted to bring a friend every weekend, she found it "too much." For three months she and Al discussed this problem, until he thought up the answer: Every other weekend his children could bring friends, on alternate weekends they came alone. Says Millie with a smile, "Finally we had a good marriage again."

Example Two: Family illnesses can produce marital tensions. Marilyn N. of Chicago recalls the time her father had a stroke just when her sister needed an emergency operation. The ensuing upset drove her mother into a psychiatric institution. During this time, Marilyn's husband was "a rock." Two years later, when his father died, Marilyn was there "just as he had been with me." Because each saw the difficult period as a chance for closeness rather than as a cause for resentment, neither felt a victim.

Seeing things through your spouse's eyes may prevent your feeling used. The following exercises may help you do this.

MARITAL EXERCISE ONE: ROLE REVERSAL

Goal: To help you understand problems from your partner's perspective

Step One: Understand your goal. You long to gain accurate empathy in a problem area. This means you want to comprehend the feeling and thinking of your partner so as to help him or her understand you in the same way. This is not a problem-solving exercise, but clarifying the problem may help you resolve it.

Step Two: Reverse roles with your partner. For the moment, you become your partner and as your partner, tell what is on your mind, your gut feelings about it, how you see things in the problem area. Your partner then corrects you—tells where you've gone wrong and what elements you've omitted.

For instance, a childless couple in their mid-thirties carries on a continual dispute on whether to have a child now. The wife wants one. The husband does not. The conflict has produced enormous dissension in what had been a very fulfilling relationship. In the following role-reversal dialogue the husband goes first.

HUSBAND   *(playing wife):* I must have the baby now. My biological
           clock is running down. It's now or never.

WIFE   *(correcting):* You don't see how important it is for me.
           Ever since I was a little girl I dreamed of having a child. If I
           don't, I'll feel that I never got out of life the thing that
           matters most to me. Each year that passes makes it less
           likely I'll have a child. I feel desperate.

HUSBAND   *(correcting himself and still playing wife):* If I don't have
           a baby, I will feel cheated out of something desperately
           important to me. I'll feel my whole life is a failure. I worry
           about being too old to have a child. I'm desperate. I must
           have the child now.

WIFE   *(correcting):* Now you're starting to get it, but I still don't
           think you really understand how important this is to me.

Step Three: Stop at this point, even if major discrepancies exist
between what you believe goes on inside the partner and what he or
she says. If you work too long on role reversal at a single session, you
may feel impatient and frustrated. Give yourself time to digest the
feelings. After a while, have another session. Reverse roles again, and
following the same procedure, correct again. Keep this up until both
of you feel that your partner has captured what is going on inside of
you, whether the partner agrees upon a certain action or not. At a
different time your mate may want to use the same technique.

MARITAL EXERCISE TWO:
THE TWO-CHAIR METHOD

Goal: To help you set up a dialogue between the different parts of
you and so clarify things inside of you.

Many times you possess doubts about whether or not your feelings
are justified. This technique is adapted from Gestalt Therapy, which
emphasizes the experience of the different parts of self that make up
the whole self.

Step One: Set up two chairs facing one another. Determine the
problems you want to discuss with yourself. When you sit in one
chair, you will take one side of the problem. When you sit in the
second, you will take the opposite side. You will keep switching
chairs, and, in each, try to convince the other side that you have the

correct point of view. Even though initially you may feel a bit foolish, this method will probably work best if you talk aloud. Keep your dialogue with yourself going until you feel you've had enough for the moment. Do this by yourself in an empty room.

Step Two: Choose a problem that disturbs you. Present one viewpoint, then move to the other chair to respond. Continue moving from one chair to the other as you continue your dialogue.

For instance, Bob P. feels victimized by Jane's constant criticism of his mechanical ineptitude around the house and his social behavior. Jane claims Bob is oversensitive to criticism and that she's really trying to help him. Despite his feelings of Jane's "unfairness," part of Bob feels Jane is right. He is a mechanical and social "klutz," and he should appreciate her criticisms rather than resent them.

In one chair Bob will take the position that Jane's criticism has a helpful purpose, and he will try to convince the empty chair of this. When he switches to the second chair, he will take the position that the criticisms are unfair and that Jane uses her problems to make him the victim. It might sound something like this:

BOB   *(in first chair, defending helpful criticism):* Look, you know you've always been a mechanical idiot. Jane has a right to be annoyed. She wants to help you. Her criticism shows respect. She knows you can do better.

BOB   *(moves to second chair and discusses unfair victimization):* That is ridiculous. Jane's own problems make her a shrew. Take the other night when I had trouble adjusting the storm windows. She had a temper tantrum, but she *knows* I never handled storm windows before. Her flareup came because she really wants the perfect man so she can feel the protection her parents never gave her. I'm tired of being the victim of her psychological needs.

BOB   *(back in first chair, defending criticism as helpful again):* Oh, come on. You know it took you ten minutes with that window and you were awkward. Jane isn't the only one with psychological problems. No matter what you do, you crave unqualified acceptance. You fantasized that after the window trouble, Jane would tell you, 'Darling, you're no good mechanically. That just makes me love you more.' Because you fail to get your fantasy fulfilled, you feel you're the victim.

Step Three: Continue your solitary dialogues at other times. You may not solve the problem, but you will gain a new perspective about yourself.

When Nothing Works

We try. We figure out the problem and venture serious attempts to adjust in a positive way. Nothing works. Either partner may feel the victim, but both want the marriage to continue.

When this impasse occurs, return to the levels concepts of Behavioral Psychotherapy.

SOMETHING MAY BE WRONG WITH YOUR PROGRAM

You may find that you're working at solving a problem too difficult for you to cope with. Start with a smaller step. For instance, you want to reveal more of yourself to your partner. Yearning for real intimacy, you try to express every thought you have or have ever had. This may prove too big a beginning. If you're a shy, tongue-tied type, you may have to increase your self-revelation gradually by first telling your feelings and thoughts about *other* people.

You may give up too quickly. Change is like dieting. At some point you will backslide. Only in this situation, instead of raiding the refrigerator, you go back to being a shrew, bully, nag, uncommitted, withdrawn. Know that this will happen. When it does, start again on the program you've set for yourself. Don't let a temporary setback get you off the track. This is a basic rule in your devictimization program.

THE ROOTS OF YOUR PROBLEMS LIE DEEPLY BURIED

When this is the case, you can't do much about your problems until the conflicts that lie buried deep inside you are brought to your awareness. To find out what it is about you that keeps a full love relationship from developing, you must work with your preconscious.

Dig up those memories. Go back to your childhood. Maybe you can't love because you have no model to emulate. Did your parents or siblings show love to each other? To you? Your parents may not have been demonstrative together, but you don't have to be that way. Nor must you feel unloved because they didn't seem to give you care in the form in which you wanted it.

For example, one woman remembers how she starred in a high school production of *Stage Door*. Every other participant received a parental corsage. She got nothing. This crystallized her feelings of being the unloved daughter. Later those feelings led into a defensive-type marital relationship. Her fear of hurt overcame the ability to show love. You should remind yourself that even if your parents did not love you in the way you wanted, another person can and will.

Here is another preconscious technique. Go back to your first days in kindergarten. Did you cry because mother left you and went home? That may have signaled separation anxiety—which you may still have. In the present, you have the goal of being taken care of rather than *loving* someone. When your partner does something independently, you feel this as threat of separation or abandonment and see yourself the victim of an uncaring partner.

Again, realize that people often have some kind of stake in not improving marital satisfaction. For example, your partner likes social situations and your shyness makes you want to avoid them. If acrimony occurs (over something different from social fun), you use the excuse, "How can I go to the party when I'm so mad at you?" Your keeping the marriage bad helps you avoid situations you fear. This represents a fear situation at Behavioral Psychotherapy Level Two.

Or you may want your partner to be authoritative and angry with you. To find the reason, you may have to reach down to Level Three, the unconscious. Perhaps you have a need to prove to yourself how dependent you are, just as when you were four years old. When your mate sets limits and lays down the law, you receive comfort from knowing that no matter how hard you fight, you can't win. You feel reassured that your partner has control. Whatever you say verbally, deep inside you feel as if your parents were taking over, and this gives you a good feeling.

Perhaps something always makes you feel inadequate. Despite his academic fame, one professor never feels desirable. In his childhood, his mother always let him know in subtle ways that he wasn't "good enough" to be loved. Now he still has those "I'll ruin it . . . Who could love me?" feelings and fails to show love to his spouse. No matter how lovingly his wife acts toward him, she cannot overcome his core feelings of unworthiness.

You may fear domination. You think that love means your partner possesses power over you. If you show your love, you place your mate in a position where he or she can use and manipulate you.

Remember, in an intimate relationship, *feeling love is not enough*. Inability to show your love serves as a major marital threat. By letting yourself show love, you strengthen yourself and the relationship.

Coping When Change Occurs

We have a committed relationship. Whether we find it satisfactory or unsatisfactory, we have reached some equilibrium. Then one partner starts to change. This upsets the balance and trouble may march in. The changed situation may be only temporary or may bring to light either partner's limited adjustment capabilities. The desirable outcome: When one partner changes, the mate should change and grow in directions that reinforce the relationship. Change can prove to be a growth experience. Instead of giving up when faced with change, partners should use their actions and love feelings to bring them closer together.

That's what Dolly did when she broke the housewife stereotype and went to work to give her husband the chance he wanted. At twenty-three, Dolly, a "fluffy" type, married Jim L., a successful public relations man. As they played their traditional roles, all went well. Seven years later Jim announced, "I hate my work. I want to teach comedy. That means my income will drop a lot. We'll have to change our style of living." At first Dolly felt betrayed, but then she determined to change her role. Somehow, despite her inexperience, she landed a job as a trainee copywriter, then moved up to creative chief. She did not let any victim feeling of "I married a different man" throw her. Through new eyes, she saw Jim as a person with limitations she had not previously recognized. But because she loved him, she made the change to being a wage earner, not a victim.

Blind acceptance of stereotyped sex roles may keep people from changing. Is this true of you?

DETERMINING YOUR RELATIONSHIP BALANCE

Goal: To see how sex role stereotypes apply to your relationship and how you might change

Step One: In your workbook make up two lists—one of "masculine" traits (often seen as the doing of things, handling of practicalities) and a second of "feminine" traits (frequently seen as the softer feelings and expression of them that bring couples closer). For the masculine list you might choose such words as *decisive, adventurous, risk-oriented.* In the feminine category, you might have traditional words for female characteristics like *soft, submissive, emotionally oriented.*

Be sure to pick items that fit your particular close relationship. (You must have the same number of items in each list; try to pick at least ten.)

As well as copying these lists, enter the date in your notebook, and allow space for your score and your partner's score.

Step Two: You and your mate take the test separately. Each of you rates yourself on your masculine and feminine qualities. Use a scale of 1 (lowest) to 7 (highest). *Note:*   Go by what each of you thinks. No cracks like "You're rating yourself wrong."

Step Three: Now try to determine what Dr. Gwendolyn L. Gerber, associate professor in the department of psychology, John Jay College of Criminal Justice, New York, terms the "satisfaction balance."

After each of you has your own score, combine your total masculine scores as a couple. Do the same for your total feminine scores. Dr. Gerber shows that *the higher the femininity score total (cohesiveness) over the masculinity total, the more satisfaction exists in the marriage.*

You can score yourself at different times in the exercise above and on a fairly regular basis. When one of you changes, how does it affect the score? How does it reflect in marital satisfaction? Remember that automatic adherence to sex stereotypes can result in marital trauma. When you recognize why and how you cling to them, you can begin to change them.

THE CASE OF THE ANNOYED HUSBAND

Martin S., a busy international lawyer, wanted Pat to be the typical corporate wife. She, too, had her law degree but stopped working to have and rear four children. The minute the youngest started school, Pat returned to a demanding full-time law job. At first Martin fumed. Then he took stock of himself and realized that he possessed an essentially selfish objective: He wanted Pat home when he got home and free to stay out late when he entertained clients from abroad. Reaching back into his preconscious, he saw that he had a competitive personality. He had always resented his younger brother, who received more parental attention than he did. These two insights helped change Martin's entire attitude.

An insightful and well-read man, Martin knew Pat's working added to what some people would define as "masculine" traits.

Intuitively, he knew he must heighten his feminine traits (cohesiveness). Abandoning sex role stereotypes, he deliberately tried to be more cheerful, sympathetic, affectionate. If, because of his competitive drive, he had maintained or accelerated his masculine traits like dominance and defense of his own beliefs, it would have increased the separateness part of the marriage. Both mates would have been less satisfied. Pat changed in one way. Martin took a different route. Now he boasts at parties, "Look, in just three years my wife has made partner." He tells Pat, "I love you for what you've done and what you are. I was wrong." At the moment they are thinking of going into practice together.

See the Overall Picture

When things get bad, look at the big picture. No such thing as the perfect relationship exists. It's continually working at the relationship that makes it possible, permanent, and almost perfect. There are two necessary credos:

1. *Don't magnify your victim feelings.* Obsessing on what you feel is wrong only compounds your problems.

2. *Don't be too quick to assume you're an unredeemable victim.* Bad things, even infidelity, can have a strengthening outcome though both partners suffer emotionally.

THE CASE OF THE WOMAN WHO NEARLY RUINED A GOOD MARRIAGE

Connie and Jim B. had met at a business event. It really was "love at first sight" and some six months later they married. There was only one trouble spot in the very happy union. Connie desperately wanted a child and could not become pregnant. She blamed Jim. They tried everything from fertility tests and programs to artificial insemination. Nothing worked. Meanwhile the painful fact of "I have no child" began to dominate the formerly tender union. Finally, Connie, a savvy woman, realized that she was permitting her obsessive reaction to childlessness to ruin the marriage. "I love Jim. What am I doing to him, to me?" she asked herself. That night she talked to Jim and they decided to adopt.

THE CASE OF THE UNFAITHFUL WIFE

Edna M. had spent sixteen years of marriage feeling, "Somehow I should be happier." When she fell in love with a neighbor, Edna thought, "This is like a Hollywood love story." However, the neighbor quickly rejected her for someone else. With no one else to turn to, Edna turned to her husband. She reveals, "He chose to wipe away my tears, stay with me, provide the emotional security I needed. He didn't think of himself as the victim. He thought of me as one. Slowly I realized the other man was a fantasy item. In some way it involved illicit sex related to my father. With my neighbor I had acted out the childhood fantasy I had repressed so long.

"If both my husband and I hadn't grown from the experience, this marriage wouldn't be alive. Either he would have walked out on me or I on him. Both of us would have been victims. But you exist through bad moments and work for better moments. You don't put yourself first. You put the relationship first. In my unconscious I knew all along this man would reject me. In my conscious I knew I had the best man in the world in my husband. By accepting the reality of rejection from one man, loving understanding from the other, *I finally grew up*. We saved the marriage. We made a second chance for ourselves."

12□Super Sex: How Victims Become Winners

Sex is at once simple and complex, biological and spiritual, a fulfilling of the individual self and a losing of identity through a merging with one another. Sex means passion and tenderness, dominance and submission, aggression and love. It is a completely automatic, natural, instinctive act, influenced by all the life experience and moral values we bring to it.

Sex influences the most sensitive part of us, the part where we can achieve our greatest feeling of self, emotional fulfillment, closeness with another. It is also the part where we can be the most frustrating or hurtful to one another, most easily become a victimizer—sometimes by intent or with awareness, at other times with no realization of what we do.

The main goals of sex consist of experience and expansion.

We *experience* our own excitements, ecstasy, passion, our very own wide spectrum of feelings—the pleasures of pleasuring our partner, the thrill of receiving through giving. In a truly close relationship, we may so merge identities that we experience our partner's sexuality as if it were our own.

Expansion serves as an aid to experience. It is the constant seeking of new ways of experiencing ourselves, of expanding our awareness of sensitivity to our partner. This comes from learning and listening, asking and constantly trying. For instance, a woman finally told her mate, "Caress my breasts more." He responded, "But you told me you don't like your breasts touched." She laughed and said, "That was fifteen years ago. I've changed."

Paying too little attention to expansion is perhaps the most common cause of sexual self-victimization. In this way we limit change. Sex becomes routine and disappointing and we vaguely know that something is missing. In this way, many people become know-not victims.

A Behavioral Psychotherapy Program for Erotic—Not Neurotic—Love

Using the levels concept of Behavioral Psychotherapy, the material that follows should help you better your sex life, get those victim feelings out of it, and substitute a whole new range of sexual sensations, freely given, freely felt.

ADVANCED SEXUAL ASSERTION: HOW TO CHANGE YOUR SEXUAL RESPONSE

Assertiveness serves as the main path to sexual fulfillment. Individual assertiveness, while necessary, is not sufficient. Sex must be a team effort in which couples act together to create a new wholeness, where the partnership becomes an entity in itself beyond the individuals who compose it. At the same time, each partner must retain a sense of individuality, because sex is a combination of self and synthesis with the partner. Successful sexual assertion means both partners' feelings and minds joining together in mutual respect and love.

In sex, the partnership takes on an identity of its own. It is the partnership that learns to be assertive. No such thing as an individual problem exists. If one of the pair has a problem in speaking up, being adventurous, letting go, it becomes the partnership's problem to resolve.

The partnership follows the general rules of advanced assertiveness. It formulates joint sexual goals, makes explicit the rights of each partner, encourages freedom of sexual talk and action. As partners, each person learns to say yes and no. Through advanced assertion, the partnership team fosters experience and expansion.

Partnership Goals

Sometimes the kind of victimization that partners bring upon one another, producing psychological impotence or frigidity, stem from either individual's having different goals. Most want to make the overall goal a super experience in every way, the most important thing in our lives—exciting and a complete fulfillment of an already good relationship.

But in setting partnership goals for change, sometimes victimization occurs because each partner has a different goal. For a mutually satisfying sex life, we want not just agreement on the overall goal but also on the sub-goals. And we need a series of successes in achieving the sub-goals. To effect this requires a *partnership pace,* setting sub-goals in accordance with what the weaker, not the stronger, member can accomplish. For example, your partner can't handle your wish to "talk more tenderly." But as a beginning step, he or she might be able to achieve it by role-playing the stereotypical French lover, complete with sexy French accent and "*Je t'aime.*" Start with something as basic as that and move up to conquering other sub-goals—more sex, more demonstrativeness in public, more experimentation—until you can reach the overall goal both want.

In setting goals, a good starting place for expansion is the definition and carrying out of sexual rights. Rights possess two components:

1. Standing up for your own rights
2. Recognition and respect for the rights of your partner

Think Through Your Sexual Bill of Rights

Use the following statement of rights as a basis for defining your sexual rights.

■ I have the right to ask for what I want. If I don't get it, I have the right to say how I feel.

■ I have the right to talk about sex freely with my partner.

■ I have the right to enjoy sex.

■ I have the right to make sex enjoyable both for my partner and myself. My partner has the right to make sex enjoyable for us—and for himself/herself.

■ I have the right to try new things and be experimental and adventurous with my partner.

■ I have the right to say no to certain sexual acts that go against my deeply held values and principles.

■ My partner has the same right to refuse to do things that go against his/her deeply held principles.

■ I have the right to say no to things I truly dislike, provided I have given them a chance in order to determine whether I'm just anxious or truly dislike the acts.

■ I have the right to expect my partner to give new things a chance, to find out whether he/she is just as anxious or truly dislikes them.

■ I have the right to grow and change sexually.

Free Your Actions with Creative Sexual Self Smarts

Take action to exercise your rights. You must remove your inhibitions about sex in general by talking about it and also by doing it in ways that make you feel right about yourself. When you learn the skills of behavior change, spontaneous sexual freedom will surely result. For example, one way of having greater sexual freedom is having sex in places other than the bed or the bedroom. Make a list of different places in order of difficulty. Start small—maybe the living room floor. Progress to the couch—or vice versa if that's easier. Then move to the kitchen table or the staircase. Use creativity.

■ *Deliberately use "dirty language."* This represents far more than use of arousal words. Because we have been brought up in a society where the uninformed perceive sex as a sinful something to be hidden behind closed doors, so-called dirty talk can teach us to loosen up, overcome sexual fears, break through societal should-nots. Often, deliberate use of those words leads not only to a reduction of inhibition about the words themselves but spreads to the entire area of sexual taboos.

Or start with something less threatening: Carry on a sexy phone conversation with your partner during the day. Then progress to in-person sex talk. When you meet your partner in the evening, continue your sexy exchanges. Your words can range from "Look how hard you made me," to exciting words or phrases that intensify the sexual experience *for you.*

■ *Set aside a definite time for sexual talk.* This is the time when you share your thoughts, feelings, fantasies, experiences, and desires about sex with your partner—not complaints or problems to solve. Arrange your discussion time in advance. It can start with as little as ten minutes and become longer as inhibitions lessen. Again, you must start at the level of the more inhibited partner.

Very low: Just read erotic passages to one another from a sexy novel like *Fanny Hill* or *Lady Chatterly's Lover.*

Medium low: Recall wonderful sexual moments you have shared. Be very specific.

High level: Share fantasies and the planning of experiences based on them.

One woman was nonorgasmic until, at a talk time session, she told her partner that she had always fantasized about being a prostitute. So they carried out her fantasy—before the act, she ordered him, "Just leave all your money on the bureau." Their talk time led to the dreamed-of act and the result was that she was able to let go of her "good girl" inhibitions. Remember: You can't just talk about sexual actions and enhancements. In my clinical practice, I see that sexual role-playing gets participants involved at many different levels of their psychological being and thus helps bring about change.

■ *Learn to handle sexual put-downs.* Surprisingly, these occur constantly in "hot" affairs, close relationships, or marriage. Because of our own feelings of insecurity or in an effort to stab the other person, we may use sexual criticism to hurt our lover in a sensitive area. These hurtful put-downs fall into two major areas and require a response.

The inadvertent put-down. Without realizing it, your partner says something that wounds you in a vulnerable area. For example, your partner exclaims, "You're cold (or detached, rough) tonight." When this happens, react as if your partner had said, "Ouch, I hurt." Your goal: to open communication. You want to clarify whether you did something to cause the problem or whether the *problem belongs to your partner*. If your partner puts you down in this manner, try the "You Message" technique of psychologist Dr. Thomas Gordon, a technique often called "active listening." Putting your own feelings aside, feed back what you believe your partner feels: "You are hurt and seem to be feeling angry." Your aim is to show that you are listening with a sensitive ear and really understand your mate's feelings.

The deliberate put-down. When your partner intentionally tries to hurt you, *you* want to say, "Ouch, I hurt." Send an "I Message," prefaced by an empathic statement: "I know you're upset but I feel very hurt when you tell me I am sexually selfish, when I know that isn't true at all." Responses to sexual put-downs differ from those to friends, acquaintances, coworkers. There you have the aim of standing up for your rights or restoration of self-esteem. Here you want to keep the lines of communication open between you and your mate.

■ *Create sexual fun.* Making love to the same person for years can create sexual apathy. Use those sexual self smarts. A few erotic action possibilities. Go public. You can sit in your mate's lap in a public phone booth. Or slip off your shoe during the soup course at a dinner party and slip it in your partner's crotch . . . or, instead of going out to dinner and a movie, rent a hotel room and spend the evening on pure sex . . . or masturbate. The renowned Dr. Ruth Westheimer terms this a "variation of sexual experience" in her book *Dr. Ruth's Guide for Married Lovers.* You can masturbate yourself in front of your partner or you can masturbate one another. Doing either may spur a sexual excitement you can't achieve through intercourse. Watch porno. Some people become connoisseurs of dirty movies. For example, when Cathy and Norman P. finally had their first sex talk after five years of marriage, she hesitatingly confessed to him that she wanted raunchier sex play. Norman was delighted. Then he revealed to her that he had always wanted a porno film for their VCR. But Cathy had to buy it. Norman didn't have the courage to walk in and ask for it.

Sexual Freedom Cautions

■ When you pick your particular experimental action, *make sure you choose something you can do successfully*. Some couples may need a very low starting point—like petting in the living room before entering the bedroom. Others can start as high as masturbating in front of one another.

■ *Don't try something only once* and say it is not for you. Stay with it until you're sure of your reaction. Then move on to an alternative or additional sex fun acts. You'll build up a sexual momentum instead of malaise.

■ *Timing matters.* Don't decide to try out a new sex act when there's a sick child in the house, who cries relentlessly. At the same time, don't wait for perfect conditions, or you'll stay in your sexual rut forever.

■ *Always imagine successful scenarios.* Your script must be "You are entitled . . . Do have fun." In this way you up your sexual psyche.

Learn to Say Yes as Partners, Not as an Individual

In sex, make it your goal to say yes as often as possible. This leads to sexual expansion and adventure. The right to say no serves as the *key element that will enable you to say yes more often*.

Observe these rules as pointers in saying yes and no:

Rule One: Make a distinction between a *temporary* no and a *permanent* no. You have a right to your own moods and the right of refusal ("No, I'm not in the mood"). You also can set limits, "Tonight I just want comforting and caring."

Rule Two: No doesn't have to be all or none. You may want to practice deferral. Your no may signify, "I'm not ready for this act yet, but with a little time I may be." A man may want fellatio. A woman may find the idea repulsive. If you refuse your mate without at least a willingness to try, you are rejecting. If you try and still feel bothered, you might ask your partner to forego it. Remember compromises exist—"I'm willing to have oral sex, but don't come in my mouth."

Rule Three: Make sure your no represents an honest expression of feeling and not blackmail or a power play—"No, unless we go to the Caribbean!" The Lysistrata technique (named after the ancient Greek wife who led the women of Athens in a sexual strike until the men would stop making war) creates antagonism.

Rule Four: Remember your no may stem from a lack of knowledge. You may need therapeutic help. If you feel you've reached an impasse but are motivated to want to overcome the problem, consider having a consultation with a qualified therapist.

THE CASE OF THE UNTRAINED NAÏF WHO ALWAYS SAID NO

Sally J. and Bill, an ex-Marine, came to me for Behavioral Psychotherapy help. They were both in their early thirties and when they married, Sally had been a virgin. This had attracted Bill, who felt her refusing of premarital sex exemplified strong moral character. However, Sally turned out not only to be inhibited but the unconscious possessor of a series of concepts she had learned as a child but did not realize. Sally believed sex should start with a minimum of foreplay. Sex, for Sally, had a set standard: "Can he make me come or not?" Everything was Bill's responsibility. "You're not man enough," she would scream at him during every sexual encounter. Both felt victimized by his "sexual inadequacy," which he saw as his inability to bring her to climax. When he suggested sexual play with her clitoris, Sally recoiled in horror.

When they came to my office, they were desperate but still in love. I started Sally on an educational program of reading and discussion. She realized that her attitude served as a defense against her sexual anxieties and the taboos she had learned in her highly rigid childhood home. At first she found the relearning was hard. After a session she would rail at Bill, "Let's see if the doctor has made a man of you yet." We moved on to the sensate focus exercises utilized by many sex therapists, in which Sally and Bill were asked to touch and fondle each other in nondemanding ways and without intercourse.

But the major part of the therapy for Sally remained education. I made up reading lists. I discussed her incorrect ideas and beliefs, increased her knowledge about sex. Sometimes I saw Sally alone, sometimes with Bill. I assigned them the "dirty talk" exercise. Surprising herself, Sally enjoyed it. Step by step, as Sally's knowledge increased, her inhibitions decreased. She changed from a no-sayer to a yes-sayer. And with her new freedom she found a whole new sexual world.

Rule Five. You must say no to any act that seems humiliating or against some deeply held belief. But question what makes the act so humiliating to you. Are you hanging on to some idea that has no validity, like "Good girls don't do certain things?" On the other hand, you have the right to say a firm no. Suppose your partner wants to whip you and you have no experience upon which to base a dislike. If this goes against your value system about cruelty, a no is perfectly in order.

When in doubt, say yes. We must try to do this sometimes even when we don't want to. We do it when saying yes is more beneficial to the other person than saying no is to ourselves. Weigh it. The other person may be troubled, vulnerable, depressed. Go the extra mile.

THE CASE OF THE WOMAN WITH A MASTECTOMY

Connie J.'s mother had died of breast cancer. Connie always feared it would happen to her. One day she found a lump. The biopsy proved malignant, and within a week Connie's left breast was gone. In the hospital and at home, she refused to cry. Instead it was husband Stan who did. Loving her as he did, he knew she felt fate and her mother's heritage had dealt her an unfair blow. He felt tense, tired, worried about Connie's future. He tried to keep this from her. Then she looked at him with moist eyes that asked, "Am I repulsive? Am I still a woman to you?" The last thing Stan wanted at that moment was sex. But he took Connie to bed and treated her with more tenderness than he ever had. Both felt good. Out of love, Stan had said yes when he wanted to say no. And Connie felt herself to be a whole woman again, not a mutilated one.

Overcoming the Blocks

Up to this point our discussion of sex has dealt entirely with behavior. The partners work at the problem, defining goals and desired changes, and experience and expansion grow. The sense of victimization decreases and we replace it with a sense of development and fulfillment. However, sometimes we cannot achieve progress. Fears, a passive attitude, some gain in refusing to be different restrain us. Then we must reach to Level Two and identify the emotional blocks that impede sexual progress and prowess.

THE SEXUALLY PUNISHING PAIR

As with all the relationships, whether professional or personal, punishing pairs exist who combine forces to maintain and perpetuate the victim relationship. When the partnership has become a punishing couple, identification of the problem serves as the key to solution of the sexual difficulty. Both partners agree that trouble exists but view it differently.

FIRST PARTNER	SECOND PARTNER
"You're not responsive."	"You're overdemanding and oversensitive."
"You're sexually repressed."	"You have no standards."
"You withhold sex to gain power over me."	"You don't respect my sexual needs."
"If you loved me, you'd want to make love to me more often."	"If you loved me, you'd leave me alone until I'm in the mood."

Here are some examples of how punishing pairs operate sexually.

Example One: Nancy B. feels she has an adult child for a spouse. She says, "He comes in with that disturbed look, and I bring him a drink but after a few days of that I feel like screaming 'I want a man!'" On the other hand, husband Marty feels Nancy treats him like a child. He exclaims, "All day I run a business with two hundred employees under me. I come home to a corporal. How can I be a passionate lover when she treats me like a six-year-old kid?"

Example Two: Ruth and Lou G. continue to play out their societally imposed sexual roles. He performs as the aggressive, expert lover with the need to impress. And she's Mrs. Grateful, performing by rote and without feeling. He must control. She has given up on her own sexuality. They're so busy existing as stereotypes that they have no concept of sexual enjoyments that go beyond the stereotype.

No matter how much we feel any bad sex is our partner's doing, we must check to see what *we* contribute to such unnecessary sexual collaboration and what *we* might gain if we change our sexual ways.

THE CASE OF THE PUNISHING PAIR WHO FEARED BEING PUPPETS

Suddenly Zelda B. turned off sex. She told her husband, Jay, that she wanted no more of it. Zelda felt that if she allowed herself to become close, she would put herself in Jay's power—become a puppet, lose her identity. They both agreed it was Zelda's problem and spent a lot of time analyzing her fear—and getting nowhere.

When they came to consult me for Behavioral Psychotherapy, I explored the situation without any preconceived idea that it was Zelda's fault. What began to emerge was that her sexual turn-off had increased as Jay had become more warm and loving to her. But they still both blamed Zelda. In therapy, we then learned that Jay had the same fear of closeness, of becoming her puppet and losing his identity. By placing all the blame on Zelda, Jay had collaborated to maintain their sexual difficulty. He had started to act warmer because he knew somewhere within him that it would turn Zelda off. Each unknowingly collaborated in making sex bad to avoid the closeness that each feared. As we worked with these fears of closeness they became able to collaborate to make sex super.

ESCAPE FROM SEXUAL FEARS

Acquired from learning, environment, and media pressures, sexual fears can create sexual victims. Some sexual fears, the fear of herpes or AIDS, for example, are realistic and you must take proper precautions against them. However, many sexual fears are unreasonable and unrealistic. Such unreasonable fears can be of almost anything—gaining or losing power through sex, infidelity or closeness, uptightness or perversion, failure or success, loneliness and separation. These fears and many others cause us to create and maintain patterns of victim behavior. Different fears can result in the same pattern. Here are examples of recurring patterns I see in my clinical practice, and the specific fear that caused each sexual reaction in these instances.

The Tester

This type sees every encounter as a test—and a possible failure. Often he or she views sex as just another job to do well. The underlying fear: *not being good enough.*

The Too Considerate Mate

These partners carry their consideration to the point where neither experiences any spontaneous pleasure. Focused on the other's response, they forget their own feelings and put on a performance. The underlying fear: *being considered selfish or too insensitive.*

The Compulsive Playaround

He or she has love in the morning, afternoon, or any time with someone other than the mate because of an underlying fear: *being in the mate's power.* Continual promiscuity serves as a way of reiterating, "I have the power, not you." Simultaneously, such an individual uses this power seemingly for sex but, in reality, to counter his or her fear. This fear of opposite sex power can extend to nonsexual relationships and limit the depths of any or all of them. There are also those who fear sexual pleasure because it will put them in the mate's power.

The partner who fears parenthood may use contraception—or a failure to use it—to gain power. A woman may "forget" to take the pill. A man may insist on not wearing a condom but promise to withdraw on time. Motivation for such behavior may be conscious but it can be completely unconscious as well.

The Occasional Playaround

The underlying fear: *being trapped*. Spasmodic affairs reassure these people of their freedom. They may also satisfy a sense of adventure. For instance, Lenore B., a bright woman with two school-age children, felt trapped in her good wife and mother role in a small New Jersey suburb; she embarked on a passionate affair with a forty-year-old widower from Long Island. Every day, Lenore packed her children off to school, drove to Long Island, trysted with her lunchtime lover at his house, and drove back home to prepare dinner for her kids and spouse. Her sex life with her husband was good. She carried on the liaison so she would not feel like "a boring housewife."

The Distant Lover

The underlying fear: *closeness, commitment, aggressiveness*. Thus he or she must push down all feelings to ensure remaining detached. Often the mate expresses this with "We need breathing space between us." The partner feels he or she is going to bed with a sphinx.

The Silent Lover

The underlying fear: *rejection*. This type is marked by the inability to say "I love you," to express tender feelings, or to ask for any form of sex. If the request was not granted, he or she would view this as rejection—a situation to be avoided at any cost.

The Stand-Still Victim

The underlying fear: *change*. Such people fear doing anything new. Sex always remains the same.

The Lover Who Fears Good Sex

The underlying fear: *guilt,* often a hangover from repressed childhood fantasies, which limits the ability to enjoy adult sexual pleasures. People create various sexual scenarios with the theme "Don't have fun. Something will happen if things get too good."

For example, after a sexual success, something comes up that makes repetition difficult. We worry about whether it will be as good as it was. Some people find avoidance excuses—like too much fatigue from working too hard or the accusation that a partner is turning on a crusade to turn off the mate.

Sometimes sexual difficulty represents a "trade-off" for success in another area. When a couple achieves enormous financial success (new house, big bank account), often the man begins to have an erectile difficulty or the woman loses her ability to have an orgasm. They are thus protecting themselves against the evil eye with the script "You can't have everything."

Whatever the specific core fear, we must realize that three variations on the fear theme affect our lives.

    1. Our fear affects our sexual relationship directly or indirectly, but we *don't know that* fear serves as its base.

    2. We have *some awareness* of the fear but feel we must hide it from our partner.

    3. We *know* the fear and *can* discuss it with our partner. As a team we can work through the fear and resolve it. At this level, identification of the fear is not enough. The *team* must realize it's not a matter of his or hers, but something to discuss, recognizing the mutual effect; then *do what you've been afraid to do.*

THE CASE OF THE MAN WHO THOUGHT HE WAS HOMOSEXUAL

Jim L., a thirty-five-year-old dentist, looked and acted like an ad for an outdoor hero. Yet, despite his seeming self-assurance, at heart Jim felt he was verging on homosexuality. He liked his wife, Linda, to play with his nipples and felt this showed he identified with being a woman and proved that basically he was a homosexual. He felt sexually tense lest Linda discover his sexual arousal in what he termed "a feminine area." He had no idea that such sensations are normal for most men and that nipples are an erogenous area for both sexes. His stress inhibited her spontaneity, and thus he trained Linda to be inactive.

Even after Jim had finally acknowledged this deep fear to me, when he had sex with Linda he avoided having her do anything that would touch him around his nipples. If she came close, he would feel guilty and push her hand away. Finally, through treatment, he became able to tell her of his fears of homosexuality.

By sharing his fear, Jim came to realize his fear was baseless and went on to an improved sex life.

THE SEXUAL STEREOTYPE RESIDUE

Be aware that continuation of sexual stereotypes can prevent change. As study after study shows, sexual roles start in childhood. Within the cultural stereotype, women learn to accept the primary responsibility for the emotional upkeep of the relationship and feel threatened by separation. On the other hand, schools and society have trained men to take the initiative, to achieve the desired goal. Many men live by the Myth of the Golden Phallus: "I can make everything right in the relationship if we have good sex." Men are conditioned to be performance-oriented and to feel threatened by intimacy and tenderness.

As this century nears its end, certain cultural changes have occurred. Now many women will admit they want sex and more of it. Younger men in particular remark, "The 'me first' attitude doesn't exist so much anymore." Maybe not "so much," but it still does exist, especially in the bedroom, where people more readily slip back into their traditional roles. Claims one woman, "Women still want to be seduced and seductive."

What we do as a team maintains the sexual stereotypes or changes them. Change in one partner will change the other. The couple who wants change in socially assigned roles must expect some stress but *be able to overcome it*.

For example, if a woman takes the initiative, she may arouse her partner's performance anxiety.

Assignment: If you are a couple experiencing difficulty because of this, approach it as a team. You must simultaneously encourage the woman's taking the initiative and minimize the man's anxiety. The woman should ask for anything she wants in sex, and her mate must agree to do this with *one limitation*—in the initial stages of this practice assignment, *no intercourse*. This reduces a man's performance anxiety.

Despite conflicts, desired change can happen.

THE CASE OF THE MAN WHO CHANGED HIS PERFORMANCE— AND HIS ROLE

Thirty-five-year-old Rob W. grew up in a family where he always felt insecure. His father and two brothers were star athletes. While Rob was successful in more intellectual areas, he placed little value on those. He wanted to hit a ball into left-field stands, and he could barely hit a ball at all. As Rob grew up, this feeling of inadequacy influenced all his relationships, particularly the sexual ones. Rob kept trying to prove his masculinity by being promiscuous. At the same time, because he felt a woman might become his sexual boss, he always made sex quick, satisfying only himself.

When he married Laurie, he told her of his promiscuity. A sexual innocent, Laurie found his experience comforting because that meant Rob would be her guide and counselor. She had her own problem. Her concept of the female role was one of passivity, complete acceptance. But as Rob continued his lifelong rabbit approach, she felt, "I don't want hop on, hop off."

Wanting to retain a basically good marriage, Rob and Laurie came to me for Behavioral Psychotherapy. Even though frightened to discuss Rob's lack as a lover—because this admission went against her own conditioned conception of sex roles—she did express herself: "I want more foreplay. I feel you're rejecting me."

In the course of the relationship Rob had grown more confident and was able to listen. He had known something was wrong and was glad Laurie spoke frankly. Frequency of intercourse increased. So did foreplay. Rob confessed to Laurie, "My family always put me down. I never felt like a man before." Together they worked to expand their sexual life. Now Laurie feels more like a woman, something she never did when she played the passive, all-accepting, supposedly feminine role. Rob feels more like a giver. Because he loved her, he could take her criticism. Because she loved him, she could give it in terms that showed love, without feeling she was demeaning his sexual prowess.

CONQUERING FALSE BELIEFS AND EXPECTATIONS

For sexual fulfillment, you want to avoid incorrect thoughts, societal or emotional ones of your own that have a sexual effect on you. This means overcoming false beliefs, false expectations.

Eliminate Your Sexual Shoulds and Should Nots

Sexual *shoulds* ("I should always have sex when my lover wants it" . . . "I should want a lot of sex" . . . "I should always get laid when I want to get laid") and *should nots* ("I should not let life pressure and events influence sex" . . . "I should not have oral sex, anal sex") run the gamut. These ideas stem from myths. Overcoming them may turn out to be a thrilling sexual experience. Deal with these myths. Take a chance. *Set new sexual house rules.*

FIVE FREQUENT SEXUAL MYTHS

MYTH:	Sexual intercourse is the one and only way to enjoy sex.
FACT:	Sexual intercourse serves as just one of the ways a couple can enjoy sexual pleasure together. Unless we want a child or insistence on no sexual activity but intercourse stems from a religious belief or principle, we don't have to live in a single sexual groove. Once we've disclaimed this myth, sexual dysfunctions (erectile dysfunction, orgasmic dysfunction) become less of a source of anxiety, frustration, and importance. As we change our way of thinking about the importance of intercourse as the only way to have sex, anxiety decreases.
THE PRICE YOU PAY:	Limiting yourself solely to reproductive mode sex makes your sex life a bore.

MYTH: A perfect lover will give his or her mate an orgasm each and every time.

FACT: Since the recent emphasis on the female orgasm, many men have become fixated on it. If they can't give a partner an orgasm, they feel they are a failure and "doing it wrong." Often they become angry with a mate. One patient asked his partner, "Did you have an orgasm?" She replied, "No, but I had pleasure." He wouldn't listen. A single woman claims, "I have a friend who thought men and women have orgasms simultaneously. She was shocked when I told her this had never happened to me. I checked with my friends, who concurred— 'No way. Maybe twenty-five percent of the time.'"

             In their pressure to prove their skill as lovers, some men, feeling sexually inadequate or that their mate doesn't love them, become impotent or seek other women. They fail to see that they may not be the cause of their partner's response. *You are not sexually responsible for all of your partner's feelings.*

THE PRICE YOU PAY: Because you turn this into a test situation, you are bound to experience anxiety and to place limits on the different kinds of enjoyment you *can* have in the sexual experience.

MYTH: "If you really loved me, you'd know exactly what I want."

FACT: We expect our partner to be a mind reader. Night after night we go to bed and never get what we want *because we don't ask.*

THE PRICE YOU PAY: People *aren't* mind readers. By expecting your partner to know your wants, you limit your learning about one another.

MYTH: Contraception can spoil sex.

FACT: For many couples the myth works actively to keep them from enjoying good sex. When employed as a health measure for the prevention of herpes or AIDS, use of condoms is usually accepted as a necessary limitation. When used for birth control, there tends to be more conflict. With many couples, making—or not making—babies is always on their mind. Some distrust contraception's effectiveness or feel it's "not worth the fuss." A woman can't let herself go because she's so busy thinking about getting to the bathroom to douche. A man can't keep his erection when he thinks his mate is ovulating. Many women don't want to interrupt passion to insert a diaphragm. A man feels the same way about putting on his condom.

THE PRICE YOU PAY: The issue of contraceptive safety and use adds anxiety to the pleasure of sex. Dagmar O'Connor, director of sexual therapy, department of psychiatry of St. Luke's–Roosevelt Hospital Center in New York, and author of the excellent book *How to Make Love to the Same Person for the Rest of Your Life*, suggests that instead we "make contraception a sensual part of sex play." When sex play has begun, insert your diaphragm in full view of your partner. That way it becomes a turn-on instead of a turn-off for you. You can take joint responsibility. Both of you put the diaphragm in together.

MYTH: To have a good relationship, we must love sex and want a lot of it.

FACT: Recently, a letter appeared in a magazine saying something like, "We've been married eighteen years. We love each other but have sex only once a month." Frequency is not the measure of sexual satisfaction. If you are happy and each provides what the other wants, your sexual relationship is a good one. The problem arises when you can't agree or measure yourself against the fantasy standards of hardcore publications, novels, and porno films.

In every mating some balance exists. In the

Woody Allen film *Annie Hall,* the screen is split. On one side sits Woody in his psychiatrist's office; on the other, his lover, Diane Keaton, is in her psychiatrist's office. Both are asked how often they make love. Woody answers, "Hardly ever. Maybe three times a week." Responds Diane, "Constantly. I'd say three times a week." People have different levels of sexual drive. Just as some people have higher energy levels, some people have higher levels of *sexual* energy. A problem sometimes arises because some people are so intent on winning the other person before marriage, they often cover up or fake the extent of their sexual intensity.

THE PRICE YOU PAY: Instead of working as a partner to find your own level of satisfaction, you let supposed standards of others needlessly affect your sexual happiness.

SENTENCE COMPLETION TEST

Goal: To surprise yourself by learning new things about your own sexuality

Step One: Copy the following sentences in your workbook and complete them:

- My greatest possible sexual delight would be _____
- My favorite sex fantasy is _____
- My partner would be shocked _____
- I would be afraid _____
- Thoughts of my partner's previous sex partners ____.
- I most enjoy sex when _____
- Over the years my sexual pleasure _____
- After good sex _____
- After disappointing sex _____
- What most interferes with good sex _____.

Step Two: Have your partner do the same thing.

Step Three: Discuss your responses. In the discussion, go only as far as you can comfortably.

Step Four: About a week or even a month later, fill out the Sexual Completion Test a second time and discuss it again. See if anything has changed during this time (you may want to do this periodically).

What You Can Learn from the Sentence Completion Test

You may surprise yourself by learning new aspects of your own fears, fantasies, sexuality. If you don't acquire new self-knowledge the first time you try the test, repeat it and answer more imaginatively. Let yourself go. As you share the test answers, remember *you and your partner must work as a team.* For instance, one mate completes the sentence, "I most enjoy sex when you wake me and caress me tenderly." The other partner is amazed: "I never realized how much you like it. I felt guilty when I woke you and hesitated to do it. This frees me to think of more exciting ways of waking you." As a sexual partnership, you undergo a learning experience in discussing highly personal sexual thoughts and answers. This sentence completion technique, often used by psychologists to uncover clients' emotional attitudes and conflicts, can clear up many misunderstandings.

Reality-Based Sexual Thinking

In today's singles society a main source of victimization occurs when one partner wants recreational sex, while the other wants relationship sex. If couples make it clear to one another that it is recreational sex, not relationship sex, that they desire, and if they feel free to decide whether they want it on those terms, they have much less risk of exposure to possible emotional victimization.

For example, Chuck Y., thirty-five, has had four lengthy relationships—with a virgin for whom he was "first love," with two experienced young career women, and now with an older divorced woman. He claims sex was "perfect" with all four but says, "They left me when they saw I wasn't ready for marriage." While proclaiming his love for the four and offering such excuses for flight as "tensions caused by death of a business partner," "too young," and "recession fear," Chuck was not open about his attitude. A victimizer who won't admit it, he fooled all four women. They all felt used because they thought he really cared about them as persons, not just as recreational sex objects.

There's also hidden agenda recreational sex—one partner acts accepting of the recreational objective but really wants to turn it into relationship sex. At times he or she succeeds; at other times he or she fails and becomes a victim of false expectations.

For example, Dirk J., married for some twelve years, has no intention of a divorce. But through his retailing jobs, he meets many pretty young women and at times becomes attached to one of them. He tells them, "No marriage . . . maybe a weekend once in a while when my wife is away" or "probably every Wednesday night," but his pretty playmates just won't listen. Their hidden agenda: "I'll get him to leave his wife!"

Participants may also play head games in one-night stands. With one-nighters there's no partnership and little chance of expansion, but one partner may think of that one encounter as relationship sex and become a victim. You must see a one-night stand for what it is. If you view it as purely recreational sex with no false expectations, you will not be a victim. Says one twenty-six-year-old woman, "I met him at a singles bar. He was stunning and I had been drinking. I have no regrets." Of course, having realistic expectations in such situations is not enough to prevent you from becoming a victim. Nowadays you *must* pay attention to your reasonable concerns about AIDS and take all necessary precautions.

False expectations can also create sexual victims when people view sex as a means to some emotional end.

For example, Pat M., a young art restorer, tried to use sex to solve an emotional problem. Because of a very painful divorce (she was "dumped"), she had doubts of her own womanliness and thus allowed her desperation to cloud her judgment. She let a new man, a real estate wheeler-dealer, invite himself to dinner. His selfishness showed immediately. She was made to wait dinner while he watched "60 Minutes"; then he mocked her cooking and when finally he took her to bed, he made her feel even more insecure. She never heard from him again. Pat was so despairing that she ignored the rebuff, called him two weeks later, and got the brush-off. Only then did she realize that her intense yearning to "feel like a woman" had made her a "kick me" victim. The minute the self-invited suitor let her elaborate dinner get cold while he watched TV, Pat should have known to look for someone else to satisfy her emotional and physical needs.

Do what you want sexually—but not through rose-tinted glasses. See recreational sex for what it is (fun and games, excitement), not as the relationship sex (meaningful over the long term) you might want it to be or become.

Develop Sexual Security

What is sexual confidence? It stems from the knowledge that we can give and receive sexual excitement. *Our goal is pleasure—not orgasm, intercourse, or any exclusive form of sex.* Most important is the concept "I can do that," which we have talked about throughout this book. You must *know* you have the ability to share tenderness and titillation, to give and take sexual enjoyment.

Here are two exercises designed to increase that gut feeling of sexual know-how.

SEXUAL CONFIDENCE EXERCISE ONE

Goal: Recall of past success

A number of times during the day, call up memories of outstanding sexual pleasures from the past. Remember the details. Pay attention to how you felt before you performed the sexual act, what you did that made it memorable. Don't limit your memories to the bedroom. One couple remembered that in the first days of their marriage, they would caress one another on plane trips under the blanket supplied by the airline. Another recalled how they used to sit in the back row at a movie, caress each other in the dark, and then rush out to the parking lot to make love. Remember the first time you had hot sex instead of the more routine sex you may now have in the bedroom.

Recollect over and over. By recalling what you've done successfully in the past, you gain the knowledge that you can be successful again. You reaffirm confidence: "I did it before. *I like myself.* I'm capable of it." A side benefit is that through recall you may be back to doing positive, enjoyable things from the past that you have stopped doing.

SEXUAL CONFIDENCE EXERCISE TWO

Goal: To practice increasing your awareness of your own sensuality

Imagine some sexual play with your partner. Get a clear image in your head. Rate the act on a scale of 0 to 100 on the amount of pleasure the image provides. Repeat. If, for example, you imagined caressing your mate's thighs and got a sex arousal score of 30, see if on a repeat performance you can bring it up to 35 or 40.

Your gain: You learn that it's passive to believe that sexual feelings just happen or don't happen to you. *You* have a great deal to say about how much excitement you will feel as you stroke your partner's thigh, buttock, or crotch. That's the active orientation. A side benefit is that through this experience you not only strengthen your awareness of your sexual feelings but strengthen the feelings themselves. Use them.

Looking Backward: Breaking Through Your Buried Barriers

Subtle blocks that go deeper than sexual stereotypes or incorrect assumptions may place an emotional barrier between you and your sexual freedom. The following brief Behavioral Psychotherapy Sexual Remembrance Guide may help you to apply the Behavioral Psychotherapy principle: *Use your past to control your present and change your sexual future.* Get out your workbook and think through the following questions. As you do, do not try to find black and white answers. Use the questions as a form of what the late philosopher William James called "passive attention." Set aside time for sexual recall (on a bus, in a car) and think about the questions. Then in your workbook write down key words or phrases to remind you of incidents you *have* remembered.

SEXUAL REMEMBRANCE GUIDE

■ *What were your sexual fantasies when you first started masturbating?* What were your feelings about masturbating? Have they changed over the years? Recall other fantasies and analyze their influence in your present.

THE CASE OF THE MAN WHO MASTURBATED AS A CHILD

Al O., a man in his early thirties, felt something missing in his marriage but didn't know what. In the course of Behavioral Psychotherapy with me, he kept saying, "I'm a victim. If only Polly were freer." As we discussed it, he became aware that after sex, he had the vague feeling/thought "I got away. I wasn't caught."

But Al couldn't understand his feeling. At first he could remember no victimizing incident from his past. One day he had a flash. Using his preconscious, he recalled a series of masturbation incidents during high school. He would come home and masturbate when he was supposed to be studying. He was terrified his mother would walk in, catch him masturbating, and berate him—not just for masturbating but for not doing his homework. This fear added to his sexual experience—Al felt he was getting away with something forbidden. As a result, in his unconscious, Al had formed the rule that sex is bad and if he were to be found out, he would be punished.

In treatment, as Al and Polly discussed his feeling, they turned it into a game. During sex, Polly would say, "You're not studying history! What if Mommy comes in?" By going back-wards in sex, Al was able to go forward.

■ *Try to recall specific incidents to determine the family feelings and attitude about sex.* Did anyone in your home talk about it directly or indirectly? For example, one thirty-year-old woman says, "My parents were very puritan. I never saw them kiss and hug. When actors kissed on TV, my father left the room. It made me very sexually conservative and has been a problem in my marriage. I'm repressed."

■ *Were you ever punished for sexual behaviors or en-couraged to engage in them?* Were there things between you and a sibling that you now recognize as sexual? Did you recognize it as such at the time? One brother and his younger sister used the upstairs of the garage to show off their nude bodies as pre-teens. They were caught and severely punished by their par-ents. Ever since, each has been uncomfortable with "good" members of the opposite sex.

■ *In retrospect, do you see yourself as being a victim or victimizer,* whether you were or not? Did you have "funny feel-ings" when an aunt or uncle held you tightly? One woman remembers that as a nine-year-old she used to visit a best friend with a very handsome, virile father. He would hug her and she would feel "something funny" going on, a sense of victimization that she didn't realize as such. The frequent childhood inci-dents left her with a fear of tall, good-looking men who radiate sensuality. The woman comments tersely, "I hear he's still sexy at seventy and on his fourth wife."

In questioning yourself, you gain perspective on your own sexuality. You recall relevant experiences that you may have forgotten and feelings that you may have ignored at the time; you may be able to pinpoint subtle feelings and thoughts that inhibit your sexual expansion. By identifying them, we often loosen their hold on us. For example, if you realize your car-ryover guilt from sibling sex play, the mere realization may make the long ago act lose its power.

Sometimes use of the preconscious leads us to remembrance and solutions of a specific problem. Many of these problems are related to guilt. Sexual feelings are a part of growing up. Guilt makes the problem. Get rid of the guilt, and you find the problem is resolved.

Some guilts relate to childhood fantasies.

THE CASE OF THE MAN WITH THE RELIGIOUS FANTASY

Gene J., a happily married forty-year-old engineer, had trouble with sexual erections. In Behavioral Pychotherapy with me, we discussed his specific sexual guilts and it came out that for years Gene had had sexual fantasies combining religion with sex. For example, in one childhood fantasy, he imagined himself as a priest (he was a Catholic) satisfying a room full of nuns. To supplement his fantasy, young Gene would buy various pieces of equipment, such as catechism beads, and hold them while masturbating. He was very ashamed of this and the shame lasted *years* after his actions stopped, continuing to inhibit his sexuality.

I used the sexual partner approach with Gene and his wife. We openly discussed sexual fantasies. She refused to tell me hers, but told Gene. He reported to me that hers made his look very minor. This made his guilt dissolve. But the point is that until he brought his shame and guilt into the open, his past continued to affect his sexual feelings and performance into the present.

Some guilts relate to childhood unconscious urges toward opposite-sex parents. Says Suzanne Prescod, editor of the newsletters *Sexuality Today* and *Behavior Today,* "Many people don't have sex with a partner, but with their mother and father and their mate's mother and father. Un-mommy your wife and un-daddy your husband."

One technique to un-mommy or un-daddy yourself is to play a game that will teach you that these guilts are natural feelings that form part of sexual development. By playing mommy and daddy games in an acceptable context, you should be able to get rid of, certainly lessen, the guilts. This kind of technique is known as *corrective emotional experience.*

THE MOMMY/DADDY GAME

Goal: To desensitize guilt feelings left over from childhood sexual fantasies involving parents

Step One: In a superficial way reestablish the mommy/daddy situation.

■ Play doctor and patient, in which each of you examines the other's body.

■ Talk baby talk.

■ Have mommy (female) caress son (male) on her lap or daddy (male) caress daughter (female) on his lap.

Step Two: Move to more adult behavior. As you go through the experience, the guilt goes away and perhaps you can have more fun in bed than mommy and daddy ever did.

Mommy and daddy can enter your sex life in many subtle ways. For example, their influence may lead to fear of sexual success. In her book *Disorders of Sexual Desire,* Dr. Helen Singer Kaplan has brilliantly analyzed this problem. In childhood, a little girl flirts with daddy. Mother responding, proclaims silently or verbally, "I'm the only one allowed to be the woman here." Thus women learn that if they allow themselves to let go sexually, they risk the loss of mother's love. A boy feels that if he competes with daddy for mother's love, daddy will castrate him. Thus in childhood many people learn that sexual feelings are sinful and that in expressing them, they risk parental displeasure and punishment, loss of love. As adults we may not readjust our thinking. Sexual success then stirs up guilt, shame, anxiety, and though we are now in mature relationships, we cling to the early guilts. Somehow we keep mommy and daddy in our sexual beds. Get them out!

At different stages in life we have different sexual attitudes. As honeymooners, sex seems perfect. (One twenty-eight-year-old claims, "We lived together for four years; we worked out everything.") Fifteen to twenty years later we may feel victimized by the aging process. A woman may feel her mother role ebbing and, without it, she believes she lacks an identity. Because he goes bald, has a career crisis, or simply feels time is passing, a man may feel a lack of virility. (One man became impotent on his daughter's wedding night.) Yet, as with everything else in life, sex is up to you. Many couples feel that as time goes by, they experience greater intimacy and ecstasy in sex because they *try* for it. They are not sexual victims because *they know what they want for themselves as they are right now.*

We are all born with the capacity for human sexual response. Later learned responses can block the intimacy we all crave. Bad sex can echo through a whole relationship. But conversely, in most instances good relationships and good sex go together. Good sex helps make a good relationship. A good relationship helps make good sex better.

As you look for super sex always keep two essentials in mind:

　　　1.　In sexual bonding, *love* serves as the greatest aphrodesiac of all.

　　　2.　As Erich Fromm wrote, "Erotic love begins with separateness and ends with oneness."

13□Don't Let Divorce Make You a Victim

Today half of first marrieds divorce. They have a choice: to wallow in emotional defeat or to use the experience as a chance for emotional growth.

Some Basic Facts About Today's Divorce

■ *Eighty-five percent of the first marrieds who divorce will remarry.* If they adapt their behavior patterns and what they've learned to new circumstances, they can make a fresh start in life and face a new and different future positively.

■ *New amicable social customs exist.* Some second wives have managed to marry off the first wife. Now ex-couples will sometimes double date with their new mates. Recently, a well-known executive left his long-term wife for a much younger woman. "My ex took it very well," he comments. She certainly did. The cast-off mate called and told him of a relatively reasonable apartment she had heard about from a friend as a housing chance for him and his new wife-to-be.

■ *Behind a seeming no-care attitude may lie pain and hurt*, sometimes right on the surface, other times buried so deep that the person involved cannot admit their existence. Usually the break-up involves far more complications than the break-up of a close unmarried relationship—because of children, interlocking relationships (like grandparents), shared possessions. Men typically fear being on their own. Women tend to fear new responsibilities. Both feel a deep sense of failure.

Comments Norman Sheresky, a well-known New York divorce lawyer and author, "Everyone who goes to a divorce court feels guilty. They [include] the alleged winners who say, 'I'll be happier somewhere else . . . I want something else out of life.' And there are the alleged losers—the spouses of the winners. Each has a fifty percent chance of being happy. Sometimes these alleged victims aren't victims at all. They want to be free and don't even know it. Or they may have been victims before the marriage and they continue as victims after the divorce."

■ *Many divorcing people make a major mistake:* They view divorce only as a personal rejection. Possessing an erroneous idea of what divorce is, they fail to recognize it as a learning experience that can mean a different future. They utilize the same victim psychology in divorce as they do in other life situations. They *need* to view themselves as victims. In this way, they absolve themselves of guilt and gain sympathy from others—"It's all my partner's fault." This may develop into a permanent personality trait.

Trauma Versus Victimization

Divorce *is* traumatic. There are feelings of pain, doubt, anger. Reactions can run the gamut of hardly any outward expression of hurt to highly expressed pain, or to camouflage, suppression, even repression of feelings. Even very brief, childless marriages that end in divorce can leave scars. For instance, when Kitty and Tom B. made the decision to break up, they divided the furniture and the money in their joint account. Tom also gave Kitty money to see her through a year of graduate school. Even so, ten years later a happily remarried Kitty still talks about that first marriage. For her it left a slowly fading, but unacknowledged, sense of failure that she doesn't dare face.

Others more openly resent the fact that they have to go through unpleasant feelings, whether sadness or fury.

Some people mistakenly expect that once they have made the decision to divorce, the trauma is essentially over—after that all will go well. They are not prepared for the delays, misunderstandings, and stressful experiences of the divorce process.

They are even less ready for the unexpected "unfairness" of others who fail to understand what they're going through. Sympathetic friends who are not empathic are the most difficult to cope with—they try to sympathize, but what they say shows they can't understand the inner feelings of the divorcing person, and that leaves the individual feeling more and more alone. There are also friends—and family—who desert you and sometimes become members of what you perceive as the enemy camp.

The divorcing person may be the actual problem. Deep within you, you keep hearing repetition of the promise, "Till death do us part." At the same time, you keep thinking "I'm rejecting" or "I'm rejected." You take the traumatic divorce situation and turn it into victimization with the goal of increasing your suffering. To cope with this "I'm a failure" feeling and the need to suffer, some people may evolve a defense: They develop unrealistic fantasies of what life will be like without that "terrible mate."

Your divorce may be a true victimization. You have left your mate. Your mate has left you. Are you going to stay focused on your emotional beating or move on to a different life?

You must achieve an emotionally helpful idea of divorce—the right idea. You will be leaving one situation for another. This gives you the chance to have a new life, which can offer you the opportunity for a freer, happier existence with more chance for you to grow. By dwelling on the trauma of divorce, you increase the reaction to your actual victimization or turn it into victimization when it is not. Go through it. Somehow you will be able to master the strength to live through it and, difficult as it may be, make yourself move on with life.

Typical Divorce Situations

OBVIOUS VICTIMIZATION

The only way to end the victim role in a relationship is to exit. Maybe you wed a difficult person and couldn't take the harangues. Or your sadistic mate used you as his whipping girl. Perhaps you grew tired of a one-sided situation in which you gave all and your mate nothing. For instance, one man put up with criticism, a do-nothing wife who boasted, "I can spend more than you make," and children trained to hate "your horrible father." But when his wife served him congealed pork chops for five nights in a row, he decided he had had it.

The relationship may change, making a victim of one partner. Sometimes you've outgrown your mate or vice versa. Or the person who initially acted as leader becomes the follower. For example, when Norma A. met John B., he had a good job as a musicologist and she a minor position as a cosmetics saleswoman. Norma rose "through the ranks" to become a successful executive. John failed at job after job. Finally, he gave up music and became a photographer. She says, "He went into my field, working for my friends. I resented it. I got tired of being his sponsor and eventually walked out. I wanted a child. I couldn't have a child. He was my child."

These cases all involve trauma. But the individuals quoted lived through the divorce with a minimum of self-agony. Usually obvious victimization cases involve a series of steps:

1. We recognize the intolerable. This is a personal intolerability. Someone else might like the idea of a husband in the same field. Norma hated it.

2. We ask ourselves, Can I live with the intolerable aspects for the sake of what is good in the marriage or do I decide to leave?

3. Prior to making the final decision, we try once again to make the relationship work.

4. We understand that decision is not enough. We must take *action*—whether merely separating "to try it" or actual divorce.

THE SURPRISE DIVORCE

In this situation, one partner announces he or she wants the divorce, and it comes as a shock to the other. Perhaps you've emerged as the liberated woman and want out of the humdrum responsibilities of homemaking and child care. More often, however, one mate meets someone else and thinks, *"This is the right one."* Madeleine J., forty-one, left for another woman, says bitterly, "Twenty years and two children don't count. He has a new girl friend with a beach house." Madeleine is very vocal about her feelings concerning the divorce, but she is acting in a helpless fashion that is subtly destructive. She does everything her lawyer tells her to do, but she doesn't strive to find extra information that might help the lawyer pursue a more favorable settlement—like the name on the house deed, whether the contents of the safe deposit box are still there. She can't cope with any of the details of the separation agreement.

Madeleine has made herself passive. Although she is a successful career woman, she can't manage her emotional life. She can't take the extra step to work through what her problem is— it's not at Behavioral Psychotherapy Levels One or Two. She is very attractive to men and has social skills. She has no fear of being on her own. Her difficulty is so subtle that pinpointing anything specific is difficult. If Madeleine would use her preconscious to try to reach Level Three, she might realize that since childhood she has had a persistent need to control. (She used to beat her younger sister when the latter wouldn't comply with her wishes.) Afraid this repressed rage will get out of control, she becomes passive. She can't bring herself to do anything to protect herself in the divorce agreement. If she worked through this conflict from the past that dogs her, not only would she achieve a better settlement, but, because she would act like her true self, she might find a mate who would not walk out on her.

THE NEVER-ENDING DIVORCE

Some people can't give up. Take Gail S. Now thirty-one, she was married at twenty-three, has been divorced three years, and admits, "It wasn't until last summer that I could even say the word *divorce*. . . . I don't know why he left me. It wasn't for another woman, though he has one now. I still love him. More than the pain of rejection, I also think about *what if*—what if I had started a family instead of concentrating on my work? I was so committed to my job. It's easier if you're like some of my friends, who go into a marriage half-heartedly. For me, it's like a continuing low-grade infection. I can't get over it." Just last week Gail sent her ex-spouse a note, suggesting they get together.

Gail keeps working to see herself as a victim and acts in many ways to develop, even glorify, that "self-perception." This is a camouflage. The divorce was a blow to her "neurotic pride" (a Karen Horney term). Again, at Behavioral Psychotherapy Level Three, Gail has an unconscious image of herself as the irresistible woman no man can fail to love. To face the fact that she has been rejected would not only challenge her fantasy but bring on tremendous self-hate. To protect herself, she settles for a made-up, lesser tragedy, and begins to live by it. Gail writes notes to the ex-husband trying for a meeting, ruminates over the past. Because she will not accept her rejection and glorifies her victimization, she protects herself from the realization that she failed to hold her spouse.

Know What You're Doing in the Divorce Process

Don't victimize yourself through ignorance. Three major areas of self-victimization in divorce are money, the children, and the negotiation of the agreement.

THE DIVORCE POOR

With very few exceptions, your standard of living will go down. The divorce poor are a new social class. While women are no longer forever on the dole with alimony (except in cases of long-term marriages and ex-wives with no capacity for employment) and most receive "spousal support" for a short retraining or training period, the fact is, *two households cannot exist as cheaply as one*. In her book, *The Divorce Revolution*, author Lenore Weitzman, a professor of sociology at Stanford University, shows that on the average during the first year after divorce, women living with their minor children experienced a decline of seventy-three percent in their standard of living.

Men also suffer financial impoverishment. One man gave so much to his ex and two children that he had to borrow money from his father. Others don't have a father from whom to borrow. They live on spaghetti and dinner invitations from well-heeled, ambitious hostesses who need an extra man to fill out a guest list. Until their children grow up, many can look forward only to impoverishment, with possible garnishment of wages. Some divorced men make huge sums of money but find that it goes into the bank accounts and comfortable keeping of their former family, not their new one.

THE CASE OF THE MONIED DOCTOR WITH NO MONEY

Bill S., an internist, had a miserable eight-year marriage to a pretty nag. The results were two children and a divorce. To save money on legal fees, their family lawyer worked out the arrangements for both. Despite the new legal codes providing alternatives to perpetual alimony, Bill obligated himself to alimony (including child support) until his former wife either dies or remarries. When his children graduate from college, the amount will be reduced. Bill bears all costs for medical bills, private schools, special lessons, camps and the ex's very costly therapy. She won't work. Bill has found a new life with Polly, a social worker, who must work despite having suffered a severe heart attack at thirty-three. She says, "I support him so he can support her. We're the new divorce poor." Despite Bill's high income, they can't afford to go out to dinner at even a halfway decent restaurant.

Before you divorce, consider the economic realities.

Divorce also creates economic victims besides the couple involved. Comments Suzanne Prescod, editor of *Behavior Today* and *Sexuality Today,* newsletters for professionals, "Lots of businesses have been destroyed because of divorce. People don't believe in the stability of the company."

In one case, a son-in-law devoted twenty years to the family firm. With divorce he got fired. He's out in the cold. All the stock is in his children's names.

In another instance, there were three daughters and all three husbands worked in the family knitwear business. Dad died and the mother inherited. When daughter number two divorced, the mother fired the ex-spouse. Fortunately he had a contract, so he got severance pay. The former son-in-law retaliated by going into a similar business and is slowly succeeding.

When married bosses split, employees feel threatened about the future of the company. Recalls one founder, "We went around and told every one of our thirty employees. It was like Mummy and Daddy telling the kids, 'Look, we're breaking up, but we still love you!'"

THE CHILDREN

"The worst victims are kids," notes Julia Perles, senior partner in the law firm of Phillips, Nizer, Benjamin, Krim & Ballon, in New York. "It's a real Oedipal thing with a teenage boy. He worries about being responsible for his mother. Another great impact is on grown children in their late twenties or early thirties with families of their own. Suddenly, they must be emotionally—if not financially—responsible for one or two parents. This takes time away from their own families."

According to a report in the March 1986 Harvard Medical School *Mental Health Newsletter,* in a study of 699 elementary school children from thirty-eight states, researchers John Guidubaldi and Joseph D. Perry found persisting effects of divorce on children (less independent, more withdrawn, less hardworking, more ill-behaved) long after the end of the marriage. Boys living with a divorced mother were unhappier than girls, had more problems with their behavior and schoolwork, and got along less well with their parents.

Often parents themselves inflict the problems on the children. They compete for attention. They taunt: "With all the money I give her, your mother dresses you in rags." They question: "Does your father introduce you to his girl friends? . . . Are they at the house when you wake up Sunday morning?" The result: You create psychological difficulties, doubts and confusions, and conflicting loyalty and disloyalty for the children you supposedly love so much. And by doing this, you create further psychological troubles for yourself. Through persistence in seeing the situation as unfair, you turn trauma into continuing victimization.

The children, too, have their own feelings: "It wasn't our fault that you couldn't get along." They, too, see themselves as victims. Sometimes the children retaliate with direct action. In one case, a divorcing couple couldn't decide what school their son should attend. The wife felt *"public* school is good enough." The husband opted for his private school alma mater. The divorce could not be settled until the judge called in the fourteen-year-old, gave him the name of three schools, and ordered him to pick. The son chose the one to which his father *had not* gone.

THE NEGOTIATION OF THE AGREEMENT

The negotiation of the separation agreement will have a tremendous impact on your life. It may be immediate; you have to change your life-style. And ten years down the line you receive a tremendous promotion and find that because you signed an escalation clause, half of the salary increase must go to your previous mate, whom you haven't seen in those ten years. Or maybe the agreement has made you a victim all along and you don't realize it until you remarry.

You must be reality-oriented. Concessions and compromises will have to be made. You are better off telling each other, "You give in there and I'll give in here." One woman wouldn't let her soon-to-be ex-spouse be fired from the family business—she wanted him to thrive financially and meet the child support payments. *Don't make victory your basic aim* in divorce negotiations. By gaining for yourself everything your mate wants, you may make it impossible for your mate to keep the agreement, and then you may lose down the line.

A settlement is a business agreement. For self-protection we must not let feelings dominate.

■ Don't perceive any compromise as a personal defeat that triggers additional victim feelings.

■ Don't react, "It's all your fault, so you aren't entitled to very much." There are always two points of view.

■ Don't bring to the negotiation the very nastiness, greed, and pettiness that may have provoked the divorce and forced your mate to search for someone with whom he or she could find happiness.

THE LAWYER IN YOUR LIFE

■ *Find a good lawyer.* You have less chance of being victimized now and in years to come if you turn to a specialist in matrimonial law, not some friend of a friend whose expertise pertains to corporate matters. Don't get a mama's boy lawyer with a need to placate women. One divorcing man did just that. His lawyer kept urging, "Give her more." The client did. The result: He was left with nothing but an ex-wife who got "more" and keeps bringing suits for "more."

You also want to avoid a lawyer who is getting a divorce at the same time as you. The lawyer may be so caught up in his or her own problems that he or she cannot handle yours.

How do you find the right lawyer? Word of mouth helps. Maybe you know someone who got divorced and can ask that person, "Whom did you use?" Or someone says, "Go to my ex's lawyer. Mine screwed me." If you lack legal contacts, call bar associations. They have lists of lawyers who specialize in divorce matters. Or call the president of the local chapter of the American Academy of Matrimonial Lawyers. Or have a consultation with the best, most famous, or most expensive matrimonial lawyer you know and get a referral.

■ *Consider your relationship with the lawyer.* Many divorce innocents view lawyers as parental figures—the lawyer will know exactly what to do, will take care, will provide. Underneath you feel your lawyer resembles your parents, he or she is an all-knowing, all-powerful figure who will get you just what you want. This distorted thinking can lead to victimization.

After the divorce you feel anger and disappointment for what you did not get. You react, "If only my lawyer had properly used his/her power, it would have worked out right for me."

Watch out for two particularly dangerous divorce traps.

The first is refusing to listen to the lawyer expert. This person tries to guide you away from future pitfalls, but your guilt makes you give too much. Or to show your independence, you pointlessly rebel against the lawyer as your imagined parent.

The second trap is to passively go along with whatever the lawyer advises. Guard against such excessive passivity. *You must do what's right for you.* You may utilize what Norman Sheresky calls the "bronze baby shoe syndrome" and emphasize possessions. The picture your aunt gave you at your wedding may matter more than money. Or you may insist on following your own priorities. In one case, a lawyer argued that Ellen J. should sell her house, a wedding present from her parents, and keep the profits to use as income. Ellen refused. She explained to the lawyer that although keeping the house would put her in a financial bind, the house was home for her two children and she wanted to keep it. Despite the financial pressure, she had to do this. But be sure the priorities you decide on are realistic— that you're not letting sentiment put you into a position of continued self-victimization.

Keep in mind that *lawyers don't always know what's best for you personally.* That's why you must do homework to avoid self-victimization. Maybe divorce mediation would be a solution— this technique works well when couples are not adversarial. Write the American Arbitration Association (140 West 51st Street, New York, NY 10020) for names of divorce mediation specialists in your area. For self-protection, it's helpful to know your state laws (are you in an equitable distribution or a community property state?) and to be familiar with settlements in that state in cases similar to yours. Dredge your memory for applicable facts about your own life. Did you put your husband through medical school years ago? Does your wife have a collection of older bearer bonds, bought by you, in her safe deposit box? What is it you really want—therapy, children's camps, a nose job, all medical and dental expenses, or half the value of the necklace you gave your spouse and a geographical restriction clause?

Try for a fair settlement. Says lawyer Julia Perles, "You do not leave the man stripped of so much money that he cannot live. You do not leave the woman with so little that she will continue to harass you for years and years. You do try to do your best for the children and help them maintain their standard of living."

Doing your homework will increase your sense of personal effectiveness. You will perform better, both with your lawyer and in the negotiations with your mate. Get that gut feeling "I know what I'm doing. My lawyer is not my father or mother. My lawyer is my adviser and I can take the advice given or leave it." Know-how spurs confidence.

■ *Be careful the lawyer does not victimize you.* The lawyer is always working for him- or herself. Except in an uncontested divorce between a childless young couple, legal fees can be staggering. Because of the complications of distribution of assets under principles of equitable distribution, costs have escalated. Sometime a lawyer must hire appraisers to evaluate everything from a business to a collection of antiques. Sometimes a lawyer can victimize a client with the so-called bonus clause, which enables an attorney to demand extra money if he or she achieves a particularly good settlement. Meanwhile, the lawyer gives no refund if he or she does not make a good deal for you.

Three Predivorce Musts for Confident Action

1. *Recognize that unconscious needs can lead to victimization.*

During divorce proceedings, money can assume an unconscious value. I see this over and over in my clinical practice. By giving too much money, a man may tell himself, "I'm still the husband." He may use excessive generosity to counter the unconscious self-image that by getting a divorce he's a bastard. By giving too much, he reassures himself he's really nice, not a bad guy. He may also satisfy a masochistic need for self-punishment and thereby relieve his feeling of "being evil" about the marital breakup. The converse may also be true. His conscious or unconscious needs to dominate or destroy may make him fight to give too little.

The wife may seek extra money to prove to herself that she's neither helpless nor powerless in the situation. She may want to be taken care of in the infantile sense. She may also covet lots of cash out of rage, anger, or a need to strike back. Conversely, she may not realize her rights and refuse to take what is legitimately due her. She may have a fantasy of how easy it will be in the singles world. She may also desire to make her mate feel guilty, punish herself because she feels guilty and undeserving, or prove to herself, "I don't need him. I can do it on my own!"

2. *Realize that when a marriage breaks up, love no longer motivates and controls the relationship.*

For your own good, you must consider divorce as a kind of joint financial venture from which each partner should be able to emerge with a sharing of the assets. At a time when you feel emotionally down, you must somehow develop the strength to negotiate the separation agreement. This will affect you the rest of your life and be more important in concete terms than any marriage certificate.

3. *As in a business deal, formulate clear goals.*

You should set goals at three levels:

Maximum—what you don't expect but would like to get if it were possible

Optimal—what you really can expect and what would be most equitable to both you and your partner

Minimal—the rock bottom level, below which you will not go

With these goals in mind, you can negotiate better.

Divorce hurts. It does not have to create permanent harm. You do not have to live in perpetual bitterness. You possess the power to convert unfortunate reality into emotional growth. Says the divorced forty-year-old mother of two, "Instead of flowing with whatever happened, *I have taken control of my life.* Divorce gave me freedom, released me from a life-style I hated, forced me back to work. I made new friends, tapped into my skills. It hurt but was a necessity."

One man learned from his first unhappy marriage what he did not want in a wife. Another learned he didn't want any kind of wife. And in the knowing, both grew up.

14□Suddenly Single

For some people divorce means an immediate re-marriage. For others, it becomes a time of change. Because you're not part of a couple any more, people will act differently toward you. You may ask yourself, "Why have they dropped me?" As a sudden single, you will feel differently about yourself. Your self-concept may grow stronger ("I had the guts to get rid of him/her") or weaker ("He/she did not want me").

We victimize ourselves in this new situation if we:

■ Concentrate only on how our ex-mate made us suffer and make no effort to create a new and victimless life for ourselves

■ Give up when the imagined Golden Goddess or White Knight doesn't materialize immediately out of the blue

■ Fear newness, so stay home and feel bad rather than say yes to new—and perhaps unfamiliar—chances to meet new people

■ Feel overwhelmed by new problems such as the stayover question or getting babysitters so we can go out . . . if we permit these problems to dominate our lives and don't solve them, don't *do* anything

■ Act out of a sense of desperation, so that the quick fix of another mate seems the only solution to our own insecurity

■ Refuse to deal with the emotional and social problems that have existed in us all along. (You married young so that they didn't show up before. Now that you're at liberty, as actors say, they do show—and hurt.)

Because so many people divorce today, those who find themselves at liberty represent an assortment of problems, needs, ages, hopes for the future. We must guard against victimization by dealing with these problems and by dealing with our own need to be a victim.

At Liberty: Four Different Reactions

The examples that follow show four typical reactions to finding oneself suddenly single.

Example One: "I feel like a frightened kid," says Laurie M., thirty-four, a legal secretary from Massachusetts, who got a divorce because "I felt I was growing more than he was, and that made me stop loving him." Financially, Laurie got what she needed (the house, child support) but confesses a problem with loneliness. "I married at nineteen. I'd never been alone. Sometimes I love it. Most of the time I hate it. My ex is supposed to have the children alternate weekends, but he told me, 'I won't take them so you can have a good time.' He also has a girl friend whom the kids like, and I resent that. I won't go to bars. The only men I meet are those who are thinking of divorce but not separated yet. They make me feel I'm going through their divorce with them. Where is the available grown-up man for me?"

Analysis: Because she has been married since her teen years, Laurie has no idea of how to start up a social network as a single. She also wants immediate results, gives up quickly, and feels herself a victim. Rather than rebuilding her life, Laurie thinks in terms of meeting men and uses her "horrible ex" to excuse her lack of action.

Example Two: Matt H., thirty-three, an architect, married right out of undergraduate school "because it seemed the thing to do." He stayed married eleven years, had no children. He and his wife grew in different ways—farther and farther apart. They also led a split existence between their country house and city apartment. One day Matt left permanently for the city. Matt claims, "I don't know how to date. Most of the time I visit old friends for dinner. Everywhere else I'm hesitant about getting involved in conversation. If I never meet someone, how can I ever marry?"

Analysis: Matt seems a counterpart of Laurie. Both married young. But Matt does have a sense of social skills. In reality, his problem is passivity. He met his wife at school and passively maintains only old friendships. Unless he changes his passive attitude and enlarges his circle, he won't develop his social skills. He's kidding himself.

Example Three: Amy L., forty, a very successful publicist, claims, "I hate myself because I chose wrong. My parents always pressured, 'Why don't you have a husband?' Marrying the man I did was a defense mechanism to get away from them. I won't remarry. Now I have a full rich life—single. It's not rebellion—I want men in my life, but only as escorts. If they want marriage, they don't want me."

Analysis: Amy was a victim of her parents and societal pressure to marry. She ended those pressures with divorce. Now she knows she wants to stay single and is no longer a victim.

Example Four: Harold T., a psychologist, says, "I've become the eligible bachelor. Even though I work until nine P.M., hostesses demand, 'Come. I'll hold a plate in the oven for you.' They introduce me to sweet young things or neurotic, bitter divorcees. I would never run an ad. How does someone like me meet a compatible woman? My friends introduce me to other doctors and social workers. I want a different world, a different life."

Analysis: Harold's problems lie in his unconscious at Level Three. In reality he's looking for a savior—a mother who will "make everything better" by providing the life he wants. But it's sinful to meet mother, so he paralyzes himself and meets the same kind of woman over and over. In that way, he handles the conflict. His fantasy dominates. Somehow he will meet just the right woman. But unless he understands his real problem, he won't. Other hard-working psychologists have managed to make time for a limited social life and to rewed.

As a newly single person with a changed life, you need a new social network. Unlike a never-married person, you have responsibilities and ghosts from your past that remain in your present. What can you do to create a more satisfying social life so that you are not the victim of fantasy, loneliness, moving too quickly or slowly, self-doubts, lack of courage, despair, or concentration on the opposite sex rather than on the quality of your life?

A Social Program for the Suddenly Single

■ *Counter your passivity.*
Two kinds of passivity exist. You may feel unable to take the initiative in the face of *external* elements. Because you don't like not knowing people or the right people for you or where to go as a sudden single, you just drift along, hoping, waiting. For new singles, attorney Norman Sheresky supplies three terse words of advice: "Join. Join. Join."

Do things that suit you as you are now—not as a just married college graduate. Make new same-sex friends. Use your job as a source for meeting new people. At twenty-four you might not have been professionally advanced enough to do that. You're more successful now. A divorced reporter interviewed the divorced head of the local school board and began seeing him socially. A divorced man stopped mailing checks to philanthropic organizations. Now he presents his checks at their semiannual banquets, where he always meets new people.

You can entertain, even if with fear. If you spent years entertaining as a married person, this is probably one area where you feel strong. If you're a male and your wife carried the load, you can learn to be a host. Remember, as with all singles, you never know. One divorced, depressed mother met her second husband at a P.T.A. meeting. She had gone to it with no expectation of meeting anyone other than her son's English teacher.

Besides passivity in the face of external elements, you may experience passivity against *internals*, your feelings, letting them control you. Sadness is natural, but you must move on with your life or you will ruin it.

One divorced man took a room at an apartment hotel, looked at the cramped quarters, and cried to himself, "Look what it has come to—life has failed me." He held on to his tearful mood for three days. Then he rented a better apartment with a kitchen, went shopping, and outfitted the one-bedroom pad completely with the stipulation that everything be delivered within two days. That Saturday he hosted a dinner party for some fifteen friends he had always liked and whom his ex-wife had not liked. He stopped crying. He says, "I had to go on living." He did not let his victim feelings hold him in an emotional clamp.

■ *Solve your new life problems.* Think them through and figure out solutions. If you're a divorced woman with young children, you may have to "kid swap" to go out at all. You will have energy problems. Can you go out after working and fixing dinner and the next day's lunch for your school-age kids? What are the priorities? If you're a man, given the right to take the children out for dinner one weekday night and have them every weekend, can you afford to date? If you have a new romantic interest, will you introduce him or her to your children early on? For their psychological health, should they know about the romantic interests in your life?

Beware of this trap: If you use your problems as a reason for not doing something you would like to do, then you will feel you are the victim more than ever.

■ *Don't give out desperation vibes.* You don't have to find that Golden Goddess or White Knight right away. Maybe you'll never find that hoped-for special person. Your attitude should be, "I'll do things and enjoy myself whether I meet someone or not." In the ten years between her first and second marriages, Dr. Helen Singer Kaplan, the noted sex therapist, was one of the most popular women in New York. Other divorcees complained of "no men." Not Kaplan. She explains the difference this way: "Many eligible women in their thirties and forties are so eager to marry that they frighten men. I was a warm person but not out for marriage. I was safe."

With men, desperation often works differently. They are so eager that they view any woman they meet as a potential spouse. On the first date they evaluate what she'll be like after twenty years and either give up or commit themselves immediately. If the relationship doesn't work out, they feel victimized. They don't allow a period for relationship growth.

■ *As well as being open to new experiences, recognize that you are changing.* If you've grown through the divorce trauma, you are different from the person you were pre-divorce. For example, one divorced stockbroker whose wife had been extremely neurotic fell "in love" repeatedly after his divorce—and then out again. Three years later he fell in love for real. He enjoys dancing, poetry, and partying, whereas his new partner opts for science, staying at home and working on her Ph.D. He comments,, "I've calmed *her* down. She has taught *me* the thinking of the common man." He pauses to reflect: "My two wives are completely different. Wife number one was dependent. Wife number two is independent." The stockbroker said yes to a new wife-style and life-style.

Remarrying Right

For some, one matrimonial try proves enough. However, despite any victimization that may have occurred, the majority of divorced people want to try again. Before you say another "I do," you might want to ask yourself and answer some important questions.

In responding, remember that no human being is perfect. Always keep this warning in mind: *Don't idealize your future partner.* Beware of the glib self-defense that you're okay—your previous partner created all the damage that produced divorce. Now you've met a new marital possibility and decided that with this person everything will be perfect. You must remember that the new person is only human and not an abstract idea. If you lose sight of that fact, because of your idealization and the inevitable disappointment at discovering that he or she is only human, you will feel the victim again.

As a divorced man who has found happiness in a second marriage, I always ask my patients considering remarriage to ask themselves the following questions:

■   *From your previous marriage, what have you learned about yourself?* Were you too moody, too mean, too selfish, too work-oriented? What have you learned that you can do differently to maximize joy, pleasure, and fun time; to minimize tension; and to add new dimensions to a future relationship?

Make sure you ask yourself, "Am I using my future mate only as a way to prove my attractiveness to myself?"

■   *From what you know of your prospective partner's moods and behaviors, can you live with them?* Are you willing to take the risk?

Be aware that during courtship you may not note any cues; you may not see the flaws. In one case, following his wife's death, a man met a woman he thought to be "Ms. Right." During courtship she was warm, loving, compassionate. After remarriage he discovered that she had continual anger spells and week-long moods and found he could not live with her. In retrospect, he could remember no warning signals. He could have learned about her only by asking her ex-husband, who had fled the same temper tantrums.

Risk always exists. We must realize that while during courtship there may *seem* to be no cues that can affect a remarriage, there are always telltale personality manifestations—temper outbursts with salespersons, inconsiderate behavior with friends, a tendency always to blame others. Evaluate these. They may or may not apply to the future relationship. Make you own decision, but do not ignore any behavioral cues you observe.

■   *Are you willing to change homes?* Could you make the shift from urban to small-town living or vice versa?

■   *What baggage will each of you bring into the marriage from your previous union?* Unlike in the first marriage, "leftovers" can complicate the relationship, and you must consider them. They may be very simple—habits you've formed in the previous union, such as always going out for dinner or always staying home, that may influence your expectations in this new marriage. Other baggage from the past may be much more serious. Can you live with it?

Can you cope with *the practical baggage* of alimony, legal bills, or whatever joint ownership of property still exists? You must know exactly what financial commitments each of you will have upon remarriage. One man thought he had told his future wife of all his obligations to a greedy ex and two stepmother-taunting children. At tax time it turned out that he had "forgotten" to reveal that he also had to pay his ex's federal, state, and city taxes. His second wife, who had thought she could live with the financial commitments, picked the tax matter and blew it up out of all proportions. The tax promise was her excuse. In reality, she found the pressures remaining from her husband's previous marriage too much. She used the tax matter as an excuse to end the marriage.

Increasingly, the prenuptial agreement, until recently used mainly by elderly remarriers who wanted to leave estates to their respective children, serves as a way to gain and settle financial facts. Not everyone agrees that this is advantageous. Norman Sheresky vetoes the prenuptial agreement except in cases of enormous wealth ("It takes the romance out"), but like Julia Perles, many legal authorities favor it. Comments Perles, "It should cover everything. What happens in case of divorce or death? Who gets the assets acquired during remarriage? *If you are mature enough to negotiate before marriage, the marriage promises to be a good one.*"

She notes that discussion of a prenuptial agreement may prevent a bad remarriage and the victimization that will accompany it. In one instance, the new wife-to-be made so many demands that the night before a man's second marriage, he called off the wedding. In another case, a female vice-president at a major investment banking firm was about to marry the divorced thirty-three-year-old scion of a rich family. To protect its assets, the family wanted the pair to enact a prenuptial agreement. The son would not tell his financially savvy girl friend what assets he had. Furious, she thought, "If he holds back before marriage, what will he do after. I don't need his money!"—and she broke the engagement.

Remember, in many cases you can start with a prenuptial agreement, review it every few years, and either renegotiate or decide to tear it up.

You should also ask yourself how you feel about *the familial baggage*—children from a previous marriage. What kind of problems and pleasures will they bring? Can you live with the guilt of a man who feels he should have asked for custody and did not? Will you resent the money, work, or time spent on your spouse's children? Can you take it if later the situation changes and, instead of being a weekend stepparent, you become a full-time parent? Recognize that the children of your future mate may have been brought up with life-style ideas that differ from yours. Can you accept that without trying to take over and pressure them to conform to your preferences?

Are you able to accept *the emotional baggage?* This includes residues of previously made commitments and love. Even though your spouse has now married you, he or she may still care about the former spouse. Or it may be that you still love your former spouse but want to remarry. You think you can do that but have not yet cut the emotional attachment. If this is the case, will you be able to make a go of another marriage? Also, if you are "the other" man or woman and feel guilty about it, can you live with this sense of guilt?

■　*Can you really take on someone who is a bad marital risk* because of addictions, neuroses, professional incapability, or a pattern that augurs badly for you? Don't assume *you* can change a lifetime pattern where another could not. Few people can take on a mama's boy or daddy's girl or a partner who will surely be as unfaithful in this marriage as in the previous marriage. Are you really one of those few?

Or are *you* the bad remarital risk because you compulsively keep repeating the same mistake? Through marriage, you keep trying to solve a problem with its roots in some other area, usually a problem you haven't consciously defined. However, it is possible that you may still have the same problem in a second marriage, but with a different mate be able to work out a different solution. For example, Jim L. always had a problem with his domineering mother, who nagged him. For his first wife, he picked a similar shrew. Unable to take her put-downs, he walked out. For his second wife, he picked a woman who never nags. She just takes over. He's happy.

■　*What is your goal in this marriage?* You may feel, "This is the person with whom I want to spend the rest of my life. I'm really in love." Or you may feel, "I want to move away from the singles scene, the loneliness." The latter does not necessarily represent a bad goal, but you must recognize it for what it is. The recognition will help you avoid disappointment.

■ *Are your goals obtainable?* Two victim traps exist in this connection:

1. You're too optimistic.

2. You're too pessimistic.

The danger in being too optimistic is that the person may be unavailable to you—or to anyone else. Or you may pick the wrong person on the rebound. Because your sense of failure is so strong, you think, "At least this person wants me." But often that isn't true.

Disregard the availability factor and you can waste years. A woman had a two-year liaison with a divorced man, expecting marriage. Eventually he sent her a "Dear Joanne" letter, explaining his forthcoming marriage to the daughter of a publishing tycoon. As in his two previous marriages, he craved status and a bank account, not a single, verging-on-middle-age TV director trying to make the good life in the big city. Though Joanne really loved him, in her naïveté she chose a man who would never marry her. (Some divorced people, incidentally, thrive on being alone for the rest of their lives.)

You also invite trouble if you're too pessimistic. When a person has a history of marital failure, it seems logical to anticipate that the next marriage may also end in divorce. This isn't always true. A divorced man comments bluntly, "You expect to have more than two jobs in your life. Why not marriages?" Some find that finally the need-fit factor works—because they have learned, mellowed, changed. You *can* achieve your goal of "marrying the person with whom I want to spend the rest of my life" the second time around.

For example, a man was rejected by his first wife, an actress. For a long time he hoped for a change in the relationship. Finally he got divorced. He was miserable, dated a succession of women, eventually fell in love again, and remarried. At the time a friend exclaimed, "It's about time!" The man: Ronald Reagan—who carried the torch for his ex, Jane Wyman—has now had an extraordinarily happy, loving marriage to Nancy Davis for over a quarter of a century.

15□A Guide for Remarried Lovers

Every evening at about 6 P.M., Carol M. returns to her Ohio ranch house from her nearby job as a lab technician at a chemical plant—and waits. But not for long. Within fifteen minutes the din begins. Her husband's former wife has arrived to perform her daily annoyance stint. For a half hour the ex honks her car's horn in front of Carol's home, where the ex had lived with the man who is now Carol's husband.

Carol did not take Len away from Mona. A divorcee with no children, Carol met Len two years after both had divorced. They married, and childless Carol assumed the job of instant part-time stepmom. Len's two children came for dinner on Wednesday nights and stayed every weekend from Friday afternoon until late Sunday afternoon. It took two years for the stepchildren (then seven and nine) to accept Carol. Even now there are "You're not my mother" outbursts. The work of hosting the children in addition to holding a full-time job was hard. Carol desperately wanted their own child. Len refused, remarking tersely, "Two are enough."

Whereas some women would not have endured or succeeded in this situation, Carol has. She has a real "love remarriage." She shrugs off the incessant honking, willingly cooks, and accepts the limits of her stepparent role with the children. Using her first failure as a growth experience, she distinguishes between what is important and what is trivial in this marriage so she can make it work. She makes many compromises, but she also stands up for herself. Just as she realizes the needs of her spouse, she recognizes her own. Whatever their money problems, she insists upon going out for dinner every Sunday night and then being alone together for privacy at home.

Solving the complexities of remarriage depends on everyone's goodwill. This goodwill is rarely present. Instead, we have a remarital melodrama in which victims and villains costar. The plot emphasizes victimization by exes who live on the periphery of the new marriages, as a result of the obligations of money, and/or through the contest for children's affection between the new mates. In addition, maybe one spouse imposes the role of "caretaker" rather than lover on the other, or there's an unnecessary self-victimization because one partner cannot relinquish the past psychologically ("I've failed once; I'll do it again") to deal with the new relationship.

Again, the statistic: Eighty-five percent of those who have been divorced once remarry. Sixty percent of these marriages end in divorce again, but forty percent, *a significant minority,* succeed.

Make yourself part of the forty percent whose repeat marriages work. Don't let the negative factors take over. Concentrate on the good in the person you love, who probably is more capable of intimacy, commitment, and giving and receiving love because of a previous divorce trauma. In doing this, expand your own love capacity. Remarriage may entail dealing with more complications, but the difficulties can bring you closer.

How to Work as a Team to Handle Outside Pressures

As in any marriage, your spousal relationship must come first, but often you must accomplish this while dealing with the remarital complications of emotional residues, hostile exes, children, and money problems.

■ *Provide emotional support. Say yes and mean it.* Do not give in to those "You're putting the kids ahead of me" accusations or to those "I'm a second wife/husband; that means I'm second best" thoughts. Oversensitivity may keep you from saying yes and meaning it, but when you promised "I do," you agreed to a remarriage contract with implicit provisos. One of those is "I will not make him/her unhappy with the remnants of his/her previous life."

For example, you and your husband have concert tickets. Then his son from his previous marriage says, "Dad, that night is P.T.A. night at school. Please come." Or someone from his previous family with whom he's still friendly is getting married and wants you and your husband to attend. You don't want to go, but your husband wants you at his side. For the sake of the relationship, say yes.

Advises Suzanne Prescod, editor of the professional newsletters *Behavior Today* and *Sexuality Today,* "It helps if you think of it as a contract in a business deal. In a business situation, you accommodate. Do it here."

Remember, it is possible for you to reduce tensions by saying yes to only part of a situation. For example, one newly married second wife wanted to form a strong relationship with her husband's eight-year-old daughter Grace. Her husband brought Grace home for lunch on Saturdays and all three would go out to eat. Since the second wife worked at home, she found this pattern disruptive, and she also felt her spouse should spend "more alone time with Grace." Her solution: "Take Grace out for lunch. Bring her home for dinner."

■ *Support your spouse but don't take over your spouse's problem.* Let your spouse handle it in his or her own style. One second wife who had been a young divorcee reveals, "Kim's kids have always been cool to me. They thought he married down. My house was a ranch, not a mansion like theirs. If they had let me, I would have supported the kids emotionally, but they didn't. They keep bringing up actions—now they say he didn't send them to private schools and should have—but I figure it is his problem and let him handle it. My aim: to show support and love."

In this context, it is essential that you allow one another elbow room for individual problem-solving.

THE CASE OF THE HARASSING EX-HUSBAND

At twenty-one, Christine L., a Southern charmer and merchandising trainee, met and married Doug J., a twenty-nine-year-old lawyer. For a while life worked well, and they had a son Craig, now thirteen. Chris did not let herself realize Doug was a roaring alcoholic. Finally she could ignore it no longer. She comments, "I'm not a savior type. I asked him to leave."

They divorced. They had only the equity of their Los Angeles house and a condo in southern California where Doug's parents lived. Chris persuaded Doug to sell the house and put her half of the money in a trust for Craig and also to turn over half of the condo ownership to Craig. She took nothing for herself.

Doug remarried quickly and never paid a penny in promised child support. Chris also remarried. Her new husband was a divorced architect. Recently, years after the divorce, Doug filed a lawsuit accusing Chris of "overreaching" to secure the house money for Craig. He also brought an action for examination of records of the trust (hard-working Chris had used none of it, spending her own earnings for Craig's schools, camps, clothes). It turned out Doug had not deeded the condo half to Craig, as had been agreed.

To cope with the problem, Chris and her husband have combined forces. The second husband provides the love and understanding Chris needs to fight her battle and also pays the extensive legal expenses. To do this, they've pared down all family living costs. Chris emphasizes, "Our expenses are horrible, but I've got a wonderful child, a happy second marriage. I got rid of that drunk, and I'll get rid of his harassment. In all this horror my second husband has been so great with me. It goes far beyond paying the legal bills. He has given me the help I need most of all—emotional support."

■ *Give practical help on everything from money to emotionally necessary retaliation against a vindictive ex.*

MONEY

Prior financial commitments and obligations create stress, but they do exist as realities of remarriage. To feel victimized by them is like saying the world should be different. Second wives find it particularly hard to realize this. Comments Julia Perles, "The second wife has to realize that a man who has been married before has an obligation to his ex-wife and children, or, if the ex has remarried, to the children. He's got a first mortgage and the bank has to get the interest and principal. If the second wife has any other attitude, she's sowing seeds for the disruption of the marriage. And the same holds true for the second husband and stepfather. Money is a terrible reality. Something has to give."

Recognize that you cannot do away with legal commitments like child support. Besides legal obligations, there are moral ones.

You can use certain protective strategies. For example, always keep count of expenditures for the children. If a husband's agreement calls for him to spend a certain amount on their clothes but Jimmy and Joan arrive in rags and he must buy them new outfits when he has already sent money for nice garb, he can send a bill to the ex or deduct the additional money spent from the next child support payment.

You may want to use the "accountability factor" and insist on records from the ex-wife so that the father knows where his money goes. One second wife claims, "We make her give us all the receipts. That way we know whether she has bought jeans for the kids or used the money to get her hair frosted."

The second wife can also take preventive actions in her own behalf to preclude being made a victim. She should keep all her money in her own name and not in a joint bank account. She can give all she wants to her husband's children, but any money given should be given via *her* personally signed checks just in case she ever needs evidence if a hostile ex-wife takes after her in court.

However, rather than making war, the answer may lie in peacemaking tactics. For example, if the children always arrive "in rags," keep extra outfits at your house. That avoids acrimony and contact with the ex, which will make the new spouse less of a victim and your remarriage better.

Always consider the possibility of changing the divorce agreement. Years later you may decide you made a bad deal. However, an agreement that you made in your eagerness to be free of a marriage gone sour usually stands unless there is something called "a change in circumstances." Such a change can produce anything from a trade-off to a reduction of payments. One woman's divorce agreement prevented her from moving to another city with the children. When she received the offer of a job in Paris, she effected an agreement change allowing the move in return for a reduction in child support. In another case a successful physician became ill and could not work. He petitioned the court and his "spousal support" was cut to nothing.

When the situation changes, you *can* change the separation agreement. Keep that phrase *change in circumstances* in your mind. Ask around. See what others have done about changing the agreement. But do nothing without consulting a matrimonial lawyer and good accountant. Through lack of knowledge you may victimize yourself with an even worse agreement and have to pay even more.

ASSERTIVE SELF-DEFENSE

For the sake of your remarriage, you may have to employ various assertive and acceptably aggressive measures.

Example One: One second wife, driven practically insane by phone calls in which her husband's ex cackled, "You mean bitch," had an unlisted number installed. Now the former wife must phone the former husband at his office. Wife number two doesn't listen to "cackling" any more.

Example Two: A remarried husband paid for an expensive private school for his son, but his ex-wife never sent on their son's report card. So he simply wrote the school, explained the situation, and asked for a duplicate card. He got more than that. The school now deals with the husband rather than the nasty ex on all matters pertaining to the boy, merely keeping the former wife informed.

What might otherwise be seen as dirty tricks, prompted by the need to limit the influence of pressures exerted by a vindictive ex, may force you to the kind of retaliation you don't like. One fortyish man recalls, "I kept to the terms of the agreement, but it didn't suit my ex. She constantly wanted more. When I lost my last job, I just put all the assets in my second wife's name. I went to court and got the child support reduced and my ex's therapy eliminated. I have nothing. My second wife even owns the car and the house. I don't like to behave this way, but my ex forced me into it."

Children often will use tactical aggression in a remarital situation. They act to remedy a circumstance that they find hurtful or unfair. Sometimes that creates pain or disruption within the "second family." However, at other times the action is aimed at a neglectful parent they feel has victimized them. A woman with a young son divorced and then remarried happily. The former husband hardly ever called; he saw his son, Mark, at most once a year. Then the remarried couple had a daughter, whom the older boy adored. He also developed a strong attachment to his stepfather. One day, when Mark was ten, the school called his mother to say Mark had switched his name to that of his stepfather on the school records. From then on he would use no other. The real father brought a lawsuit and the new family fought back. Mark won. In court he attacked his real father for his neglect and 'the judge sided with him. Mark was the victim who took assertive action and devictimized himself.

An Emotional Change Program to Make Remarriage Work

In your unconscious, certain needs left over from previous relationships linger on and interfere with the new partnership that's been established. These needs vary from person to person, but here are three to think about:

1. *Dependency.* You fear your spouse's ex-family will prevent him or her from giving you things you need or that you'll be abandoned again, helpless and alone, feeling a victim again.

2. *Narcissism.* As a second spouse, you find that any contact your spouse has with his or her ex-family lowers your self-esteem and intensifies your victim feelings. Or because of infantile self-love, you may simply have a need for exclusive possession. You don't realize the unconscious forces behind your attitude.

3. *Remnants of sibling rivalry.* Perhaps your spouse's contact with the ex-family stirs up feelings of jealousy and rage—the same feelings you had whenever your brother or sister won parental attention, leaving you ignored.

Various forms of these inner feelings may interfere with your remarriage. Do not let them.

■ *Do not distort.* One thirty-five-year-old divorcee married a divorced man whose two children lived with their mother. When new IRS laws were put into effect, he called the ex for her Social Security number, which he was now required to list on his income tax return. Overhearing, the second wife threw a tantrum: "You still love her. How dare you call her on our home phone!" She turned a simple matter into a fight by thinking she was a victim when she was not.

■ *Don't think all the complications come from you.* A man with three daughters became divorced. Thinking they'd have daddy all to themselves, the girls weren't at all upset. But then daddy remarried. The girls viewed this as rejection. Because they aren't the love of his life, as in their fantasies they thought they would be, now they won't speak to him. They don't realize they've made themselves victims. In this case, the second wife has not focused only on her own hurts. She's playing a waiting game, hoping the girls will grow up and see things more maturely.

■ *Don't blame your partner for obligations committed to in the separation agreement.* That's now a fact that must be lived with. Don't harp on the sacrifices or injustices imposed on you. Wait patiently for "circumstances" to change.

■ *Make the most of sex.* For example, Margy M. married for the first time at twenty-two. ("I made myself a victim. He asked me. I took him. I was passive. Even then I realized the lack of sexual passion.") Ten years and one child later, she and her husband divorced. Then Margy met and married lawyer Larry M. She says, "This time I didn't make the same mistake again. I went for passion and I have it."

In remarriage, sex can prove one of the strongest bonds. You know you're a sexual team and have probably proved it before you marry, but special vulnerabilities and victimizations do exist. In the first marriage, a couple has time to build a relationship. In the second marriage, it may be that there are not just children, but two sets of them . . . not just families, but ex-families and houses and apartments to make arrangements about. In the middle of this turmoil you must cement the bond between you, and the main place to do so is sex.

Certain factors may make teamwork in remarriage difficult. In the initial stages you may tend to glorify the sexual relationship. One second wife exclaimed, "When I married my second husband, I was like a nymphomaniac." That period lasted just five months. When realities intrude, you may feel victimized and think, "This isn't as great as I originally thought."

You may find you have shifted sexual goals. Now, instead of giving and receiving pleasure, you want to prove you're better than the ex. So, you try too hard, demand too much, become oversensitive to trivialities. If your mate isn't in the mood, you think, "He's getting ready to leave me just the way my ex did." An imagined danger signal flashes: "Maybe I'm not as good."

If you've been part of a losing marital team, use the knowledge you've gained from failure to make yourself part of a winning sexual team. Always remember that *you are first and foremost a couple*, not, for example, a couple with kids. Your marital relationship must come first, the children and step-children second. After all, eventually they will grow up and move away.

You must schedule alone time—in bed as well as socially. One remarried mother has a technique: "If one kid says she's going to a party and the second says he's meeting a friend, I encourage the third to meet a friend. That leaves the house open for me. I ask, 'How long are you going to be out?' The kids think we're concerned about them. We can't wait to get into that bed."

■ *Set ground rules for the children.* All parents should do this, but with remarrieds it matters more. One second wife acquired a teenaged family who ran in and out of the bedroom and had no set bedtimes of their own. She told them, "You don't have to go to sleep, but you must be in your rooms at a certain time, and if our door is closed, you must knock." She adds, "Until we made rules, there was no time for sex."

When you set limits, understand that you may have to deal with conflicting loyalties. When Polly married Dirk B., a divorced man with two children who slept over every weekend, the ten-year-old boy insisted on sleeping in Dirk's study, just off the master bedroom with a door in between. They refused— "No, you have your own bedroom." The younger girl felt defensive of her mother. One night Polly and Dirk walked into their bedroom, which had been that of Dirk and his ex, and found the daughter in the middle of the bed. She told her new stepmother, "It's not your bedroom." Polly answered firmly, "It is now."

■ *Check out your repetition compulsion pattern.* It may be a simple matter of asking yourself, "Am I maintaining a 'poor innocent me' attitude?" A woman felt blameless when her husband deserted her for his assistant. Her second husband asked, "What did you do wrong?" Upon reflection she realized that she had preferred her own friends to those of her husband and working at night to being at home with him. She vowed she would not repeat these mistakes in marriage number two. Now when she finds herself beginning to slip in the old pattern, she catches herself.

Sometimes we act the same way out of fear that "the bad thing will happen again."

THE CASE OF THE REMARRIED WOMAN WHO COULDN'T FORGET

Marcia Z., a social worker, and Kent D., a hospital director, had each had bad marriages that failed for the same reason: an unfaithful spouse. In Marcia's case, her ex-husband had had a one-night stand with a buyer on a business trip. She walked out on the marriage. Now in their early forties and in their eighth year of marriage, with all children from previous marriages away at school, Marcia and Kent felt more and more in love. Then Kent drank too much at an office Christmas party and in his alcoholic stupor took a pretty secretary home to her fold-out bed for a quick sexual encounter. When he finally arrived home, Marcia queried, "Where have you been?" He confessed. All hell broke loose.

In a minute, Marcia's eight years of remarital security were undermined. Her only thought: "It's starting again. If he really loved me, he would not have done this."

Kent did love her. He felt terrible about his boozy aberration, wanted to keep the marriage going, and tried in every way to do so. But at first Marcia turned terribly critical. She spoke of leaving him, made him stop his weekly poker game, and declared a ban on sex. Then she started thinking about her first marriage. She had always had some regrets about her immediate dumping of her first husband. Slowly Marcia changed her attitude. She didn't think what Ken had done was right, but she wanted this marriage to succeed. So she rescinded all the bans. Her confidence came back. Occasionally Marcia thinks of the Christmas party scene and wonders, "Will it happen again?" but she forces herself to push down the thought. Through the hurt, Marcia and Kent have learned how important they are to each other.

In first marriages, communication difficulties often form the core of marital troubles. If you let it, the inability to talk to one another openly can cause stresses in the remarriage. A man acknowledges that bad communication in his first marriage "was my fault. Now when I find myself retreating, I force myself to say what's on my mind."

Does lack of communication create emotional barriers between you and your mate?

REMARITAL COMMUNICATION EXERCISE

Goal: To compare the way you exchanged good, bad, and fighting feelings in the past and how you do so now

Step One: Make two columns in your Behavioral Psychotherapy workbook. One should be headed *Former Marriage,* the other *Remar-*

riage. Grade yourself on the following statements concerning communication, using the score:

> 0 — terrible   2 — fair
>
> 1 — poor   3 — good

1. Saying positive and/or affectionate things
   - I can do so to my partner.
   - When I do so, my partner seems to get the message.
   - I feel pleased when my partner says good things to me.
2. Saying negative things or disagreeing
   - I can and do do this with my partner.
   - My partner seems to understand what I am saying.
   - When this is done to me, I usually understand what my partner is saying.
3. Fighting with each other
   - I am/am not afraid to fight with my partner.
   - Who "wins" the fight is very important to me.
   - Most of the time fighting seems to clear the air and bring us closer.
   - We fight too much.
   - Too much of our fighting concerns ex-families.

Step Two: Look at your answers to see if you repeat the same "terrible" or "poor" communication of your previous marriage. If you do, realize that your current marriage may end in the same unfortunate way. And if it does, you can't put the blame on your present partner—*you* have now gone wrong in two marriages. Figure out what you do to set up bad communication.

- *Try your own Behavioral Psychotherapy for remarital change.*

First, agree upon a *specific* behavior you want to change. Don't pick general categories like "I want a pleasanter home atmosphere." Select something that affects the remarriage. It can be anything from "I'd like us to spend some alone time over the weekend instead of letting his kids intrude so much" or "I want her to be as nice to my children when they visit me as she is to hers, who are on the spot every minute" or "I want him/her to stop talking about his/her ex so much."

Second, agree on what either of you can deliberately do to effect actual change in behavior and emotional reaction.

Third, evaluate whether change in the problem pattern has taken place. For example, *count* how many times your mate mentions his or her ex in a day. Have your spouse do the same for you. Remember, if *you* feel your partner spends too much time with his or her ex-family, *you* must decide whether the "too much time" behavior has decreased. If *your partner* feels you should be nicer to his or her visiting children, then *your partner* must rate your behavior.

If this behavior change (Level One—Actions) does not show signs of working quickly, perhaps you've picked something too difficult. Perhaps you had a mistaken idea of what you could do; perhaps your partner is too impatient. Try to change another behavior.

Sometimes the remarital difficulty is so subtle that to find your trouble you must reach deep into your unconscious.

THE CASE OF THE WOMAN WHO PICKED THE WRONG MAN TWICE

When Mary K. wed John M., their happiness did not endure long beyond the "I do" stage. John had a lifelong pattern of regarding himself as a victim when he wasn't. His response to this misconception was to engage in continual fighting with his wife. He picked on Mary a lot. They split. Next Mary married Tom T., who seemed John's opposite. They never fought. Tom constantly placated Mary, but she lacked any feeling of real contact or communication with him. Another split.

At first Mary felt blameless. But then in Behavioral Psychotherapy with me, she came to realize that her two ex-husbands weren't that different. Each had a need to see himself as a victim, but they coped with that need differently. John hit out. Tom would say to himself, "It's my fault. I'm doing something wrong and deserve to be the victim." By blaming himself, he felt less helpless.

In thinking through why she chose such basically similar men, Mary realized that her mother had been a victimizer, constantly harassing her mate, children, and friends. Mary identified with her mother and possessed a strong unconscious urge to be a victimizer herself, but she found this wish intolerable and had to repress it from her consciousness. She resolved the conflict by unconsciously selecting men who made victims of themselves. Thus *she* had no need to victimize—they did it for her—and could say, "I'm blameless." She had had no idea of her identification with her mother.

Once Mary realized her mother identification and its effect upon her behavior, she no longer had to choose between being a victimizer and marrying a self-made victim. Therapy helped her see that when her husbands made victims of themselves, she gained a feeling of dominance and power without having to turn into the kind of victimizer her mother had been. By understanding her problem, Mary resolved it. She made a good third marriage. She has no need to hide her need to victimize from herself. Her new husband has no need to see himself as a victim. They live with love.

Stepparenting Without Too Much Hurt

As more and more men gain joint or full custody, an increasing number of women become catapulted into the role of instant stepmother. Their husbands expect them to be instant mothers, even if they've had no previous training, thus often setting them up for failure. Often the part-time stepmother feels betrayed, victimized, that it's all giving and no getting on her part. But much of the negative feelings stem from unrealistic expectations.

SOME STEPMOTHER BASICS

■ *If you're a weekend stepmother, act like one.* You are not the children's mother, although you may end up in the role of loving aunt, special friend, or trusted counselor. While you ache and feel the victim because the children "have no feeling for me," *they* may be afraid to show liking even if there's growing attachment. They have a mother. They live with her. She may not like it if they show they like you. Fail to realize this, and you make the children the victim of your fantasies.

■ *Know your cans and can'ts.* You can't impose *your* standards on the child. One woman forced herself to say nothing when a fourteen-year-old stepdaughter told her father, "Give me your credit card. I want to go to Bloomie's and get a dress like my friend Suzie's." The father gave his daughter the card. It was *his* problem. But you don't have to hand over *your* card.

You can't mold and control every weekend. Don't try. But you can certainly speak up about what's yours. One woman says, "Bert's kid used to come and jump on the furniture. When I protested, he said, 'My mother lets me.' I said, 'Then do it at your home.' He stopped."

You cannot properly question the child about what goes on in his mother's home: "Does your mother have a boy friend? Does he sleep over? . . . Does your mother call a doctor when you have a sore throat? What did your mother give you for your birthday?" Remember you are your husband's wife, not in competition with the ex-wife. You have him now. Talk over the discipline problems with him, and, if necessary, let him be the disciplinarian.

■ *Don't be a victimizing stepmother.* One woman owned ten new cashmere sweaters and wouldn't donate one as a present to her stepdaughter. Out of jealousy and resentment, she said, "That child gets too much as it is." You need to be constantly aware that your husband has an obligation to his former family.

■ *You must overcome your victim feelings about the financial burdens you carry.* You knew what you were taking on. One professional woman with two children of her own from a previous marriage complains about her stepson, "That child has more per capita income than any member of our family—at nine!" This stepmother might have tolerated the boy's income better if he hadn't had so much and her own children so little, but she would do better to stop dwelling on the injustice she perceives. Tell yourself, "It's like having the painters. It's finite. Someday the child support will end." One woman who felt a terrible victim of her husband's monetary obligations went out and studied and became a star real estate salesperson. She's so successful that her spouse's financial obligations no longer matter.

■ *In your stepmother role, it helps if you can gain a perception of the ex-wife as a person who has her own insecurities and resentments.* Because she feels threatened, she may teach her child to say and do nasty things. Or she may attempt to keep the children friendly, but they absorb her underlying attitude nevertheless. Or she may not be insecure at all and may try to promote a friendly relationship, but because of *their* problem, the children act up just the same. In many cases the ex tries for friendliness and neither the father nor new wife want it—the father may be an unloving man; the new wife, wrapped up in her own problems, may not want to be nice to her mate's children from a former union.

■ Even though you try hard, *you may have to accept the fact that nothing may work.* Some stepmothers give too much and sometimes receive only ingratitude and rejection. One second wife claims, "I took his unhappy teen daughter to lunch and asked, 'How can I help?' She answered, 'No way.'" You may have to concede that the children do not like you. It is quite possible they never will. You are the victim of a situation drama.

■ *Ask yourself if your stepchildren are really the problem.* If you have difficulty with your stepchildren, do they represent the real trouble source or are they your attempt to avoid seeing other marital problems? You may be feeling the victim of the children when, in reality, it's your husband who asks too much of you. As Carol did at the beginning of this chapter, compromise for the sake of the children, but stand up for what you want in the marriage.

SOME STEPFATHER BASICS

Historically, the stepmother, sometimes "wicked," sometimes "good," has received all the attention and the stepfather exists as the forgotten man. He lives in a bind. He's supposed to be boss and have a certain paternal responsibility for the children, but he is *not* the father. Often the real father contributes nothing, and the stepfather must assume financial support of his wife's children. This becomes an added burden, particularly when his own children live elsewhere with his ex-wife. As a result, the stepfather experiences the same emotions as does the stepmother. He feels unappreciated and unloved by the ungrateful children for whom he tries so hard.

A man who has never had children needs guidance when he becomes an instant father. A stepfather should set three goals: to be an authority figure, give love, communicate. One re-marital veteran advises all stepfathers, "The most important element is the mother, the natural parent, who must support the stepfather. He should learn *her* values with the children concerning discipline, politeness, spending of money."

■ *You can play the part of the father in day-to-day living, but you must understand that you are not the biological parent.* One remarried stepfather says, "I've replaced the father. On the other hand, I'm not my stepson's father. I love him, but he still loves his own father best—a man who sees him twice a year, sends no support and never writes." An experienced stepfather advises, "When father indifference occurs, keep your focus on making a go of your present marriage and other matters will fall into place."

■ *Recognize the conflicts between your two roles—father and stepfather.* For example, when your own children come to visit, encourage your stepchildren to make them feel wanted. On these visits—sometimes all too rare—ask your stepchildren to think up activities, food, and pleasures that your children will like. Because this is your stepchildren's home turf, they can contribute to making the visit a real family get-together, not a victim situation. It also helps if your wife understands that in all probability, you will always love *your* kids more.

■ *Etiquette matters will arise.* Be prepared for com-promise. For example, your wife's elder daughter—your step-daughter, whom you've raised since she was three—plans to marry and wants her real father to escort her down the aisle. You may feel hurt, but you must consider the girl's desire. Try to work out a special role for yourself—perhaps you can host a dinner for the groom's family. Do not reveal any resentment you may feel. No acrimony must turn your stepdaughter into your victim on that special day.

■ *Don't be the wicked stepfather.* At all costs, refrain

from taunts like "your bad real father" or from showing favoritism for the child you and your wife may have together. However, remember that what unknowing onlookers believe to be wrong can serve a good purpose in reality. One successful stepfather refused to pay for his stepson's college. However, the bright boy managed to win a full scholarship to a top school. Explains the stepfather, "Of course, I could have done it, but he had been so spoiled by his mother and sisters. I wanted him to do something on his own—and he did."

■ Again, remember that *in remarriage, the husband-wife role is primary.* If that changes—the marriage goes wrong—the good stepfather can turn bad.

THE CASE OF THE BOY WHO BECAME THE VICTIM

Brought up to be a princess, Massachusetts-born Alice A. grew up in a marriage-oriented household, so right after college graduation, she married Bob L. Ten months later they had a son, Tom, born with serious hearing problems. Shortly afterward Alice got divorced and subsequently married Alex L., a Washington, D.C., businessman who seemed to love Tom. Meanwhile Alice had started her climb up the management ladder. Except for an occasional check for Tom, Alice got nothing from Bob. However, trying hard to be a good stepfather, Alex helped Tom with homework, took him rowing, and attended P.T.A. meetings.

Then the real father wooed Tom, now a teen, to Texas, where his new young stepmother introduced him to marijuana. Tom became a high school dropout. He eventually called Alice, pleading, "Can I come home?" He went home, but, recalls Alice, "Alex took out his jealousy of my business success on Tom. He abused him verbally and didn't keep his promise to adopt him. Tom felt so hurt." Alice and her second husband divorced. One night, high on acid, Tom fell off the balcony of a movie theater and required months of hospitalization.

Now in her forties, with Tom a recluse in faraway Nepal, Alice says bitterly, "Everyone shortchanged Tom. I wasn't blameless. I was busy working. His real father was no good. His stepfather accepted, then rejected him. All of us made Tom a victim."

Alice may see her story that way, but she distorts the picture. She tends to blame, focusing too much on the real father. It seems unlikely that a visit to his father would have caused so major a change in Tom. It is far more likely that because Tom had so many unfortunate problems, Alice paid more attention to him than to her second husband. This not only spoiled her relationship with Alex but caused him to resent the boy. Following her pattern, Alice accepts some responsibility ("busy working") but also blames husband number two. She fails to see that if she had given priority to her relationship with Alex, they could have worked together as a team to help the boy.

The problems with stepchildren don't disappear overnight. You love some, hate some, win some.

For the sake of your spouse, try to keep things smooth. In one case, for example, the real father and stepfather play golf together occasionally—for the sake of the son who lives with the stepparent.

Stepfamilies have emerged only recently as a burgeoning and major institution, and stepparenting as yet lacks firm rules or norms. Special groups are forming. A leading group with regional branches is the Stepfamily Association of America (602 East Joppa Road, Baltimore, MD 21204). Whether you are a stepmother or stepfather, you serve as a pioneer in a relatively new form of family that is just now creating its own code for togetherness.

Happy Changes in Remarriage

Nothing stays the same. For example, not so long ago a divorce was something of a social stigma, a confession of failure. Now repeated remarriage seems to be a growing trend. Says Julia Perles, "When they marry the same wrong choice as before, it can be as traumatic as the first. With each failure, it's a horror. The participants bring it on themselves because they repeat their mistakes. However, when they choose someone different, even a fourth marriage can be a glory."

THE CASE OF THE
MULTIPLE MARRIER

Ted R. serves as consultant to many advertising firms. His *fourth* wife, Eileen, at thirty-seven, is twenty-five years younger than he. Married ten years and the parents of a young son, they glow with happiness. Ted explains his much married history with "I'm a minister's son—I always marry the girl." His capsule versions of his marriages:

Marriage One—"I was a virgin. She was a nice girl. We were just unsuited."

Marriage Two—"It was an affair that should have stayed an affair. Pretty soon I had two children and a host of reasons why I was unhappy."

Marriage Three—"I married an artist. That marriage was hell, lasted for two years, and I determined I must never marry again. Now I had double alimony with my second and third wives."

Then he met Eileen, who was the age of his daughter, at his office. They fell in love. Ted recalls, "Eileen ruled out age as a factor, and since she is Catholic and I am not, I found a Jesuit-trained father who would marry us. Money was the worst problem. I made a settlement with wife number three to be paid over a ten-year period."

Eileen's side of the story: "In my twenties, I wasn't meeting my match. I wanted a man brighter than I was. But I don't think for a minute I married my father. With Ted's children there's no resentment. My only role with them is as their father's wife. All during the courtship Ted would say, "If we were married and had a baby . . ." And then we did both. I resented that settlement with wife number three. I used to say, 'Wouldn't it be wonderful if she died!' Ted told me, 'You don't understand. I'd have to pay her estate.'"

She adds, "When I knew how I loved this man, I knew why I had been born. Whatever happens, all my life, I'll be able to say, I was married to Ted _____."

Ted sums it up, "I always had a roving eye, but now I feel fulfilled."

Exes and children change. Harassing exes do find other mates. Difficult situations can improve with time. One man had paid alimony for years to an ex who went from being homemaker to business tycoon. He wrote her, "I've supported you for years. Now that you don't need it, can you let me off the hook?" She did. In many cases, hostile stepchildren have turned into friends. A seventeen-year-old girl asked her stepmother, "Will you drive me to college?" That request made up to the stepmother for years of humiliation. One woman walked out on her husband for another man, taking their three little girls with her. Eventually the husband remarried and had a son. That son has four mothers—his own and the three young stepsisters.

Second marriages *are* harder. But instead of feeling victimized by obligations and vestiges of past failures, you must think of the rewards. One second wife tells herself, "I did it. I made it work." A remarried man happily claims, "I've become the person I want to be. I'm not what I was at twenty-four when I married my first wife. Then I didn't know what I wanted." As Samuel Johnson wrote, for a man and woman, a second marriage represents the triumph of hope over experience. When it works, it can be a triumph for both. *You have that second chance.* You don't have to play a role in a second marital melodrama. You can be victor instead of victim.

Many repeaters reveal insecurity by wondering deep inside themselves, "I'm second choice . . . Does he/she view me as second best?" That insecurity can be assuaged if both partners understand that in remarriage, as in first marriage, *the most important success factors are mutual support, understanding, and the expression of feelings by either partner.* One remarried man demonstrated this knowledge when he gave his second wife a watch for Christmas. On it was engraved, "To my own *first* love."

Stop obsessing about the past—your mate's, your own. Work together to change behaviors. Use this second chance to make your remarital life right this time, not wrong again. Adopt the personal battle cry "This time I can do it."

16 Portraits of Two Ex-Victims Who Took Control of Their Lives

        This is an account of two victims who changed their lives. The first is famous and male. The second is poor and female.

  I did not treat the first. I did treat the second. Both used the principles of Behavioral Psychotherapy to change their lives and become happy, fulfilled human beings.

Portrait of Keir Dullea

        If you're under thirty, unless you're a theatrical buff, you won't even know the name of the famous actor who created the role of the mixed-up boy in *David and Lisa* and then went on to stage, screen, and TV fame and took the part of the blind hero in Broadway's *Butterflies Are Free*—and then became a theatrical dropout, living in a self-induced limbo.

Keir Dullea admits, "I wrote a life script. I made myself a victim." However, unlike many self-victims, Dullea faced his problems, began the struggle to come back, and now is making it.

A handsome, blue-eyed, six footer, now fifty-one, Dullea grew up in New York's Greenwich Village. His parents owned a bookshop, and when he was five, his mother read him *Macbeth*.

The memories aren't all good—"Growing up I was an outsider. I tested bright but I wasn't a good student." He had a history of childhood disease, including rheumatic fever, which left him with a heart murmur until he was nineteen. He was overweight. His very name caused problems—"Instead of Keir, at school they called me 'queer.' They weren't thinking gay. But it was painful."

The first sign of success came when, with the financial aid of an uncle, he was sent to the private George School, which had an excellent drama department. Keir shone—"I could put on a mask and escape my loneliness." After graduation, Dullea attended Rutgers briefly, then fled to San Francisco "to find myself" and got a job as a carpenter's apprentice. His parents, a remarkable, life-oriented couple, visited and asked, "Have you ever thought of being an actor?"

Keir recalls, "It was like a cartoon of a light bulb going off. Acting was it. I had searched for an identity for so long." He enrolled at San Francisco State College for a year to begin learning the rudiments of his craft and then returned East to continue his studies at the Neighborhood Playhouse School of the Theater with famed teacher Sanford Meisner. Success came quickly: television roles, the part of the young hoodlum who dies in the electric chair in *The Hoodlum Priest,* the fabulous hit as the confused boy in a private sanitarium for youngsters in the film *David and Lisa.* He had film hit after film hit—*Bunny Lake Is Missing, 2001: A Space Odyssey.* Then came the Broadway success *Butterflies Are Free,* in which he played the blind boy who strikes out for himself.

Keir went on to London with *Butterflies Are Free.* It failed. Keir dropped out. Why? He knows the reasons only too well.

■ Success too young—"I escaped into acting. I was so deeply lacking in self-esteem when I was young and not on stage. The part of me that was successful didn't believe I was.

I wasn't able to own my successes. They belonged to someone else, not me."

■ Two unsuccessful marriages—"I was so inexperienced in relationships, so young emotionally. When I married at twenty-four, I was like eighteen. It didn't work. In my second relationship I chose a relationship in which I allowed myself to be dominated. I created mistrust. I philandered."

■ Lack of confidence—"I always ran scared. In this business you have to keep moving. I hit the midlife crisis when I was thirty-five."

Dullea stayed in London, realized his lifelong fear of being "a has-been," felt out of control, got about "a job a year." He did meet and marry Susie Fuller, a divorcee with two children. In 1974 Keir returned to New York and performed in two plays back to back, thinking, "That will fix my career." It didn't. He recalls, "People are fickle. It was as if I'd been blacklisted."

More years of failure. He and Susie moved to Los Angeles— "That move was soul-destroying. There it's 'What have you done lately?'" Keir's confidence completely disappeared. "I wouldn't read the *Hollywood Reporter*. I didn't want to hear who was working." He did manage to survive economically, doing three films in Hollywood in seven years and four for TV, but the glamorous star image had faded away. He was asked to read for parts "I wouldn't have taken in the past. I lived waiting for the phone to ring."

Dullea felt more and more of a victim. Then a major shift occurred. He had always felt that when good things happen, *he* had nothing to do with it. But somehow—probably because of his parents' strengths (they are still active as volunteers in their eighties)—he had a core of strength. Despite his surface despair, he began to use that strength. Two things contributed to his turnaround: Therapy helped mobilize him, and finally he had the right wife—"Susie and I are a remarkable team. In this marriage I discovered the joys of fidelity."

Building on these two pluses gave Keir a sense of confidence, his own strength, the desire to make things happen, the feeling of personal effectiveness—"I can do it if I try."

Dullea and Susie moved back East—this time to suburban Westport, Connecticut. He made it back to Broadway in the comedy *Doubles*—"This time I didn't play a weirdo." He's in demand for soaps and active in the Theater Artists workshop of Westport (where *Doubles* tried out prior to Broadway).

Now, even when doing things he did before, he does them *deliberately*. This makes him feel his life is under his command. For example, he has a yoga room. "I concentrate on putting myself in a certain emotional state. I try to free my mind. Tension is an enemy. It would scare me if there were no stage fright. I like to think I'm master rather than have fear master me. Of course, I'm nervous. I turn nervousness into excitement."

Because of his new confidence from that "I can do it" feeling, he does things more assertively in every area, from speaking up about politics to making career decisions. He says, "Most actors turned down don't push on. Now I *push*." For example, he heard about a new TV mini-series but was told he was too old. Undeterred, he called the producer. "Let me come in. I might be right for something in the future." He did the same thing with Peter Hinds, director of *2010*—"I think it would be mutually good if we met." He got the part.

He has made a deliberate effort to conquer his shoulds. "I always felt I should be the polite, good little gentleman my parents wanted me to be. Now I'm not that good little boy any more. I'm a lot looser."

After fighting his way back from the depths, Dullea now has the confidence of "owning" his own success. Because of his sense of personal effectiveness, he knows it's nice to win but realizes winning isn't everything. The important thing is challenge and growing with it. "I want to be an individual, not a carbon copy of someone else. Enjoying my work is of prime importance. I would have made lots more money in mediocre pictures and teleplays, but I want to produce a film, do comedy, be more and more responsible for my own career."

Because he fought his way back from his own self-victimization, he has both confidence and a sense of peace. He adds, "I now have more self-esteem and joy in life than at any other period in my life. More than ever I enjoy who I am. I wouldn't trade places with Robert Redford."

The Story of Dorothy

One day a former patient called me and said, "I have the most wonderful cleaning woman. She's so bright and so depressed because she hates her life. Will you help her?"

I agreed to see Dorothy M. at the clinic. When she came, under the apparent depression I could immediately see smouldering resentment. At thirty-two, the mother of two, she had left Trinidad and married to get a green card. Now Dorothy felt confined. She was willing to work hard to change but didn't know what to do or what she had the right to do as "a poor woman with hardly any education."

She had no feeling of control over her life. She did have the sense, "There has to be more to life," and yearned desperately to be more than a maid to three wealthy women.

With Dorothy we started at Level One. Sometimes a patient needs a guide in addition to a therapist. I asked my former patient to help. She said, "I'll do anything I can and pay for what I can. She deserves more." So for Dorothy's birthday present, the ex-patient drove her and her children to Stratford, Connecticut, to see Christopher Plummer and James Earl Jones in *Othello*. The patient followed my suggestion that the elder daughter, then fifteen, read the play in advance and explain it to the others. Dorothy herself had a core fear of reading.

The expedition turned out to be a terrific success. The next day they all took turns playing Othello killing Desdemona.

My ex-patient loved helping Dorothy, who caught on very quickly to the fact that another life-style *could* exist for her. The ex-patient treated Dorothy to inexpensive lunches. "I can afford this!" exclaimed Dorothy, who had always thought the only restaurant available to her was McDonald's. In contrast to a punishing pair, the ex-patient (a childless, warm-hearted woman) and Dorothy became the cooperative couple. Dorothy gave the ex-patient love. The ex-patient provided Dorothy with a role model.

I wanted to increase Dorothy's sense of "I can do it" thinking. She was having psychological trouble with one daughter; I got them into family therapy. She had the courage to move through situations she feared rather than avoid them. For example, she was terrified to do things alone. I sent her to the Brooklyn Museum, and she managed not only to spend the day there but to join—"I can afford this." At my instigation, she began a high school equivalency course. When she didn't like some of the reading assignments *(Anna Karenina)*, I suggested others full of the love and escape type of tale I knew she would enjoy *(Rebecca, Gone with the Wind, Cheri)*. Dorothy became a reader. She wanted to buy a pair of argyle socks for a present. I sent her to Brooks Brothers. With a not wholly misplaced fear of mistreatment, she went to this good store, made her $5.95 purchase, and stayed for hours—"They were so nice to me!"

But Dorothy was still a domestic. At one session, she confided, "My other two employers treat me as if I'm not a person, but I am a person." I told her, "If you stay a domestic, that is what they will always think." Dorothy got more and more angry and depressed and practically stopped trying.

At that point I made Dorothy go back to her preconscious Level Three. She had been the fourth of seven children. As she delved back into her memories, she recalled that the older children got special privileges and the younger three got special attention. She was ignored. Not only did she feel resentful, but her distorted thinking led to the feeling "I should be given things," in her case meaning the privileges of middle class life.

Once Dorothy realized this, she knew the education and better job she wanted would not come from loving parents. Terrified as she was of entering what was a new world to her, she had to go through the anxiety and work for what *she* wanted, not simply follow her lifetime pattern of meekly accepting whatever came her way. "I see. I have to do it for myself," she exclaimed. That was her starting point for important change.

Dorothy quit her two morning jobs and decided to take a word processing course. On her own she got a grant. She has recently earned her high school equivalency diploma. Her elder daughter will soon graduate from college (my ex-patient helped get her a scholarship). In a year Dorothy will complete the word processing course and through this training will be able to get the white collar job she wants. Her future goal: to attend college.

Recently, her pretty face shining, Dorothy made me a speech: "I always knew what I wanted, but I didn't know how to get it. You taught me how. The most important thing is that inside I know I can do it—whatever it is. If it doesn't work out, I know I've tried. I'm nobody's victim any more. I've got a future."

Both Keir Dullea and Dorothy took themselves out of the emotional victim category.

So can anyone else.

Say yes to life.

Do as superstar athletes do—think to win.

Develop that sense of personal effectiveness. Know that you can do it. Repeat that all-important affirmation: "I can do it."

Use the preconscious techniques explained in this book.

When necessary, employ acceptable aggression.

In intimate relationships and friendships, aim to be part of a cooperative couple, working for mutual good. Don't be part of a punishing pair bringing on the consequence of mutual destruction.

If something goes wrong, take the proper measures. Pick yourself up and start all over with the knowledge you can do it.

Apply the guiding principle of Behavioral Psychotherapy: *Remember your past to control your present and change your future.*

Don't permit yourself to become or stay an emotional victim. You can achieve this—if you want to, if you try!

☐ About the Collaboration That Produced This Book

      Making Life Right When It Feels All Wrong marks the third collaborative effort for Dr. Herbert Fensterheim and Jean Baer, who in private life are husband and wife. Their first was *Don't Say Yes When You Want to Say No* (which received an award from the American Psychological Association for its "noteworthy contribution to the public's understanding of psychology") and their second, *Stop Running Scared!*

  Dr. Herbert Fensterheim received his M.A. in psychology from Columbia University and his Ph.D. from New York University. He spent twenty years as an analytically oriented therapist before becoming one of the first clinicians involved with Behavior Therapy. Currently in private practice in Manhattan, he is clinical professor at Cornell University Medical College and attending psychologist at Payne Whitney Clinic—The New York Hospital. He has taught psychology at undergraduate, graduate, and postdoctoral levels at leading universities and medical colleges. In addition he has written about one hundred professional papers, coedited three books on Behavior Therapy, and is the author of *Help Without Psychoanalysis*. His last professional book, *Behavioral Psychotherapy*, presented the clinical integration of behavioral and psychoanalytic methods, and he serves on the board of advisers of the Society for the Exploration of Psychotherapy Integration (SEPI). A recognized leader in his field, Dr. Fensterheim has given many talks to and conducted workshops for the professional community at meetings of such groups as the American Psychological Association, American Psychiatric Association, and the American Group Psychotherapy Association, thus enabling other therapists to learn behavioral techniques and teach them to others. For four years he served as sports psychologist for the United States Olympic fencing team.

Jean Baer has written extensively on contemporary problems, especially those concerning male-female relationships. In addition to conceiving *Don't Say Yes When You Want to Say No* and *Stop Running Scared!*, written with Dr. Fensterheim, her other books include *Follow Me!*, *The Single Girl Goes to Town*, *The Second Wife*, *How to Be an Assertive—Not Aggressive—Woman in Life, in Love, and on the Job*, and *The Self-Chosen*. She is a frequent contributor to the major women's magazines. Daughter of a well-known newspaperman and a graduate of Cornell University, she has worked for the Mutual Broadcasting Company, the United States Information Agency, and spent many years as senior editor and special projects director of *Seventeen* magazine. She also hosted the syndicated radio series "Youth on Youth" and is a frequent lecturer at national organization meetings.

□ Bibliography

ARKOWITZ, HALL, AND STANLEY B. MESSER (editors). *Psychoanalytic Therapy and Behavior Therapy.* New York: Plenum Press, 1984.

BAER, JEAN. *How to Be an Assertive—Not Aggressive—Woman in Life, in Love, and on the Job.* New York: New American Library, 1976.

BAGAROZZI, DENNIS A., AND STEVEN ANDERSON. "The Evolution of Family Mythological Systems: Considerations for Meaning, Clinical Assessment, and Treatment." *The Journal of Psychoanalytic Anthropology,* vol. 5, no. 1 (winter 1982), pp. 71–90.

BANDURA, ALBERT. "Self-Efficacy: Toward a Unifying Theory for Behavioral Change." *Psychological Review,* vol. 84, no. 2 (1977), pp. 191–215.

BANK, STEPHEN P., AND MICHAEL D. KAHN. *The Sibling Bond.* New York: Basic Books, 1984.

BARNETT, JOSEPH, M.D. "Narcissism and Dependency in the Obsessional-Hysteric Marriage." *Family Process,* 1971, pp. 75–83.

BECK, AARON T. *Cognitive Therapy and the Emotional Disorders.* New York: International Universities Press, 1976.

BEM, SANDRA LIPSITZ. "The Measurement of Psychological Androgyny." *Journal of Consulting and Clinical Psychology,* vol. 47, no. 2, 1974, pp. 155–162.

——————. "Gender Schema Theory: A Cognitive Account of Sex Typing." *Psychological Review,* vol. 88 (1981), pp. 354–364.

BERNE, ERIC, M.D. *Games People Play.* New York: Ballantine Books, 1964.

BRENTON, MYRON. "Calamity Strikes Again." *Cosmopolitan*, May 1983.

CHIAUZZI, EMIL, AND RICHARD G. HEIMBERG. "Legitimacy of Request and Social Problem Solving." *Behavior Modification*, vol. 10, no. 1 (January 1986), pp. 3–18.

ELLIS, ALBERT. *Reason and Emotion in Psychotherapy*. New York: Lyle Stuart, 1962.

FERNSTERHEIM, HERBERT, PH.D., AND JEAN BAER. *Don't Say Yes When You Want to Say No*. New York: Dell Publishing Co., Inc., 1975.

——————. *Stop Running Scared!* New York: Dell Publishing Co., Inc., 1977.

FENSTERHEIM, HERBERT, PH.D., AND HOWARD I. GLAZER, PH.D. (editors). *Behavioral Psychotherapy: Basic Principles and Case Studies in an Integrative Clinical Model*. New York: Brunner/Mazel, Inc., 1983.

FREEDMAN, ALFRED M., M.D., HAROLD I. KAPLAN, M.D., AND BENJAMIN J. SADOCK, M.D. (editors). *Comprehensive Textbook of Psychiatry/II*. Baltimore: The Williams & Wilkins Company, 1975, p. 2600.

FREUD, SIGMUND. *Standard Edition of the Complete Psychological Works of Sigmund Freud* (edited by James Strachey). London: The Hogarth Press, 1964.

FRIED, EDRITA, PH.D. *Active/Passive*. New York: Grune & Stratton, 1970.

GERBER, GWENDOLYN L. "The Relationship Balance Model and Its Implications for Individual and Couples Therapy." In *The Dynamics of Feminist Therapy* (D. Howard, editor). New York: Haworth Press, 1986, pp. 19–27.

GOLEMAN, DANIEL. "Two Views of Marriage Explored: His and Hers." *The New York Times*, April 1, 1986.

GREER, WILLIAM R. "The Changing Women's Marriage Market." *The New York Times*, February 22, 1986.

JACKSON, ANNE. *Early Stages*. Boston: Little, Brown and Co., 1979.

HORNEY, KAREN, M.D. *Neurosis and Human Growth*. New York: W. W. Norton & Co., Inc., 1950.

HATTERER, DR. LAWRENCE J. *The Pleasure Addicts*. South Brunswick, N.J., and New York: A. S. Barnes and Co., 1980.

KAHN, STEPHEN; GARY ZIMMERMAN; MIHALY CSIKSZENTMIHALYI; and JACOB. W. GETZELS. "Relations Between Identity in Young Adulthood and Intimacy at Midlife." *Journal of Personality and Social Psychology*, vol. 49, no. 5 (1985).

KAPLAN, HELEN SINGER, M.D., PH.D. *Disorders of Sexual Desire*. New York: Simon & Schuster, 1979.

——————. *Sexual Aversion, Sexual Phobias, and Panic Disorders*. New York: Brunner/Mazel, 1987.

KEMPEL, JOHN K., AND JOHN G. HOLMES. "How Do I Trust Thee?" *Psychology Today*, February 1986.

LARZELERE, ROBERT E., AND TED L. HUSTON. "The Dyadic Trust Scale: Toward Understanding and Impersonal Trust in Close Relationships." *Journal of Marriage and the Family*, August 1980, pp. 595–603.

LAZARUS, ARNOLD, PH.D., AND ALLEN FAY, M.D. *I Can If I Want To*. New York: Warner Books, Inc., 1975.

LEIGHTON, FRANCES SPATZ. *The Search for the Real Nancy Reagan*. New York: Macmillan Publishing Company, 1987.

LOWENTHAL, MARJORIE FISK; MAJDE THURNHER; DAVID CHRIBOGA; and ASSOCIATES. *Four Stages of Life*. San Francisco: Jossey-Bass Publishers, 1976.

MASLOW, ABRAHAM H. *Toward a Psychology of Being*, second edition. New York: D. Van Nostrand Company, 1968.

MUNROE, RUTH L. *Schools of Psychoanalytic Thought*. New York: Holt, Rinehart and Winston, Inc., 1955.

O'CONNOR, DAGMAR. *How to Make Love to the Same Person for the Rest of Your Life and Still Love It*. Garden City, N.Y.: Doubleday & Company, Inc., 1985.

ORLOVSKY, JACOB L.; JAMES E. MARCIA; and IRA M. LESSER. "Identity Status and the Intimacy Versus Isolation Crisis of Young Adulthood." *Journal of Personality and Social Psychology*, vol. 27, pp. 211–219.

PERLS, FREDERICK S. *Gestalt Therapy Verbatim*. Lafayette, Calif.: Real People Press, 1969.

STERNBERG, ROBERT J. "A Triangular Theory of Love." *Psychological Review*, vol. 93, no. 2 (1986), pp. 119–135.

——————. "Explorations of Love." Volume 1 in *Advances in Personal Relationships* (Jones, Warren, and Dan Perlman, editors). Greenwich, Conn.: J.A.I. Press, 1987.

STERNBERG, ROBERT J., and SUSAN GRAJEK. "The Nature of Love." *Journal of Personality and Social Psychology*, vol. 47, no. 2 (1984), pp. 312–329.

STOKES, JOSEPH; LAURENCE CHILDS; ANN FUEHER. "Gender and Sex Rules as Predictors of Self-Disclosure." *Journal of Counseling Psychology*, vol. 28, no. 6 (November 1981).

SUINN, RICHARD M., PH.D. *Seven Steps to Peak Performance*. Toronto: Hans Huber Publishers, 1986.

TESCH, STEPHANIE A., and SUSAN KRAUSS WHITBOURNE. "Intimacy and Identity Status in Young Adults." *Journal of Personality and Social Psychology*, vol. 43, no. 5 (1982), pp. 1041–1051.

WACHTEL, PAUL L. *Psychoanalysis and Behavior Therapy*. New York: Basic Books, Inc., 1977.

WACHTEL, ELLEN F., and PAUL L. WACHTEL. *Family Dynamics in Individual Psychotherapy*. New York: The Guilford Press, 1986.

WATKINS, DR. DALE. *Sisters.* New York: Arbor House, 1984.

WEITZMAN, DR. LENORE J. *The Divorce Revolution.* New York: The Free Press, 1985.

WESTHEIMER, DR. RUTH L. *Dr. Ruth's Guide to Good Sex.* New York: Warner Books, Inc., 1983.

——————. *Dr. Ruth's Guide for Married Lovers.* New York: Warner Books, Inc., 1986.

WHITE, KATHLEEN M.; JOSEPH C. SPEISMAN; DORIS JACKSON; SCOTT BARTIS; and DARYL COSTOS. "Intimacy Maturity and Its Correlates in Young Married Couples." *Journal of Personality and Social Psychology,* vol. 50, no. 1 (1986), pp. 152–162.

WINNIK, H. Z. "Victimology and Psychoanalysis." *Israel Annals of Psychiatry and Related Disciplines,* vol. 17, no. 3 (1979), pp. 241–254.

WOLPE, JOSEPH. *The Practice of Behavior Therapy* (2nd edition). New York: Pergamon Press, 1973.

Index